Women, Sustainable Entrepreneurship and the Economy

When a woman decides to become an 'entrepreneur,' she starts her business with a sense of excitement, freedom, wealth, happiness, prestige; however, these feelings can soon turn to fears over debt, difficulties, unpaid invoices, stress, and uncertainty.

Being an entrepreneur means taking risks, making decisions, adapting management styles in line with developmental needs, clashing with rivals, being more agile than competitors, negotiating risky scenarios, following business trends, capturing new opportunities before, and being better than the competition.

If a woman wants to be successful as an entrepreneur, she needs to have a business education, undergo continued professional development, and have patience and emotional intelligence.

Supporting women in their entrepreneurial activities has been shown to positively affect the economy, which is why governments pay special attention to opening new funding opportunities and training programs for women who want to start or develop a business. Female entrepreneurship has individual characteristics because of those aspects of the business which are affected by cultural, technological, legislative, social, and historical developments. This book discusses the relationship between female entrepreneurship and the economy, and academic authors from developing countries such as Brazil, Turkey, Albania, Kosovo, Portugal, and Malaysia analyze the developments encompassing women and entrepreneurship in their respective countries.

The authors discuss the regulatory frameworks of each country to show how these either help or hinder female entrepreneurship, and consequently, the place of women in the economy.

Women and entrepreneurship is an emerging theme, and this book is a must-read for researchers from both developing and developed countries.

Prof. Dr. Kıymet Tunca Çalıyurt, CPA, CFE, is the founder of the International Women and Business Group (IWBG) and International Group on Governance, Fraud, Ethics and Social Responsibility (IConGFE & SR). She teaches accounting, auditing, fraud examination, sustainability, to women in business in Trakya University, and ACCA-accredited master program on accounting and auditing in University of National World and Economy, Sofia.

Liliane Segura is a professor at the Mackenzie Presbyterian University, Brazil, and she teaches accounting, firm valuation, and corporate social responsibility. She is a postdoctorate in business from the University of Salamanca, Spain; Doctor in Finance from Mackenzie Presbyterian University, Brazil, and Accounting Degree and Master in Strategy from the University of São Paulo, Brazil.

Women and Sustainable Business
Series Editor: Kıymet Tunca Çalıyurt

Women in Agriculture Worldwide
Key Issues and Practical Approaches
Edited by Amber J. Fletcher, Wendee Kubik

Women and Sustainability in Business
A Global Perspective
Kıymet Tunca Çalıyurt

Women, Sustainable Entrepreneurship and the Economy
A Global Perspective
Edited by Kıymet Tunca Çalıyurt and Liliane Segura

Women, Sustainable Entrepreneurship and the Economy

A Global Perspective

Edited by
Kıymet Tunca Çalıyurt and
Liliane Segura

Routledge
Taylor & Francis Group
LONDON AND NEW YORK

First published 2020
by Routledge
2 Park Square, Milton Park, Abingdon, Oxon, OX14 4RN

and by Routledge
605 Third Avenue, New York, NY 10017

First issued in paperback 2021

Routledge is an imprint of the Taylor & Francis Group, an informa business

Library of Congress Cataloging-in-Publication Data
A catalog record for this title has been requested

ISBN 13: 978-1-03-208603-3 (pbk)
ISBN 13: 978-0-815-38162-4 (hbk)

Typeset in Sabon
by codeMantra

Contents

Figures

Tables

Contributors

Dafina D. Abdullahu, graduated master programme from the University of Prizren, Economic Faculty.

Maria Do Livramento De Aguiar, specialist in fashion design from the Federal University of Pernambuco – UFPE (2006), specialist in art education from the Federal University of Pernambuco – UFPE (2005), graduated in psychology from the Faculty of Human Sciences of Olinda – FACHO (1986). She has experience in the social area, with emphasis on children and adolescents and their families, and has been working in several NGOs since 1982. Currently, she is State Councilor for Cultural Policy in Pernambuco; Counselor for Children and Adolescents Law in the city of Recife, and Municipal Counselor for Social Assistance in Recife. She develops activities with women from vulnerable communities, strengthening actions in a network, with a focus on the market. She was a consultant at the Solidare Institute for Vocational Training of Women – 2015/2017, and Program Psychologist: 'Family: Children's Law' of the Lar do Nenen from 2006 to 2014 – Recife/PE. She worked at the Casa Menina Mulher as an advisor on product development for young women's professional training – 2007 to 2017 – Recife/PE. She was a consultant at the Dom Helder Câmara Institute in the Project Productive Unit for Families – 2010/2012 – Recife/PE. She was a consultant for the Project Tailoring My Dignity by Senac, in the area of professional training for women – 2009/2010 – Quipapá/PE. She coordinated productive unit for the Altino Ventura Foundation in the Project Imprimindo um novo olhar – professional training for women – 2009- Recife/PE. Coordinated projects at Casa de Passagem for professional training for adolescents and young people in fashion, decoration, and handicrafts – 1998/2007 – Recife/PE. She serves as political representation in the boards: COMDICA (2012/2014), CMAS (2015/2017), FORUM DCA – coordination (2016/2017), FORAP – State Forum of Learning, Fepetipe – State Forum for the Eradication of Child Labor, MNDH-PE (National Human Rights Movement – Pernambuco), National Movement for Family and Community Living).

Luljeta Aliu is a teaching assistant at the University of Prishtina 'Hasan Prishtina.' Ms. Aliu is pursuing PhD studies in the field of economics at University of Prishtina, in the program developed in cooperation with University of Nice Sophia Antipolis, France; Johannes Kepler University Linz, Austria; and University 'G. d'Annunzio' of Chieti Pescara, Italy. She has profound experience on project development, mainly European Union-funded projects. Her experience is related to curriculum development, quality assurance; research and development, and accreditation process. She has been part of the working groups for development of the strategic documents for the private and public universities in Kosovo. Additionally, she is engaged as local expert by UNDP to support University of Prishtina in establishing first scientific journal. Her research interests are in economics of development and transformation and digital economy.

Caio Venâncio De Araújo earned his bachelor's degree in business administration and entrepreneur; he has worked as a volunteer at Junior Achievement. He is currently Executive Director – Next Academy. Has experience in Administration, focusing on Entrepreneurial Education, acting on the following subjects: entrepreneurship, social entrepreneurship and financial administration.

Micilane Pereira de Araújo is currently attending a masters degree in education, at Federal University of Pernambuco – Brazil (UFPE) and is a public school teacher with broad experience in training young in a situation of social vulnerability. She is presently member of a group that develops researches on educational policies. She has been coordinator of the Gender Study and Coping with Violence against Women Unit, where she worked on the inclusion of the gender perspective and its interfaces within the schools.

Micilvânia Pereira de Araújo is an administrator of companies, works in the State Secretariat of Agriculture and Agrarian Reform of the State of Pernambuco in the position of administrative analyst. She has extensive experience in teamwork, mainly in NGOs related to the field, presentation skills, conflict resolution. She has a master's degree in sustainable local development management from the Faculty of Management Sciences of Pernambuco/University of Pernambuco – Brazil (FCAP/UPE) and a degree in business administration from the Faculty of Olinda – Brazil (FOCCA); is currently a postgraduate student in neuroscience, music, and inclusion at the Federal University of Pernambuco – Brazil (UFPE), and a graduate student in pedagogy at the Federal University of Pernambuco – Brazil (UFPE).

Izabele Barros, graduated in fashion design from the Federal University of Ceará in 2005, has a postgraduate degree in Teaching the History of the

Arts from the Federal Rural University of Pernambuco, concluding in 2006. Since 2007, she has been assistant professor at the University of Pernambuco/Faculdade de Ciências da Administração de Pernambuco in the marketing field. In 2011, she created the Modateca University Extension Program (formed by the Modateca Social and Modateca Ambiental Projects), in which she is also the coordinator. For four years, she was general extension coordinator of the University of Pernambuco, where she managed, at extension level, thirteen university campuses and three university hospitals. She was a member of the Environmental Actions Committee of the Institutions of the Government of Pernambuco. She received a master's degree in Sustainable Local Development Management from the University of Pernambuco in 2013. Izabele is a researcher member of the Sustainable Local Development Management Research Group in the line of research for people for Sustainable Local Development and is responsible for the investigation 'Modateca Social: Analyzing the Practice of Social Entrepreneurship.' She has experience and performance in the areas of marketing, sustainability, fashion design, creative economy, and social entrepreneurship, highlighting the work of education aimed at the economic empowerment of women and the development of communities in risk situation. She is the author of several academic articles and book chapters in the areas mentioned earlier, and is also the organizer of the book Linhas da Moda. She is a winner of several prizes: Friend of the Environment (State Agency for the Environment/CPRH/2010), UNIJUS de Inteligência Ambiental, (Ins Unijus/2010), Women Connected to Agenda 21 (Secretary of Environment and Sustainability of the Government of Pernambuco/2011), Vasconcelos Sobrinho Prize (Environment and Sustainability Secretariat of the Government of Pernambuco/CPRH/2012), Income Generation for Women (Instituto Lojas Renner/2016). In 2018, she completed a master of business administration in marketing from the University of Pernambuco.

João Batista, graduate student in business administration and entrepreneur.

Bekim Berisha has graduated from University of Prishtina – graduated economist in 1987. He worked as KFSRB Kosovo – Statutory Auditor and SCAAK Kosovo – Certificated Accountant in 2002 and 2003. Bekim has postgraduated from Academy of Advanced University Studies ASAU Prishtina. His master degree is from Academy of Advanced University Studies ASAU Prishtina – postgraduate study – master by research – PhD-VI level ISCED/1997. His doctorate study is from University of Skopje in 2013. He can speak Albanian, Serbian, Turkish, Russian, Macedonian, and English. He is acting as auditor in Prizren.

Ibsen Mateus Bittencourt has a PhD in business administration (Mackenzie-SP), a master in Brazilian Education in Information and Communication

Technology (UFAL), an MBA in Tourism Management (UBM-RJ), a specialist in Mathematics (UFPE), a bachelor in Companies (UFAL), and bachelor in Tourism (CESMAC). He is Adjunct Professor II of the Federal University of Alagoas – UFAL, and researcher of the Center of Excellence in Social Technologies – NEES/UFAL/CNPq, acting as Professor of the Master in Intellectual Property and Technology Transfer for Innovation – PROFNIT of Business and Computer Science. He has published more than 100 academic articles in national and international periodicals and congresses. He is the managing partner of IT4LIFE, a company that develops software based on human recommendations and consulting in complex business management. He has worked in the Commercial Management of VARIG Linhas Aéreas S/A and Contecny Contruções Ltda and in ICE Equipment that worked in the import and export of equipment SOREDEX in Finland and QR s.r.l. in Italy.

Berenice Carpigiani is a psychologist and licentiate in psychology from the Pontifical Catholic University of São Paulo (1979). She is a psychoanalysis specialist (1986); theory of communication and didactics of higher education specialist (1995), and clinical psychology specialist (CRP/06.2004). She did her masters (1996) and doctororate (2007) from UMESP. She teaches the discipline psychoanalysis, and she is supervisor of the area of clinical psychology, and the director of the Biological and Health Sciences Center.

Publication of books: Psychology of the roots to the contemporary movements (São Paulo, Cengage Learning. 3ª. edition 2010); Places of Psychology. Org. (São Paulo, 2008); Theories and techniques of attendance in a psychology practice (São Paulo, Vetor, 2011), and Training space of the psychologist in Brazil: 20 years of the psychology clinic Alvino Augusto de Sá. Org. Mackenzie. (2014).

Chapters of books in areas of historical psychology, health psychology, clinical psychology and psychopedagogy. She has been teaching in higher education for 35 years, 30 years of them at the Presbyterian University Mackenzie in the courses of psychology, pedagogy, and postgraduate (Lato sensu e Stricto sensu).

Research Line: Evaluation and intervention in psychology. It guides PIBIC, PIVIC, and TCC in this line.

Administrative duties in the Institution: Psychology General Department (2001–2006)

Substitute of the Direction of the Faculty of Psychology (2001–2005). Coordinator of Extension (2007–2009); member of the Standing Disciplinary Committee of the psychology (2005–2006); Rapporteur of the Commission for Studies on the Academic Regiment – Appointed by the Rectory (2007); Rapporteur of the Commission for care of the environment – appointed by the Rectory (2008); Idealizer and Coordinator of the Orientation and Attendance Program for Psychology (1987 to 2007). Coordinated the psychology course – biological science and health – vice-director Presbiterian Mackenzie University (2007 to 2011), and, from the second semester of 2014, she took over the direction of the Center of Sciences Biological and Health Sciences of UPM-SP. She has helped teenagers, adults, and the elderly people in the perspective of psychoanalysis, since 1981.

Ana Maria Porto Castanheira is coordinator of the Academic Collection and Registration of Diplomas-CARD Mackenzie Presbyterain Mackenzie.

She has a bachelor's degree in mathematics from Mackenzie (1974), master's degree in business administration-emphasis: HR (1995), and doctorate in business administration-(1997) from Universidade Presbiteriana Mackenzie-UPM (1997). She has done specialization in Higher Education Didactics and a specialization in Institutional Evaluation from UnB-Catedra UNESCO. She is the member of the editorial board of the *Journal of Engineering Teaching* – ABENGE (2004–2010). Professor at the UPM, she teaches calculus for mathematics and engineering (1974–2018). She is the coordinator of the Academic Collection and Registration of Diplomas-CARD linked to the Secretariat of the High Councils and Academic Control-SCCA of the UPM (2014, the present date). She is the advisor of the rectory and coordinator of Institutional Evaluation and CPA-Evaluation Committee UPM (2001–2014), and director of the Faculty of Biological, Exact and Experimental Sciences of UPM (1991–2001). She worked as effective teacher of mathematics in basic education of the State Network of SP (1973–1979). She was Professor of FAAP (1985–1989) and Faculty Osvaldo Cruz (1975–1982). She has experience in the area of management and education. She works mainly in the following subjects: evaluation, regulation, quality, teacher training, pedagogical projects, teaching, learning, and curriculum guidelines of higher education. She participated in the Research Group: Higher Education: Pedagogical Didactic Projects and Teaching from 2000 to 2013 and the Education, Management and Society group from 2007 to 2013.

She is the institutional evaluator and course evaluator of Ministry of Education and e-Culture of Brazil / INEP (since 2008), and institutional evaluator of the Education Departamento São Paulo.

Mary Rosane Ceroni is Brazilian, divorced, 63 years old, with 45 years of experience in education. She was born on December 21, 1954, in São Paulo / Brazil, studied at Universidade Presbiteriana Mackenzie-UPM / São Paulo/SP/Brazil: 1997–1999 – PhD in business administration; 1994–1996 – masters in business administration; 1993 – postgraduate Course in business administration; 1992 – postgraduate course in higher education didactics (1992) from UPM.

She holds a bachelor's degree and license in languages and pedagogy. She is coordinator of pedagogy course PARFOR/CAPES/MEC

(Ministry of Education of Brazil) in UPM since 2011. She has been responsible for School and Challenges of Teaching Theme in Distance Education – (Educação a Distância – EaD), in the pedagogy's course at UPM´s Education, Philosophy and Theology Center. She has been the leader of the Research Group Education, Management and Society since 2006 at UPM/ Brazil, conducting research on teacher´s training, corporations, and social and educational management in the contemporary era. She has been an active member of the EmprendeSUR Network-Entrepreneurship and innovation in Latin America since 2014. She was the International Representative of CEFT/UPMackenzie and Member of the Standing Committee of Internalization/CEFT/UPM in the period of 2016–2018. She has been teaching in pedagogy and language courses at UPM since 1993 and she taught business administration and foreign trade courses (1993–2003) also at UPM. She has been teaching higher education didactics in postgraduation courses at UPM (since 2003) as well as in courses such as higher education teaching, corporate pedagogy, and educational management (since 2001) at Faculdades Metropolitanas Unidas-FMU/São Paulo/Brazil. She was also a member of the FMU´s Pedagogical Advisory Board (2005–2007). She was the coordinator of the pedagogy course (2008–2012) as well as the FOPEPE Program (2007) – Permanent Forum of Education, Research and Extension at UPM´s Education, Philosophy and Theology Center. She was a member of the Executive Board (People Management) on NGO (non-governmental organization) in Brazil action ethics and citizenship (2000–2003). Mary also has experience as both teacher and manager in basic education (1975–1996).

But Dedaj, dean of the Faculty of Economics, University of Prishtina 'Hasan Prishtina,' Kosovo. Prof. Dedaj is a published author, producing scientific research papers in the field of economics and higher dducation. Prof. Dedaj is a member of several professional bodies and working groups that develop strategic documents relating to higher education.

Jade Demettino, graduate student in business administration. She works at Red Bull.

Carolina Sandra Giang is a lecturer in Marketing at Swinburne University of Technology, Sarawak Campus, Malaysia. Carol has extensive background working in the area of human resource development and organizational consultancy in business development, delivery, and consultancy works. She has 15 years of experience as a trainer in the areas of leadership and management, self-management (motivational), communication, problem solving, teambuilding, presentation skills, women and NGO related programs. She is currently undergoing her doctoral of business administration program from the Universiti Teknologi MARA. **Ekrem Gjokaj** has over thirteen years' experience in management of the administration department as director of Economic Analysis and Agricultural Statistics. Additionally, he has more than ten years' experience in teaching and wide experience in training and research for various studies in the field of rural development, environment, agribusiness, and food security. His work so far has certainly covered a wide range of topics in management of rural development, environment, agriculture, agribusiness, agricultural policies, markets, and trade policies. Gjokaj is a researcher and lecturer at International Business College, University of Prishtina and University of Prizren. He has conducted several researches and contributed in large number of scientific publications.

Seyhan Bilir Guler is an assistant professor at Trakya University, Faculty of Economics and Administrative Sciences, Edirne, Turkey. She obtained a bachelor's degree from Inonu University, Faculty of Economics and Administrative Sciences; a master's degree from Trakya University, Department of Business Administration; her doctorate degree from Ankara University, Department of Business Administration. Her main research and interest are in gender, organizational theory, organizational culture, organizational design, and change management.

Kapllan Halimi has over ten years' experience in management of the administration as state secretary of Ministry of Agriculture, Forestry and Rural Development. Additionally, he is doing his PhD in Leibnitz Institute for Economic Development in Transition Economies in Germany. During this time, he has developed and acquired skills on managing and researching. Mr. Halimi is a researcher in Leibnitz Institute for Economic Development in Transition Economies, based on Halle (Saale) in Germany. He has conducted several researches and contributed in large number of scientific publications.

Prof. Ass. Dr. Hamdi Shaban Hoti was born in 1964, in Carralluke, Malisheve, Republic of Kosovo. His bachelor degree is from University of Pristina 'Hasan PRİSHTİNA' in Year 1991. He has graduated from Magistrature (Mr. Sc) of Economic Sciences, Faculty of Economic, management direction from University of Prishtina 'Hasan PRISHTINA,' Kosovo, in 2008. He did his PhD in economic science, Faculty of Economic at the State University of Tirana, Management Department, in 2013, Tirana – Albania. His research and teaching areas are human resource management, corporate governance, principles of human resource, change management, accounting and auditing, research methods at University of Prizren 'Ukshin HOTI.' For the period 2008–2014, he worked as a director for Budget and Finance Ministry of Culture, Youth and Sports, Prishtine, Kosovo.

Dr. Corina Joseph is an associate professor at the Faculty of Accountancy, Universiti Teknologi MARA, Samarahan Campus, Sarawak, Malaysia. Her research expertise is in CSR and sustainability reporting, corporate governance, public sector accounting and governance and website reporting. At present, Corina is serving as the co-chief editor for the

International Journal of Service Management and Sustainability and the as editorial board member for other several international reputable refereed journals.

Artë Kastrati was born in 1992. She is a PhD candidate in economics at the University of Prishtina 'Hasan Prishtina.' She attended a semester at Université Côte d'Azur in Nice (France) under the Erasmus + Programme. She earned both her bachelor's and master's degree from the University of Prishtina, with a specialization in economics. Her research interest is in macroeconomic field, especially in fiscal policy. She has worked in this field from 2015 to 2017 at the Ministry of Finance of the Republic of Kosovo. She has presented a paper titled 'Migration of Labor Force and Its Effects on Economic Development: The Case of Kosovo,' at The 3nd International Conference on Research and Education – 'Challenges Toward the Future' (ICRAE2015).

Pinar Keles has graduated from Entrepreneurship Master Program in Trakya University and working in municipality.

Diana Kopeva is a full-time professor at the University of National and World Economy (UNWE), Sofia, Bulgaria. She gives lectures on strategic management, entrepreneurship, business planning, cost-benefit analysis, and project management. She has more than 100 scientific publications, based on her research interests. She is one of the leading researchers in the area of business economics and entrepreneurship in Bulgaria. Her research interests are in the field of entrepreneurship, start-ups, corporate social responsibility (CSR), and circular economy. She participated in numerous projects (national and international) focused on CSR and transition from linear to circular and regenerative economies.

Nilson Leão is assistant professor at the Federal University of Alagoas, graduated in business administration and masters in production engineering. He is currently a PhD student in business administration.

Emanuel Leite holds a bachelor's degree in business administration from the Federal University of Pernambuco (1982), a master's degree in administration from the Federal University of Paraíba (1992), a PhD in engineering sciences from the University of Porto (1999), and a postdoctoral degree in innovation and entrepreneurship from the University of Aveiro. He is currently an associate at the University of Pernambuco, Professor Emeritus of the Autonomy of Higher Education of Garanhuns. He was a guest lecturer at Universidad del Mar (Chile). He was Professor of Innovation and Business Creation at Fernando Pessoa University – Porto – Portugal. He is a full professor of the Faculty of Humanities of Pernambuco (Pernambuco Society of Culture and Education – SOPECE), author of the books The Phenomenon of Entrepreneurship Creating Wealth (Belmiro Siqueira Prize 2001 – Entrepreneurship), Business Innovation and the Law of Innovation and The Phenomenon of Entrepreneurship (Editora

Saraiva), a text work in the partnership Editora Saraiva/Hoper. He has experience in administration, with emphasis on administration, working mainly on the following topics: entrepreneurship, administration, technology-based company, innovation, and entrepreneur. He was coordinator of the CEAG Office in the city of Garanhuns. He was awarded the Innovation Award for Luck in the Marketing and Technology Categories, he was a full professor of the subject advanced management in the Faculty of Sciences Humanities Pernambuco and was a member of the Editorial Board of the Director's Magazine of the Business Development Center of Pernambuco. It is premier – Prize Entrepreneur Professor Emanuel Leite sponsored by the Faculty of Administration of Garanhuns (FAGA) – Autonomy of Higher Education of Garanhuns (AESGA). He was a member of the panel of evaluators of papers submitted to the magazine Desenvolvimento em Questão, e-reviewer of articles of the journal *Industrial Engineering of the Higher Polytechnic Institute*? José Antonio Echeverría (Cujae – Cuba).

Maria Elisa Pereira Lopes graduated in pedagogy at Pontifícia Universidade Católica de São Paulo (1982), postgraduation in psychopedagogy at the Sedes Sapienta Institute, and master's degree in developmental disorders from Universidade Presbiteriana Mackenzie (2005). She is currently teaching at Mackenzie Presbyterian University. She has experience in education, with emphasis on education, working mainly in the following subjects: teacher training, didactics of higher education, literacy, literacy and process of reading and writing acquisition, youth and adult education, and education psychology. She is coordinator of the Open University of Time of the Mackenzie Presbyterian University.

Angelo Antônio Martins, bachelor of business administration, postgraduate in tourism science in England (1996–1998) from the University of Birmingham and Sheffield Hallam University, master of business administration from the Federal University of Paraíba (1988), and PhD in business administration from FEA-USP (2006). He is currently professor at Federal University of Alagoas-UFAL, Faculty of Economics, Administration and Accounting-FEAC.

Ilke Oruc is an assistant professor at Trakya University, Faculty of Economics and Administrative Sciences, Edirne, Turkey. She obtained a bachelor's degree from Abant Izzet Baysal University, Faculty of Economics and Administrative Sciences; a master's degree from Trakya University, Department of Business Administration; her doctorate degree from Anadolu University, Department of Business Administration; and her postdoctorate from the University of South Africa (UNISA), Graduate School of Business Leadership. Her main research and interests are in gender, organizational behavior, corporate social responsibility, ethical behavior and management, and the sociology of work.

Ana Rita Valverde Peroba, PhD student in Design by PPGDesign – Mestrado e Doutorado Escola de Artes, Arquitetura, Design e Moda da Universidade Anhembi Morumbi Laureate International Universities (2014/2018). Master's in Design from Universidade Anhembi Morumbi (2008), graduated in industrial design habilitation in visual programming from the Federal University of Pernambuco (UFPE/2003). She has experience in the field of arts, with emphasis on fashion and graphic design. She trained ten years at the Senac Pernambuco College in the course of Technology in Fashion Design, in Fashion Production and Styling Postgraduation, in Ead Visual Arts Culture and Creation Postgraduation and was Assistant Professor of the University of Pernambuco (UPE) in the Bachelor of Business Administration with emphasis on Fashion Marketing in Caruaru. She was a professor at the Superior Course of Fashion and Styling at the Faculdade Maurício de Nassau, ESBJ, between 2007 and 2011. Since 2004, she has been working with the development of fashion collections for the clothing industry in Recife and Pólo do Agreste Pernambucano. She worked in advertising agencies and design offices (Ampla publicidade e propaganda, Sucesso propaganda e promoções, URT publicidade, ArtCor, etc.) by developing visual identities for various events and clients in addition to marketing and advertising campaigns. Since 2006, she has been working in NGOs (Centro Social Josué de Castro, Casa de Passagem, Casa Menina Mulher, Lar do Nenen, Aldeias Infantis, etc.) providing workshops, courses, and lectures for women's groups aimed at generating employment and income. Beside this, she develops graphic pieces for the fashion and interior design products created in these initiatives. She researches the following themes: fashion design, socio-environmental design, crafts, creative economy and globally integrated capitalism. Currently, she collaborates with the University of Pernambuco (UPE) in the Extension Program MODATECA FCAP, and participates in the PPG Design research group at UAM-SP: CUIDE-SE [o cuidado de si: conexões entre Design, processos de subjetivação e Arte contemporânea], coordinated by Dr. Cristiane Mesquita.

Dr. Gluma Saban is a senior lecturer at the Faculty of Business Management, Universiti Teknologi MARA, Samarahan Campus, Sarawak, Malaysia. His research area is in strategic marketing export, international and global marketing entrepreneurship, training and development motivation. Currently, Dr Gluma is the head of Quality Management Unit, Universiti Teknologi MARA, Samarahan Campus, Sarawak.

Samire Sahiti was born in 1992. She did MSc in economics and obtained the degree in 2015 from the University of Prishtina 'Hasan Prishtina.' Also, she was graduated in 2013 from the University of Prishina 'Hasan Prishtina.' Her research interest is in small and medium-sized enterprises (SME), and she has worked in this field from 2017 to 2018 at KIESA (Kosovo Investment Enterprises and Support Agency). She has attended some conferences, seminars, trainings, and study visits in some important fields such as business, migration, management, political academy, and finance. She currently works as a researcher at INPO (Initiative for Progress).

Roshima Said is an associate professor at the Universiti Teknologi MARA, Malaysia. Her research interest is in corporate governance, corporate social responsibility, corporate reporting, ethics and financial criminology. She has conducted several researches that were presented at international and local seminars, conferences, and colloquium, and published in proceedings and journals. She also has published papers, book, and book chapters, both nationally and internationally. She also acts as Editorial Advisory Board for *Social Responsibility Journal* published by Emerald Group Publishing Limited. She also acts as Members of Board in issues in *Social and Environmental Accounting* (Issues in SEA) and the Editorial Board Members for other several international reputable refereed journals.

Nayade Kennedy Sales dos Santos holds a degree in business administration from the Faculty of Management Sciences of Pernambuco, University of Pernambuco (FCAP/UPE/2016), a master's student in administration from the Federal University of Pernambuco in the research line Organization and Society (PROPAD/UFPE). She participated as collaborator in the development of the research project 'Residential Libraries, Schooling and Sustainable Local Development' in 2013, with an article published in the *Journal of the Science of Administration*. In 2015, she was a science initiation fellow at the FCAP/UPE in the research 'Knowledge Industries: Case Study,' with an article published in the *Perspectives in Information Science* Magazine. She was a Fellow of the Modateca Social Extension Project in 2015 and 2016, guided by Professor Ma. Izabele Sousa Barros, where she also worked on the research 'Modateca Social: Analyzing the Practice of Social Entrepreneurship.' As a collaborator, she participated in the Brazilian Team in the International Project 'Elaboration of a System of Synthetic Indicators for the Quality Measurement of Airports,' carried out by Universidad Autónoma de Madrid/9th Call for Inter-University Cooperation Projects UAM-Santander with Latin America in 2015 and 2016.

Lígia de Araújo Sarmento graduated in social communication with emphasis in advertising and propaganda by Faculdade Maurício de Nassau – Pernambuco – Brazil; approved monograph on gender violence in the Recife-PE-Brazil Carnival, an analysis of the awareness campaign on violence against women carried out by the Recife Women's Secretariat; acts as digital marketing analyst at CERS Online Courses; does volunteer work with children and the elderly people in the social project Contando Cantando História (CCH), in Recife – Brazil.

Nikolay Shterev is full-time professor in organization and management of marketing at the University of National and World Economy – Sofia (UNWE), Bulgaria. He is head of Industrial Business Department at the Business Faculty. He is chairman of Association of Professors of Industrial Economics and Management (APIUI). His main research fields are industrial growth, leadership and marketing leaders, start-ups and entrepreneurship, CSR in industry, industrial marketing management.

Eraldo Souza is a graduate in business administration and entrepreneur.

Mjellma Carabregu Vokshi, assistant Msc. Mjellma Carabregu Vokshi is working in Faculty of Economy in University of Pristina. She has bachelor in economics from University of Prishtina in 2006. She has done MSc in management from University of Prishtina in 2011, and her PhD in the field of Economics from University of Prishtina.

Editors' Biographies

Prof. Dr. Kıymet Tunca Çalıyurt CPA, CFE, graduated from the Faculty of Business Administration at Marmara University, Istanbul, Turkey. Her master's and PhD degrees are in Accounting and Finance Programme from the Social Graduate School, Marmara University. Her research interests are in accounting, auditing, fraud, social responsibility, corporate governance, finance, and business ethics, with a special interest in aviation management, NGOs, women rights in business. She has been a visiting researcher in Massachusetts University Amherst Business School. In 2009, she founded the International Women and Business Group to organize global and annual conferences.

Liliane Segura is a professor at the Mackenzie Presbyterian University, Brazil, and she teaches accounting, firm valuation, and corporate social responsibility. She is postdocorate in business from the University of Salamanca, Spain; Doctor in Finance from Mackenzie Presbyterian University, Brazil, and accounting degree and master in strategy from the University of São Paulo, Brazil.

Preface

We get new results from Global Entrepreneurship Report (GEM)[1] 2017–2018. This report helps us to make decision on how to develop women entrepreneurship in the future. Globally, the female entrepreneurs to male entrepreneurs ratio is up by 6%, comparing the same set of countries (48) which participated in the GEM survey in both 2016 and 2017. Almost 70% of the adult population across 52 economies believes that entrepreneurs are well regarded and enjoy high status within their societies. About 61% of adults in all three economic development groups[2] believe that entrepreneurs garner substantial media attention (up from 60% in 2016). Across the board, men are more likely to be entrepreneurs than women. In just three economies, women report equal or higher entrepreneurship rates than men:

- Ecuador 28.7%
- Vietnam 21.7%
- Brazil 19.8%[3]

The reason we publish this book series is to reveal the problems of women in business world, especially in underdeveloped and developing countries. Before starting to publish book series, we organized several conferences by International Women and Business Group (IWBG) since 2010 in different countries; 9th conference in India 2018, 8th conference in Canada 2017, 7th Malaysia conference in 2016, 6th Brazil conference in 2015, 5th Serbia conference in 2014, 4th Bulgaria conference in 2013, 3th Bosnia and Herzegovina conference in 2012, 2th Turkey conference in 2011, and 1st Macedonia conference in 2011.

IWBG was established by Prof. Kiymet Caliyurt from Trakya University and Prof. Jovanka Biljan from St. Kliment Ohridski University, Macedonia, in 2010. IWBG had a big step in 2014, and started to publish book series titled *Women And Sustainability In Business* by Gower Publishing in United Kingdom. We have received very good critiques in the first two of our series.

Empowering women to participate fully in economic life across all sectors and throughout all levels of economic activity is essential to:

- Build strong economies;
- Establish more stable and just societies;

- Achieve internationally agreed goals for development, sustainability, and human rights;
- Improve quality of life for women, men, families, and communities; and
- Propel businesses' operations and goals (UN).

Many academicians believe that there is huge potential in highly educated, professional. and talented women that is still unused or it is irrationally used by employing highly educated women in less demanded positions. It is obvious that the educational component of women is not the cause of their inequality when gaining leading positions, so it is necessary to conduct additional research and to find the real reasons which prevent women from overcoming this gap (Vinnicombe, 2015, 3[4]).[5]

After a very successful conference in National Law University in New Delhi, I will meet with more than 50 academicians around the word and listen to excellent researches in 10th conference in Bergen, Norway. We hope to see you there...

Prof. Dr. Kıymet Tunca Çalıyurt
Book Series Editor

Notes

1 Babson College is a founding institution and sponsor of the Global Entrepreneurship Monitor (GEM). Located in Wellesley, Massachusetts, USA, Babson is recognized internationally as a leader in entrepreneurial management education. U.S. News and World Report have ranked Babson #1 in entrepreneurship education for 21 consecutive years. The 2017 Global Entrepreneurship Monitor (GEM) report is the 19th consecutive global report that the GEM consortium has published as part of its worldwide research project since it was founded in 1997 by academics from Babson College and the London Business School. GEM provides a primary data based measurement and assessment tools of all forms of entrepreneurship and other socio-economic renewal derivatives, culminating in policy decisions and relevant recommendations for participating countries.

2 Adapted from the World Economic Forum (WEF) Economies in transition from factor to efficiency-driven have been grouped with the factor-driven economies, while those in transition from efficiency, to innovation-driven have been included in the efficiency-driven category.

3 Global Entrepreneurship Monitor, rev-gem-2017-2018-global-report-revised-1527266790-1548584425-1549359513.pdf, Accessed on May 27th, 2019.

4 Vinnicombe S., Doldor, E., Sealy, R., Pryce, P., Turner, C. (2015) The Female FTSE Board Report 2015: Putting the UK Progress into a Global Perspective. Cranfield International Centre For Women Leaders, UK.

5 6th International Women and Business Conference, São Paulo – Brazil 21 to 23 September, 2015, www.mackenzie.br/fileadmin/user_upload/Proceedings Abstract_book.pdf, Special Chapter Special Article: Women In Business And Sustainable Business, p. 28.

Acknowledgments

I would like to thank members of **International Women and Business Group** (**IWBG**) and conference series presidents, Prof. Dr. Lilian Segura from Brazil, Prof. Dr. Harpreet Kaur from India, and Prof. Dr. Nauman Farooqi from Canada for their support and hospitality.

INTERNATIONAL WOMEN AND BUSINESS GROUP

The role of academician in women entrepreneurship

Liliane Segura and Kıymet Tunca Çalıyurt

The role of academician in "women entrepreneurship" is to search and publish trending and necessary topics to determine, dig, and share with the public. Academicians should focus on current, beneficial issues to research and publish instead of oldfashion, accustomed, repeated issues in women entrepreneurship. The results of the research carried out by academicians are used by many environment. This is more important for women's entrepreneurship. "There is an economic crisis because women is working." "Let women work part time." We live in a world called. In order to be effective and useful in decisions to be taken by the legislators, parliamentarians, and senior executives, academicians should benefit from current reports. This is the primary task of the "women's research centers" established in universities. Cultural, social, technological, and legal developments on women entrepreneurship should be determined by academics and presented to the public and business world through research.

The number of women-owned businesses increased nearly 3,000% since 1972 according to the "2018 State of Women-Owned Businesses Report" commissioned by American Express. Not only that but between 2017 and 2018 women started an average of 1,821 new businesses per day in the U.S. With women now making up a whopping 40% of new entrepreneurs, it's clear that more women are turning to entrepreneurship than ever before (Castrillon, 2019). This development is an exciting research subject for academicians. Entrepreneurship is a common theme throughout the academic debate these days.

Entrepreneurship is the topic of global debate because of not only its contribution to the development and economic growth (Schumpeter, 1934), but also its new business development methods and innovative production processes. However, the debate about entrepreneurship cannot be complete without a debate on the role of women in companies' management and as an entrepreneurial leader.

As a recent development, International Labour Organization (ILO) organized a research. In 2014, brief reviewed 6 meta-evaluations and 23 rigorous impact evaluations of Women Entrepreneurship Development (WED) interventions in terms of outcomes for women-owned business startup and survival; business knowledge and practices; business growth (i.e. revenues, profits, number of employees); and women's agency, or decision-making capacity within their business or household. This review examines those outcomes, as well as other interventions such as mentoring, peer groups/networks, and enabling environment factors within the evidence published in the years since the last brief (i.e. from 2014 to 2017). To be easily usable for practitioners and donors designing WED programmes, findings are laid out by type of intervention and resulting impacts on women-owned enterprises and women's incomes. Figure I.1 summarizes the areas of intervention, and specific strategies within those, that have been shown to work for WED.

From the figure, academicians who studies on women entrepreneurship should focus following current issues for their researches.

- Mentorship and support networks: appear to work best in the short-term. Mentoring following a training may help to increase business performance in the short-term but that the impacts are not sustained over time.

Figure I.1 Intervention areas and associated strategies that have worked for WED.

- Business training: most effective in combination with access to finance.
- Access to finance: products that help women "label" money for specific business uses.
- Enabling environmental factors: supporting improvements in; electrification, access to childcare, security of land rights.
- Bundled services: It is not uncommon for WED interventions to combine several services or intervention strategies; in recent years, some programs have tried to build a "package" of several (usually three to five distinct but related) services that address different challenges women face in starting and growing a business. The importance of a comprehensive "suite" of services is reinforced by studies from agriculture that find that interventions tackling only one dimension of the challenges that female farmers face – whether it be improved inputs (Beaman et al., 2013; Karamba & Winters, 2014), better market information through mobile phone platforms (Aker & Ksoll, 2016; Van Campenhout, 2013), or land rights (Mendola & Sitomwe, 2015) – are not sufficient on their own to sustainably improve women's incomes

The International Women and Business Group started working on this debate in 2009. Several conferences have been held since the group was founded. This book has been elaborated using papers presented in the 6th International Women and Business Conference held in São Paulo, Brazil, in 2015; from 7th International Women and Business Conference held in Canada in 2016; from 8th International Women and Business Conference held in Malaysia in 2017; and from 9th International Women and Business Conference held in India in 2018.

In this book, we have published some of the papers presented at these conferences, as well as others discussed by the International Women and Business Group at other conferences around the world. The debates that take place in the conferences are extensive, outlining the leading research in the world so that the most important topics can be brought to all conferences.

However, there is still a rather broad debate about the development of and opportunities for women entrepreneurs (Leitch, Welter, & Henry, 2018). Over the last few years, despite tremendous and significant developments in relation to the role of women in companies and their characteristics that can help to develop the business, significant differentials were not obtained in relation to women's access to credit, public policies that were formed to develop women's entrepreneurship, and the difficulties that exist in accessing entrepreneurial finance (Leitch et al., 2018).

According to Naguib and Jamali (2015), research shows that several variables affect female entrepreneurship such as personality traits, age, education, motivations, marital status, business characteristics, type of activities, development of government policies, financial resources, and sociocultural factors.

The most emergent themes in literature, to date, according to Leitch et al. (2018), continue to suggest that women-run startups are smaller than that of men's, less capitalized, and less likely to get debts. Also, according to Leitch et al. (2018), these issues are more exacerbated for women in less number and in developing countries, as an earlier study by Blanchard, Zhao, and Yinger (2008) also proved.

According to Segura, Formigoni, David, and Abreu (2016), the presence of women on the board of a firm has already been investigated in accounting and financial literature. Also, the authors affirm that it is known from some studies that gender diversity can make an excellent contribution toward performance, transparency, and ethics, and thereby increase the value of a firm's shares.

At the same time, there is also a significant movement in Europe and the United States regarding the participation of women in business decisions. Large companies in several European countries are already required to have 30% of women on the board. In Norway, the requirement is 40% of seats. In Brazil, there is a similar discussion, and in the public administration, a bill has been passed to raise the quotas of women in management positions to 30%. These measures by governments have changed the picture of the board of large corporations and the public sector. We will study if these measures can help to improve the indices of entrepreneurship around the world.

Part I of the book, 'Regulations and Institutions on Women Entrepreneurship and Economy in the World' includes articles by Roshima Said, titled 'Community Engagement Activities as Relationship Marketing Practices: the Sarawak Women Entrepreneurs Context,' and also a Kosovo case study by authors Kastrati Artë and Samiri Sahiti, titled 'Women In Business and Management: Case Study Of Kosovo.' Both provide insights into how entrepreneurs relate to each other in the community.

Part II of this book discusses the theme of women entrepreneurship: country cases, with articles by Brazilian authors Izabele Barros, Ana Rita Valverde Peroba, Maria do Livramento Aguiar, and Nayade Kennedy Sales dos Santos, titled 'Modateca Social FCAP: Apprehending Entrepreneurship,' which brings to light a vision of feminist entrepreneurship in northeastern Brazil. Next we have the article by Dafina Abdullahu, titled 'Challenges Faced By Female Entrepreneurs,' another article by Diana Kopeva, Nikolay Shterev, Ekrem Gjokaj, and Kaplan Halimi, titled 'Women's Entrepreneurship – Source For Livelihood Opportunities in Rural Areas of Kosovo and in Bulgaria,' yet another article by Ibsen Mateus Bittencourt, Jade Demettino, Caio Venâncio de Araújo, Eraldo Souza, and João Batista, titled 'Female Entrepreneurs: an analysis of the entrepreneurial profile of female university students at the Federal University of Alagoas' – UFAL. From these articles, it is possible to understand diverse entrepreneurial points of view in rural areas and in various different countries.

Part III of the book is dedicated to the 'Learning and Choosing Type of Entrepreneurship,' with articles by Ibsen Mateus Bittencourt, Jade Demettino, Caio Venâncio de Araújo, Eraldo Souza, and João Batista, titled 'Female Entrepreneurs: an analysis of the entrepreneurial profile of female universe,' followed by another article by Ibsen Mateus Bittencourt, Angelo Antônio Martins, Nilson Leão, Jade Demettino, and Caio Venâncio de Araújo, titled 'Entrepreneurial Women in the Generation of High-Impact Business in the State of Alagoas,' and the work of Mary Rosane Ceroni, Berenice Carpigiani, Maria Elisa Pereira Lopes, and Ana Maria Porto Castanheira, titled 'Some Thoughts on Leadership and Entrepreneurial Education of Brazilian Women,' focused on entrepreneurial education in Brazil. In this part of the book we also can read chapter titled "Kosovar Women's Role in Development of Local Business" by Hamdi Hoti, Bekim Berisha. Next chapter' authors Luljeta Aliu, But Dedaj, Mjellma Carabregu Vokshi are from Kosovo give details from Kosovo about women in higher education with a chapter titled "Gender Inequality in Higher Education And Employment in Developing Countries: Evidence From Kosovo". The last chapter in Part III is from Brasil and title of the chapter is "The Role Of Women in Construction of Sustainable And Social Entrepreneurship" written by Micilvânia Pereira de Araújo, Micilane Pereira de Araújo, Lígia de Araújo Sarmento, Emanuel Leite.

As editors, we hope to receive critics and comments from our audience.

References

Aker, J. C., & Ksoll, C. (2016). Can mobile phones improve agricultural outcomes? Evidence from a randomized experiment in Niger. *Food Policy, 60*, 44–51.

Beaman, L., Karlan, D., Thuysbaert, B., & Udry, C. (2013). Profitability of fertilizer: Experimental evidence from female rice farmers in Mali. *The American Economic Review, 103*(3), 381–386.

Blanchard, L., Zhao, B. J., & Yinger. (2008). Do lenders discriminate against minority and woman entrepreneurs? *Journal of Urban Economics, 63*(2), 467–497.

Castrillon, C. (2019). Why more women are turning to entrepreneurship. https://www.forbes.com/sites/carolinecastrillon/2019/02/04/why-more-women-are-turning-to-entrepreneurship/#42a4218a542a. Accessed on Sep 12th, 2019

Karamba, W. R., & Winters, P. C. (2015). Gender and agricultural productivity: Implications of the farm input subsidy program in Malawi. *Agricultural Economics, 46*(3), 357–374.

Leitch, C., Welter, F., & Henry, C. (2018). Women entrepreneurs' financing revisited: Taking stock and looking forward: New perspectives on women entrepreneurs and finance (Special Issue). *Venture Capital, 20*(2), 103–114. doi:10.1080/13691066.2018.1418624

Mendola, M., & Simtowe, F. (2015). The welfare impact of land redistribution: Evidence from a quasi-experimental initiative in Malawi. *World Development, 72*, 53–69.

Naguib, R., & Jamali, D. (2015). Female entrepreneurship in the UAE: A multi-level integrative lens. *Gender in Management, 30*(2), 135–161. doi:10.1108/GM-12-2013-0142

Schumpeter, J. A. (1934). *The Theory of Economic Development.* Cambridge, MA: Harvard University Press.

Segura, L., Formigoni, H., David, F., & Abreu, R. (2016). The influence of women on earnings management: Public companies in Brazil. *Women and Sustainability in Business: A Global Perspective.* doi:10.4324/9781315546834.

Van Campenhout, B. (2013). *Is There an App for That? The Impact of Community Knowledge Workers in Uganda.* IFPRI Discussion Paper 01316. Available at SSRN: https://ssrn.com/abstract=2405695.

Part I

Regulations and institutions on women entrepreneurship and economy in the world

1 Community engagement activities as relationship marketing practices

The Sarawak women entrepreneurs context

Carolina Sandra Giang, Gluma Saban, Corina Joseph and Roshima Said

Introduction

Small and medium enterprises (SMEs) are conceded as playing an important role in most economies of the world. Even though SME setups are small, they are, however, cognizant as one of the main contributors to economic growth. They create jobs, thereby reducing unemployment, boosting the economy through revenue generation, alleviating poverty through business opportunities, and providing communities such as women to acquire wealth (Kelly, Brush, Greene, & Litovsky, 2010). Entrepreneurship is an important field as it contributes to a nation's economy through various business ventures. Similarly, it is also important to women because owning a business allows them to improve work-life balance, be self-sufficient, and be able to have the autonomy to manage their lives and the livelihood of their families (Huq, 2012; Adema, 2014).

Community engagement, which involves networking and working with the community has been a standard feature for women who play multiple roles, as a nurturer of family and, at the same time, as owners, managers, and members of the community (Buttner & Moore, 1997; Ahl, 2006). According to Blomback and Wigren-Kristoferson (2014), entrepreneurs often see themselves as being accountable and look upon themselves to engage with the community. Economic activities of firms tend to be influenced by business networks, and encounters with social organization and institutions are unavoidable (Johannisson & Monsted, 1997).

However, previous literature on community engagement focused on addressing health problems or issues the communities face (Minkler & Wallerstein, 2003; Ahmed & Palermo, 2010; Silberg, Cook, Drescher, McCloskey, Weaver, & Ziegahn, 2011). Also, two streams of studies that have similar characteristics as that of community engagement are commonly known as corporate social responsibilities (CSR), which are conducted from the perspective of large organizations (Gupta, Sukhmani, & Kalra, 2012; Agrawal & Sahasranamam, 2016), and social entrepreneurship (Austin, 2000; Austin, Stevenson, & Wei-Skillern, 2006; Crisan & Borza, 2010), which focus on community works from the perspective of the non-governmental or not-for-profit organization. Although research on community engagement is generally found in businesses, limited studies were conducted about how women entrepreneurs (WEs) can utilize community engagement as a relationship marketing (RM) tool (Arnold, Briggs, Landry, & Suter, 2013). In addition, more studies tend to adopt quantitative method when investigating community engagement and the marketplace (Briggs, Yang, Yong Harmon-Kizer, & Arnold, 2016).

This study attempts to expand research on WEs from the perspective of WEs who are constructing their lives and their businesses by leveraging their innate feminine quality, as argued by Ahl (2006). Since there is a dearth of research on how WEs utilize community engagement as a RM tool to self-brand and publicise their products and services, this study contributes to how women incorporate their innate feminine ability into their business.

Literature review

Buttner and Moore (1997) defined 'Female or Women Entrepreneur' as woman that initiates a business, operates and manages the overall business owning at least 50% of the firm, and has been operating as a business owner for at least a year. WEs through their feminine nature almost always regard their enterprise as comprising one part of a broader structure which includes family, community, and friends. Women's main concern has always been about juggling responsibility between work and family (Buttner & Moore, 1997; Kargwell, 2012), and being an entrepreneur provides the flexibility to balance family life and career.

The personal traits of women are commonly highlighted as being particularly good at developing interpersonal relationships (Aida, 2008), have often achieved results by adopting the people-oriented approach, and have a preference for working as a team rather than as an individual (Alam, Jani, & Omar, 2011). Inherently, WEs prefer relationships that are inclusive, reciprocal, collaborative, and socially related. These social behaviors are evident through their networking activities – a typical gender-related behavior – and these activities, in turn, motivate them to be entrepreneurially ambitious (Hampton, Cooper, & McGowan, 2009). Interpersonal skills are crucial because relationships are important for WEs to succeed (Brush, 1992; Gundry & Welsch, 2001). WEs are inclined to grow their businesses using their strong interpersonal skills to achieve personal goals (Manolova, Brush, Edelman, & Shaver, 2012).

Relationship marketing orientation

Gronroos (1994) described 'relationship marketing,' or RM, as a reciprocal beneficial concept aimed at producing significant long-term relationships with customers. McKenna (1991) iterated that the customers are important, and therefore they must be included by involving them. Meanwhile,

Sheth and Parvatiyar (1995) and Parvatiyar and Sheth (1999) described RM as a continuous process of creating mutual business relationships, focusing on the intention to interact closely with customers, suppliers, and other partners within the marketing activities of the firm. However, as explained by Harker and Egan (2006), the definition by Gronroos (1994) is more appropriate as it includes the underlying conceptualizations of RM which is comprehensive. Moreover, it encompasses the overall definition of RM as it identifies and brings into existence the relationships with customers and stakeholders profitably and meets the company's objectives through mutual exchange and fulfillment of promises. Additionally, RM is further defined as a composition of activities to attract, maintain, and enhance customer relationships (Berry & Parasuraman, 1993). However, Cardwell (1994) explained RM as developing closeness to the customer, understanding his needs and wants, building a relationship, and developing customer dedication, which are all essential for the survival of the firm (Cardwell, 1994).

Chaston (1997) suggested that relationships that exist in marketing are fundamentally important for entrepreneurial practice, while Hill and Wright (2000) iterated that personal interactions and building of relationships play an influential part in SMEs. In addition, Carson, Cromie, McGowan, and Hill (1995) stated that the owner-managers are found not to define 4Ps Marketing Mix, but are shown to practice and adopt more of interactive marketing.

Community engagement

CSR is closely related to corporate sustainability, corporate citizenship, and socially responsible behavior that define ethical business (Perrini, 2006; Dillard & Murray, 2013). CSR is further described as charitable activities that a firm implements as mandatory within their business operation (Blowfield & Murray, 2008; Arya & Zhang, 2009; Sheth & Babiak, 2010). Moreover, involvement in CSR activities gives a firm an advantage in that it provides outcomes such as enhancement of the business' reputation and brand image (Ibe, Min, Ling, & Yii, 2015).

Findings by Bevan and Yung (2014) suggested that small to medium-sized enterprises (SMEs) practice a rather informal type of CSR. In various literature related to CSR, the term CSR encompasses social behaviors and practices (Carroll, 1999), green practices (Mehran & Azlan, 2013), corporate citizenship (Mehtap & Kokalan, 2013), corporate responsibility (Wood, 1991), social opportunity (Sajjad & Eweje, 2014), responsible business practices (Southwell, 2004; Arslan & Zaman, 2014), corporate social entrepreneurial activities (Agrawal & Sahasranamam, 2016), and community engagement (Silberg, Cook, Drescher, McCloskey, Weaver, & Ziegahn, 2011). In this context, this article describes CSR as community engagement through the involvement and participation in addressing specific issues within a community (Silberg, Cook, Drescher, McCloskey, Weaver, &

Ziegahn, 2011). The key processes of community engagement focus on building relationships and coalitions, fostering cooperation and collaboration, and using local organizational and interpersonal networks. Community engagement is about decision-making, relationship development, and capacity building (Butteriss, 2016). Community engagement prioritizes fostering and enhancement of trust as a critical element in the long-term, for sustainable engagement and effective governance.

From the perspective of marketing, community engagement is measured in terms of the goodwill of a firm. It relates to the state of the firm's relationship with the community and the level of relationship congeniality between the firm and its community or stakeholders which could result in social upliftment and financial benefits to firms, especially SMEs (Gupta, Sukhmani, & Kalra, 2012). From the social perspective, community engagement is a social partnership, in which the firms are committed to working with the public or non-profit organizations (Waddock, 1988). Further, the outcome of community engagement practices of firms encourages them to make an effort to improve their relationships with the community by meaningful and practical ways such as improved work practices, culture, governance, and transparency, as well as taking the responsibility to assist the community to improve the quality of lives (Butteriss, 2016).

According to Blomback and Wigren-Kristoferson (2014), community engagement activities are conducted in the name of the firm, but initiated by individual as well as business-oriented concerns. Community engagement is the development of economic relationships and different types of social relationships where an exchange is assumed to occur when each party controls goods, commodity, and condition, which are valued by both groups (Crisan, 2013). As such, community engagement is relevant to the social exchange theory, where the relationship itself becomes the main influential factor and the rewards obtained may potentially result from other relationships. According to this theory, all relationships exist because they help in exchange of gains and rewards (Nath, 2010). Firms involved in collaboration or partnership for social purposes (donations, sponsorships, and fundraising) deal with profit maximization constraints, but at the same time are strategically altruistic in dispersing funds (Gan, 2006). With reference to collaborations and partnership, it must be emphasized that the strength of this relation relies on the benefits obtained by both parties (Crisan, 2013). This concept relates to the understanding of social capital which refers to the interaction among people through social networks that are built based on reciprocity, trust, sharing information, and cooperation (Putnam, 2000; Audretsch & Keilbach, 2004; Timberlake, 2005). Crisan posits that for a long-term relationship, the benefits for both parties (entrepreneur and the community involved) must be mutual and there must be a healthy business model to enable self-sustainable. As such, SMEs' role needs to be acknowledged for social and sustainability development of a community.

In general, studies on CSR were scanty for SMEs compared to large firms (Morsing & Perrini, 2009). In addition, the literature review revealed the concept of CSR or community engagement in the context of RM has yet to attract the attention of many academics. Consequently, very few studies have been conducted on community engagement from the perspective of WEs and on its adoption as a marketing tool. Most of the previous studies demonstrated their comparative nature which generalized CSR practices (Sajjad & Eweje, 2014), exploring the SMEs' perception of the concept of CSR (Herwina & Zarith, 2012; Mehran & Azlan, 2013), with limited studies conducted on community engagement as a RM tool used by WEs. Hence, the current research aims to build an understanding of community engagement practices used as RM tool. Therefore, the research question for this paper is to explore how WEs use community engagement as a RM tool.

Research methodology

This study attempts to explore the adoption of community engagement concept as an integral part of RM practices by WEs. According to Creswell (2013), the phenomenological research's main aim is to study the common meaning of lived experiences of different participants in the study of a concept or phenomenon. It occurs within the natural settings where entrepreneurs operate, and in the multifaceted, subjective experiences of individual WEs (Lee, Mitchell, & Sabliynski, 1999). The study of phenomenological experiences provide rich resources of 'life-worlds' and intensely personal perspectives (Moustakas, 1994), especially as there is limited available literature on WEs in Sarawak. Inductive perspective is adopted to ensure the accuracy of the description of the phenomenon, reducing the likelihood of preconceived framework and allowing the researcher to focus on the trueness of the subject involved. As such, the study uses a qualitative phenomenology method, and therefore takes an epistemological interpretive approach, seeking to explain the phenomenon from the perspective of the specific gender –the WEs.

The researchers conducted 22 interviews spread over a period of four months, from the month of November 2015 until February 2016. Before conducting the interviews, the participants were informed to focus on their reflection of the meaning of RM and how community engagement was embedded into their business activities. The study adopted Moustakas' (1994) method of bracketing or epoche while collecting data by holding back any preconceived knowledge or personal opinions about the context of the study. This was conducted by letting the participants narrate their stories, with little interference or interruption by the researchers.

This study employed Seidman's (1991) 'phenomenological based interviewing' to gather the data (p. 9). The interviews were conducted in English, and each participant was adviced that they could withdraw from the study at any time they wanted. Some of the participants responded in English mixed with the local dialect. Permission was requested to record the conversation. The interviews lasted between 45 and 90 minutes, and were then transcribed verbatim and saved into Microsoft Word documents for safe-keeping. Respondent validation as stipulated by Bryman (1988), or 'member checks' as mentioned by Lincoln and Guba (1985), cited in Maxwell (2005), was conducted. It was a necessary process to avoid misinterpretation of the actual meaning delivered by the participants. Based on the 'validity check' of the participants, some minor modifications were made to ensure the essence of the interview was maintained. Also, the validity check allowed the researchers to delete the sensitive responses from the transcripts upon the request of the interviewees. Each participant was given a pseudo name (for example, WE1 to WE22) as identification to ensure complete secrecy and confidentiality.

The data coding process uses Atlas.ti7 program for creating primary documents from the transcripts. According to Seidel (1998), three components were involved, noticing, collecting, and thinking about the data, as basic elements common to data analysis. Before attempting to code, the researchers spent time reading the transcription, 'digesting and reflecting' on the data collected (Clarke, 2005, p. 84), which then moved to a phase of categorizing the data into meaningful analytical units.

Results and discussions

Several themes emerged from the data based on the revelation of the experiences of the WEs practicing community engagement as a RM tool. In addition, the descriptions of the 22 participants' personality extracted from the textual transcripts showed some interesting findings. The findings demonstrate that the participants came from various backgrounds, work experiences, and business fields, with some running a second business. At the time of the study, the data revealed that the participants' age ranged from 31 to 63 years, and they were involved in the overall operation of the business for at least 3 to 26 years. Besides managing the business, the participants juggled with multiple responsibilities, as wife, parent, nurturer, and carer for their dependents and loved ones. As part of their daily business routine, the participants interacted directly and indirectly with those around them such as employees, customers, competitors, suppliers, government agencies, and politicians. Through regular interactions, the participants revealed their rich experiences as WEs, which revealed a meaningful phenomenon of community engagement and marketing practices.

Appendix 1 shows a comprehensive description of the demographic profile of the WEs in this study.

In all, 54.4% (12) of the participants were found to be aged 50 or more. A total of 77% of the participants were married, 14% were single, 4.5% or 1 participant was divorced and a was single mother, and 4.5% or one participant was widowed. In terms of the level of education, the findings further revealed that 27.3% (six) of the WEs were postgraduates, 31.8% (seven) had tertiary education, and 40.9% (nine) of the participants had completed their secondary school or high school education.

In this study, the participants described their marketing activities as mainly community engagement. The participants optimized their community activities effort not only as an approach to contribute toward the community but also as a marketing tool to publicize their firms and products. Hence, as revealed by their stories, the business activities were seen as being embedded within their community works, and eventually created 'self-branding' in their own right. The community engagement concept used in RM by the participants is described in the following ways.

Provide free-of-charge (FOC) lecture

Eight or 36.4% of the participants accepted invitations to provide lectures free of charge to organizations or non-governmental organizations. Moreover, the participants were willing to share their personal and business network with those involved in business, an example practiced by WEs. The FOC lectures thus provided them with the opportunity to publicize their business to a larger audience. In addition, they also used the event to interact with the attendees and to know them closely.

> Three months ago, someone told me to give a talk as well. Share with the female program, about personal grooming, clothes and everything.
>
> (W22)

> I have been called by various universities locally to give talks to the students. I never say no. That's what I said, whoever called you to ask such favour, never expect any financial returns.
>
> (W5)

> So we give talks like...a corporate talk, free talks to teach the audience on how to use perfumes for example. That in itself helped to get our names out there. It takes a lot of late work but being in a locality like ours...it's good because we can reach out to quite a lot of people.
>
> (W8)

FOC lecture presentation by the participants was a good initiative and serves as a compensation for the lack of tangible resources to market the business of the WEs. Not only were the WEs able to utilize FOC lectures as their promotional tool, but these lectures also provided them with an efficient and effective approach to give back to the society in terms of their time and expertise. Moreover, for WEs, FOC lectures worked to promote business, initiate a relational or social exchange activity with the community, and build trust and be part of the community (Cook & Emerson, 1978).

Sharing of entrepreneurial experiences and business knowledge

Nine or 40.9% of the participants recognized that information and knowledge should be shared with others. According to WE12, sharing experiences of her journey in developing her business would provide tips and guidance to those who had the intention to start up a business. Consequently, they might be able to avoid some of the pitfalls of business ventures which the participants experienced.

> I feel that I should help a lot of people because I know how it feels. Therefore, I want to share my success with others, guide others and also to teach others. That is for me so that others can feel what I feel too. That is the satisfaction that I will gain by helping others so that they can be successful.
>
> (W12)

Similarly, WE16 concurred that knowledge should always be shared and one should avoid being calculative and selfish by keeping it to oneself. She explained that if the knowledge that had been earned, when taken to the grave, becomes useless. Therefore, by sharing knowledge with others, especially with clients, she would be appreciated even after she was gone.

> I share…what I know. I mean in business. What I know I share with you all. I don't keep. I will be honest with them (customers). I say "Anything wrong with me, you will think of me…because who you are, what you are today." Also, it's no point to keep this knowledge to myself and bring it with me to the grave…At least if I shared all the knowledge with my customers, at least they know that I have shared with them. That's how I see thing…
>
> (W16)

The concept of sharing in the context of the aforementioned findings could be illustrated in two ways. Firstly, and based on the description by WE12, sharing of business experiences was to create an awareness of the challenges faced by women in operating their business. She felt it was important to share the experiences with potential WEs to avoid major pitfalls. Secondly, sharing was illustrated by WE16 as a collaborative relationship with customers for the purpose of providing knowledge about the products and services that the customers purchased (Sheth, Parvatiyar, & Sinha, 2015).

Sponsorships

Only one participant utilized sponsorship as part of an engagement with the community or as a corporate social responsibility (CSR) effort with the community. She had chosen sponsorships through giving donations due to time constraint and her limitations and the inability to be involved and participate directly in community works. She believed that if a person wanted to be involved in any NGO activity, the person needs to be doing it full-time and should not be done half-heartedly. As shared by participant WE15,

> I try to avoid joining associations, like those uh…women entrepreneurs all this. Because I find that I'm too busy, you know. My time is really so limited, so I try not to join all these NGOs. I used to be invited to join, but then when I think over, I can't. Because joining all this, you have to be really um…devoted. No half-half. You need time, you need your commitment… Most of these associations, they get their fund from the government so indirectly I contribute in terms of money wise, we sponsor. I have to say, we don't have the time, but we contribute in kind.
>
> (W15)

According to participants WE8 and WE16, sponsorships were interpreted as working together with associations by conducting programs, such as cancer awareness programs, beauty pageant competitions, and subsidizing training programs for youth.

> So, because I believe in giving back to the society…for example… we work on cancer awareness program. We are actually sponsoring programs to create an awareness for children suffering from cancer. Things like that…I felt it does impact the business as well because you are getting yourself out there and like…my involvement with like the pageant and all that and how we actually sponsor you know all these…programs that we…you know…that we can get ourselves into.
>
> (W8)

> I have trained maybe thousands and thousands of girls and boys. They pay part and my company subsidise some. To help these young girls, for them to get a job in the supermarket. A lot of them. Because the certificate is very important for them. I heard from people that a lot of training centres said that you have to learn this four, Windows, Excel and PowerPoint, months and months. For me no. Two months enough. Once you learn all these, it will stick to you forever, that's what I tell them.
>
> (W16)

These findings suggest that WEs in this study created social and economic value through various social entrepreneurial activities. Apart from assisting in promoting the firms, these social entrepreneurial activities provided the WEs with explicit and implicit benefits in managing the prevailing social issues within the community. Explicit benefits include the creation of new market opportunities and new channels of revenues through their social works, while implicit benefits include political and social legitimacy, trust, goodwill, and new collaborations (Agrawal & Sahasranamam, 2016).

Fundraising and partnership activities

With regards to time and resources, 13.6% (three) of the participants took advantage of their core business expertise by providing services to assist NGOs in raising funds either by charging a minimum fee or by working together with the NGOs on a profit-sharing basis.

> It Is like this, for example, if they have a program on...right...we would have a certain time allocated, for examples...the sales for this period will take a certain percentage of the profit, and you would actually put upfront...ok...certain percentage of these sales will go to this program.
>
> (W8)

> I'm holding a fund-raising program with our ethnic NGO, and as a businesswoman also, I'm also taking the opportunity to do my business, and I'm giving them a 10% of the profit. That also goes for the members. You can't do it without them and, also, you can't do it on your own. It's equal
>
> (W22)

WE22 reiterated that, even though she had been in business for 26 years, there were areas that she needed support, especially in promotional activities in which she lacked the necessary expertise. Therefore, it was only wise to work with those who could assist her in areas in which she had no knowledge or skills. She further mentioned that this was also an opportunity for her to do her part to raise funds for the community.

Meanwhile, participant WE1, who only had four years of business experience, acknowledged the lack of relevant resources, network, and experience, but worked with NGOs by rendering her event management services as her way to contribute to the community. On the other hand, the NGO recognized she was new in the business and that this would provide her the opportunity to publicize her business.

> ...we took part or participate in the community like...there is this one NGO that conducted this SPM (Public Exam) workshop, or they called it a clinic...so we took part as a company by assisting them. We will... you know...being an association we will charge minimal...
>
> (W1)

Overall, the participants revealed that social work is their passion despite the challenges they face to create a better place for the community. They admitted it is difficult work, but, by the end of the day, they found peace in their ability to help others who were less fortunate. They accepted feeling good that they could give back to the community. As demonstrated in this study, the WEs viewed the business not only for its ability to manage their lives and the flexibility it provided in juggling their family and business career, but also for allowing them to help others whom they considered as less fortunate. The majority of the participants stated that giving back to the community is one of the most satisfying and motivating factor to further succeed in their business. The findings agree with a study conducted by Wang and Morrell (2015), where the majority of their participants shared similar sentiments.

Moreover, getting involved with the community positively impacted the personal image of the WEs, described as self-branding. This finding supports a study conducted by Esmaeilpour and Barjoei (2016). Therefore, we can conclude that WEs' engagement in community could result in their positive image in the minds of customers, increasing their belief toward the products and services offered by them.

Conclusions

This paper aims to explore the use of community engagement concept in RM practices by WEs. Through the act of giving FOC talks, knowledge sharing, sponsorship, and partnership activities, WEs engage with the community. Overall, the study revealed that the participants were passionate in social works despite facing numerous challenges, so as to create a better place for the community. Several positive values were a result of using community engagement as the RM tool. Firstly, it provided an intangible value, such as social capital and trust obtained from the community and government agencies. Secondly, it enhanced their self-branding, which helped create a positive image of their firms. Finally, community engagement provides the opportunity to be exposed to potential customers and expand their customer base, resulting in financial gains.

The findings of this study demonstrated that community engagement is a suitable tool for the implementation of RM concept. Moreover, community engagement is also a tool to bridge the resource gap experienced by most WEs. Their 'innate feminine' ability in developing a relationship with the community was the most priced resources available to WEs. As a result, community engagements helped in the enhancement of their self-branding, building trust, and bonding and bridging relationships with the community, as reflected in their business. Moreover, the frequent connections that they had with members of the community helped built their social capital in terms of being better informed about and sympathetic to the issues in their community, which, in turn, motivated them improve policy efforts to advance not only women's status, but also that of the community. Moreover, the findings could provide a better understanding of community engagement or CSR initiatives implemented by SME that could be linked to sustainable development.

This study is expected to provide an in-depth understanding of the practices of community engagement as RM tool. This research achieved its objective to fill the gap in the literature about practical tools used in implementing RM activities among WEs, within the field of SMEs. The whole society could benefit from collaboration with WEs, more systematically, with the objective to improve the lives of the people in the community. From the perspective of the policy-makers, this study could assist in the designing of a more focused developmental program, specifically for WEs.

The main limitation of the study is related to sample size and distribution. A sample of 22 WEs of SMEs could not be generalized to the whole Malaysian SMEs. Besides, the majority of the participating SMEs were based in Sarawak in East Malaysia, which limits the geographical distribution of the samples. In the context of future academic research, this paper may provide a basis for further investigation on community engagement as a RM tool for SMEs, using quantitative method.

References

Adema, W. (2014). A Better Work-Life Balance for Both Fathers and Mothers. In *Family Futures* Jacqui Griffiths (Ed.), Leicester: Tudor Rose., p. 59. http://digital.tudor-rose.co.uk/family-futures/files/assets/common/downloads/publication.pdf (Accessed on March 6, 2019).

Agrawal, A., & Sahasranamam, S. (2016). Corporate Social Entrepreneurship in India. *South Asian Journal of Global Business Research*, Vol. 5, No. 2, pp. 214–233.

Ahl, H. (2006). Why Research on Women Entrepreneurs Needs New Directions. *Entrepreneurship Theory and Practice*, Vol. 30, No. 5, pp. 595–621.

Ahmed, S. M., & Palermo, A. S. (2010). Community Engagement in Research: Frameworks for Education and Peer Review. *American Journal of Public Health*, Vol. 100, No. 8, pp. 1380–1387.

Aida, I. (2008). A Profile of Innovative Women Entrepreneurs. *International Business Research*, Vol. 1, No. 2, pp. 3–10.

Alam, S. S., Jani, M. F. M., & Omar, N. A. (2011). An Empirical Study of Success Factors of Women Entrepreneurs in Southern Region in Malaysia. *International Journal of Economics and Finance*, Vol. 3, No. 2. doi:10.5539/ijef.v3n2p166

Arnold, T. J., Briggs, E., Landry, T. D., & Suter, T. A. (2013). The Development of Core Retalier Community Functions. *Journal of Marketing Theory and Practice*, Vol. 21, No. 3, pp. 243–255.

Arslan, M., & Zaman, R. (2014). Impact of Corporate Social Responsibility on Brand Image: A Study on Telecom Brands. *Developing Country Studies*, Vol. 4, No. 21, pp. 84–89.

Arya, B., & Zhang, G. (2009). Institutional Reforms and Investor Reactions to CSR Announcements: Evidence from an Emerging Economy. *Journal of Management Studies*, Vol. 46, No. 7, pp. 1089–1112. doi:10.1111/j.1467-6486.2009.00836.x

Audretsch, D. B., & Keilbach, M. (2004). Does Entrepreneurship Capital Matter? *Entrepreneurship Theory and Practice*, Vol. 28, No. 5, pp. 419–429.

Austin, J. E. (2000). *The Collaboration Challenge How Nonprofit and Businesses Succeed Through Strategic Alliances.* London: Peter Drucker Foundation.

Austin, J. E., Stevenson, H., & Wei-Skillern, J. (2006). Social and Commercial Entrepreneurship: Same, Different, or Both? *Entrepreneurship Theory and Practice*, Vol. 30, pp. 1–22.

Berry, L. L., & Parasuraman, A. (1993). Building a New Academic Field-the Case of Services Marketing. *Journal of Retail*, Vol. 69, No. 1, pp. 13–60.

Bevan, E. A. M., & Yung, P. (2014). Implementation of Corporagte Social Responsibility in Australia Construction SMEs. *Engineering, Construction and Architectural Management*, Vol. 22, No. 2, pp. 295–311.

Blomback, A., & Wigren-Kristoferson, C. (2014). Corporate Community Responsibility as an Outcome of Individual Embeddedness. *Social Responsibility Journal*, Vol. 10, No. 2, pp. 207–315.

Blowfield, M., & Murray, A. (2008). *Corporate Responsibility – A Critical Introduction*. Oxford: Oxford University Press.

Briggs, E., Yang, Z., Harmon-Kizer, T. R., & Arnold, T. J. (2016). How Do Different Community Engagement Strategies Affect Consumer Responses to a Retailer? *Journal of Marketing Theory and Practice*, Vol. 24, No. 1, pp. 109–127.

Brush, C. G. (1992). Research on Women Business Owners: Past Trends, a New Perspective and Future Directions. *Entrepreneurship Theory & Practice*, Vol. 16 (Summer), No. 4, pp. 5–30.

Bryman, A. (1988). *Quantity and Quality in Social Research*. London: Routledge.

Butteriss, C. (2016). What Is Community Engagement, Exactly? www.bangthetable.com/whatis-community-engagement/ retrieved on 23 May 2017.

Buttner, E. H., & Moore, D. P. (1997). *Women Entrepreneurs*. Thousand Oaks, CA: Sage Publications.

Cardwell, M. (1994). *Customer Care Strategy for the '90s*. Cheltenham: Nelson Thorne.

Carroll, A. B. (1999). Corporate Social Responsibility Evolution of a Definitional Construct. *Business and Society Review*, Vol. 38, No. 3, pp. 268–295.

Carson, D., Cromie, S., McGowan, P., & Hill, J. (1995). *Marketing and Entrepreneurship in SMEs, An Innovative Approach*. Englewood Cliffs, NJ: Prentice-Hall.

Chaston, I. (1997). How Interaction Between Relationship and Entrepreneurial Marketing May Affect Organisational Competencies in Small UK Manufacturing Firms. *Marketing Education Review*, Vol. 7, No. 3, pp. 55–65.

Clarke, A. (2005). *Situational Analysis: Grounded Theory After the Postmodern Turn*. Thousand Oaks, CA: SAGE.

Cook, Karen S., & Emerson, M. (1978). Power, Equity and Commitment in Exchange Networks. *American Sociology Review*, Vol. 43 (October), pp. 721–739.

Creswell, J. W. (2013). *Qualitative Inquiry and Research Design: Choosing Among Five Approaches* (3rd ed.). Thousand Oaks, CA: SAGE Publications, Inc.

Crisan, C. M. (2013). Approaching Corporate Social Responsibility Through Cross Sector Social Partnership – Case Study of Bufab Romania. *Management & Marketing Challenges for the Knowledge Society*, Vol. 8, No. 4, pp. 623–636.

Crisan, C. S., & Borza, A. (2010). The Role of Corporate Social Responsibility in Social Entrepreneurship. *Management & Marketing Challenges for Knowledge Society*, Vol. 5, No. 2, pp. 63–76.

Dillard, J., & Murray, A. (2013). Deciphering the Domain of Corporate Social Responsibility. In K. Haynes, A. Murray & J. Dillar (Eds.), *Business Schools and their Contribution to Society*, pp. 10–27. London: SAGE.

Esmaeilpour, M., & Barjoei, S. (2016). The Impact of Corporate Social Responsibility and Image on Brand Equity. *Global Business and Management Research: An International Journal*, Vol. 8, No. 3, pp. 55–66.

Gan, A. (2006). The Impact of Public Scrutiny on Corporate Philanthropy. *Journal of Business Ethics*, Vol. 69, No. 3, pp. 217–236.

Gronroos, C. (1994). From Marketing Mix to Relationship Marketing: Towards a Paradigm Shift in Marketing. *Management Decision*, Vol. 32, No. 2, pp. 4–20.

Gundry, L. K., & Welsch, H. P. (2001). The Ambitious Entrepreneur: High Growth Strategies of Women-Owned Enterprises. *Journal of Business Venturing*, Vol. 16, pp. 453–470.

Gupta, S., Sukhmani, & Kalra, N. (2012). Corporate Social Responsibility: Relevance in Indian SMEs. *Productivity*, Vol. 52, No. 4, pp. 258–268.

Hampton, A., Cooper, S., & McGowan, P. (2009). Female Entrepreneurial Networks and Networking Activity in Technology-based Ventures: An Exploratory Study. *International Small Business Journal*, Vol. 27, No. 2, pp. 193–214. doi:10.1177/0266242608100490

Harker, M. J., & Egan, J. (2006). The Past, Present and Future of Relationship Marketing. *Journal of Marketing Management*, Vol. 22, No. 1–2, pp. 215–242. doi:10.1362/026725706776022326

Herwina, R., & Zarith, D. A. A. (2012). Exploring Corporate Social Responsibility among SMEs in Malaysia. *IEEE Symposium on Business, Engineering and Industrial Applications*, pp. 250–253.

Hill, J., & Wright, L. T. (2000). Defining the Scope of Entrepreneurial Marketing: A Qualitative Approach. *Journal of Enterprise Culture*, Vol. 8, pp. 23–46.

Huq, A. (2012). Influences of Gender Labelling of Entrepreneurship on the Entrepreneurial Career Aspirations of Educated Women in Bangladesh – A Comparative Study of Employed Women and Housewives. *Journal of Business Diversity*, Vol. 12, No. 3, pp. 54–66.

Ibe, C. M., Min, W. Z., Ling, K. C., Yii, D. S. K. (2015). Exploring Performance Based Practice of CSR in Sustaining the Relationship Between Business and Society: A Literature Review. *Asian Social Science*, Vol. 11, No. 5, pp. 181–192.

Johannisson, B., & Mønsted, M. (1997). Contextualizing Entrepreneurial Networking: The Case of Scandinavia. *International Studies of Management & Organization, Entrepreneurship Research in Europe*, Vol. 27, No. 3, pp. 109–136.

Kargwell, S. A. (2012). Women Entrepreneurs Breaking Through: Push and Pull within UAE Cultural Context. *International Journal of Business and Social Science*, Vol. 3, No. 17, 122–131.

Kelly, D. J., Brush, C. G., Greene, P. G., & Litovsky, Y. (2010). *Global Entrepreneurship Monitor 2010 Women Report.*

Lee, T. W., Mitchell, T. R., & Sabliynski, C. J. (1999). Qualitative Research in Organizational and Vocational Psychology. *Journal of Vocational Behavior*, Vol. 55, pp. 161–187.

Lincoln, Y. S., & Guba, E. G. (1985). Naturalistic inquiry. Beverly Hills, CA: SAGE.

Manolova, T. S., Brush, C. G., Edelman, L. F., & Shaver, K. G. (2012). One Size Does Not Fit All: Entrepreneurial Expectancies and Growth Intentions of US Women and Men Nascent Entrepreneurs. *Entrepreneurship & Regional Development*, Vol. 24, No. 1–2, pp. 7–27.

Maxwell, J. A. (2005). *Qualitative Research Design: An Interactive Approach* (2nd ed.). Thousand Oaks, CA: SAGE.

McKenna, R. (1991). *Relationship Marketing: Successful Strategies for the Age of the Customer.* Cambrigde, MA: Perseus Publishing.

Mehran, N., & Azlan A. (2013). Corporate Social Responsibility Terminologies in Small Businesses: Insights from Malaysia. *Business Strategy Series*, Vol. 14, No. 1, pp. 11–14. doi:10.1108/17515631311295668

Mehtap, O., & Kokalan, O. (2013). The Relationship Between Corporate Reputation and Organisational Citizenship Behavior: A Comparative Study on TV Companies and Banks. *Quality and Quantity*, Vol. 47, No. 6, pp. 3609–3619.

Minkler, M., & Wallerstein N. (2003). *Community-Based Participatory Research for Health*. San Francisco, CA: Jossey-Bass.

Morsing, M., & Perrini, F. (2009). CSR in SMEs: Do SMEs Matter for the CSR Agenda? *Business Ethics: A European Review*, Vol. 18, No. 1, pp. 1–6.

Moustakas, C. E. (1994). *Phenomenological Research Methods*. Thousand Oaks, CA: SAGE Publications.

Nath, K. (2010). Faculty Forum: Interpersonal Relationship. Silchar Medical College and Hospital. *Dysphrenia*, Vol. 1, No. 1, p. 3.

Parvatiyar, A., & Sheth, J. N. (1999). *The Domain and Conceptual Foundations of Relationship Marketing*. Thousand Oaks, CA: SAGE Publications.

Perrini, F. (2006). SMs and CSR Theory: Evidence and Implications from an Italian Perspective. *Journal of Business Ethics*, Vol. 67, pp. 305–316.

Putnam, R. (2000). *Bowling Alone: The Collapse and Revival of American Community*. New York: Simon and Schuster.

Sajjad, A., & Eweje, G. (2014). Corporate Social Responsibility in Pakistan: Current Trends and Future Directions. In G. Eweja (Ed.), *Corporate Social Responsibility and Sustainability: Emerging Trends in Developing Economies*, pp. 163–187. Bingley: Emerald Group Publishing Limited.

Seidel, J. V. (1998) Qualitative Data Analysis. *Qualis Research*, Qualis@qualisresearch.com

Seidman, I. E. (1991). *Interviewing as Qualitative Research: A Guide for Researchers in Education and the Social Sciences*. New York: Teachers College Press.

Sheth, H., & Babiak, K. M. (2010). Beyond the Game: Perceptions and Practices of Corporate Social Responsibility in the Professional Sport Industry. *Journal of Business Ethics*, Vol. 91, No. 3, pp. 433–450. doi:10.1007/s10551-009-0094-0

Sheth, J. N., & Parvatiyar, A. (1995). The Evolution of Relationship Marketing. *International Business Review*, Vol. 4, No. 4, pp. 397–418.

Sheth, J. N., Parvatiyar, A., & Sinha, M. (2015). The Conceptual Foundations of Relationship Marketing: Review and Synthesis. *Journal of Economic Sociology*, Vol. 16, No. 2, pp. 119–149.

Silberg, M., Cook, J., Drescher, C., McCloskey, D. J., Weaver, S., & Ziegahn, L. (2011). *Principles of Community Engagement* (2nd ed.). Washington, DC: NIH Publications.

Southwell, C. (2004). Engaging SMEs in Community and Social Issues. In L. J. Spence, A. Habisch & R. Schmidpeter (Eds.), *Responsibility and Social Capital: The World of Small and Medium Sized Enterprises*, pp. 96–111. Basingstoke: Palgrave MacMillan.

Timberlake, S. (2005). Social Capital and Gender in the Workplace. *Journal of Management Development*, Vol. 24, No. 1, pp. 34–44.

Waddock, S. (1988). Building Successful Partnerships. *Sloan Management Review*, Vol. 29 (Summer), No. 4, pp. 17–23.

Wang, Q., & Morrell, E. (2015). Gender and Entrepreneurship Revisited from a Community Perspective: Experiences in A New Immigrant Gateway and Beyond. *Environment and Planning*, Vol. 47, pp. 2645–2662.

Wood, M. (1991). Corporate Social Performance as a Competitive Advantage in Attracting a Quality Workforce. *Business and Society*, Vol. 39, pp. 254–280.

Appendix 1

Demographic characteristics of Sarawak Women Entrepreneurs

No	Particulars	Frequency	Percentage (%)
1	*Age*		
	31–40 years old	2	9.1
	41–50 years old	8	36.4
	51 years old and above	12	54.5
	Total (N)	22	100.0
2	*Marital status*		
	Single	3	14.0
	Married	17	77.0
	Divorced	1	4.5
	Widowed	1	4.5
	Total (N)	22	100.0
3	*Level of education*		
	Secondary school	9	40.9
	Tertiary education	7	31.8
	Postgraduate	6	27.3
	Total (N)	22	100.0
4	*Type of business*		
	Event management services	1	4.53
	Bookstore and health supplement **	1	4.53
	SPA management & modern handicrafts **	1	4.53
	Handicraft retail outlet and supplier	2	9.17
	Fashion boutique & homestay **	1	4.53
	Corporate gifts & restaurant **	1	4.53
	Graphic design and multimedia & fitness center **	1	4.53
	Perfume boutique	1	4.53
	Construction and homestay **	1	4.53
	Food restaurant	1	4.53
	Tour operator	1	4.53
	IT services	1	4.53
	Health and wellness	1	4.53
	Traditional and modern embroidery	2	9.17
	Hair, beauty, and fashion (one-stop centre)	1	4.53

No	Particulars	Frequency	Percentage (%)
	Education, training and development	1	4.53
	Oil and gas services	2	9.17
	Construction contractor	1	4.53
	Food manufacturer and distributor	1	4.53
	Total (N)	22	100.0
5	*Number of years in business*		
	<5 years	4	18.2
	6–10 years	8	36.4
	11–20 years	6	27.2
	>21 years	4	18.2
	Total (N)	22	100.0
6	*Legal form of business*		
	Sole-proprietor	11	50.0
	Partnership (with spouse)	2	9.5
	Partnership (with non-family member)	2	9.5
	Private limited	6	27.0
	Private limited and partnership	1	4.0
	Total (N)	22	100.0

Note: **WE who had two businesses in operation at the same time.

2 (Wo)Men workers and unions in Turkey

The reproduction of gender

Seyhan Bilir Guler, Ilke Oruc, and Pinar Keles

Abbreviations

BASK	Conference Of Independent Public Official Unions[1]
DISK	Confederation of Progressive Trade Unions of Turkey[2]
EGITIM-SEN	Confederation of Education[3]
EoC	ethics of care
ETUC	The European Trade Union Confederation
HAK-İS	Fair Job Trade Union[4]
ITUC	The International Trade Union Confederation
KADER	The Association for Supporting Women Candidates[5]
KESK	Conferedation of Public Employees Trade Unions
KRISTAL-IS	Glass, Cement, Ceramic and Soil Industries Workers' Union of Turkey[6]
MEMUR-SEN	Conferedation of Public Servants Trade Unions
PETROL-IS	Oil, Chemistry, Tire Workers' Union[7]
TISK	Turkish Confederation of Employer Association
TURK-IS	Confederation of Turkish Trade Unions[8]
TURKİYE KAMU-SEN	Public Workers Unions Confederation of Turkey
TUSIAD	The Turkish Industry and Business Association

Introduction

The traditional division of labor is one of the primary and most chronic problems of underdeveloped capitalist societies with inegalitarian labor markets. Under the influence of social structure's sexist approach, trade unions develop as dominant male structures. Sexist social structure and its determiner patriarchal sociocultural tradition expect from woman primarily housework and childcare. Thus, either she is pushed out of the market or has to take low-status jobs and work as a subordinate. Thinking that balancing domestic and work lives would only be possible if a professional fitting to this sexist social role was chosen pushes women to make sexist choices anyway. While professions like teaching and nursing are regarded as appropriate for women, engineering, inspectorship, and specific leadership roles are considered as branches of occupation-for-men.

In Turkey, only one-third of women in are actively involved in business, and only one-third have wage-earning jobs (Toksöz and Sayılan, 1998, p. 303). Employment ratio of women working as executives in the public realm is 9.3%. A study of the occupational groups shows that women instead take a backseat at engineering and manufacturing jobs, while women employment ratio is much higher in off-the-books segments. With regards to women's work life, notable differences are seen between women of urban and rural areas. Women in rural areas work as unpaid family workers, while in cities they work in industry or service sectors that predominantly belong to informal employment category.

The sexist social structure, which demands housework and childcare from women and lays those down as a condition for social and ethical acceptance, is considered as the main problem that not only hinders women from joining work but also prevents them naturally from participation in organizational activities. The male-dominant view of organizational activities, which have been woven with patriarchal tradition and formed by those prejudices, creates an organizational structure that excludes women from union activities and gives them almost no single place in management positions.

A study on 347 unionized women who work in banking, textile, and commerce – office sectors – shows that 5% of these women had already had active duty in the trade unions, but 24% of them, who hadn't been active yet, actually wished to be active (Koray, 1991). According to another study by Türk-İş in which 1116 women were surveyed (1989), the rate of women who were willing to have an active role increased to almost a third. This situation, which contradicts with such commentaries of trade union leaders as 'We can't find female candidates,' proves that only a little encouragement would be enough. In all, 28% of women, who refuse to take part, argue that they don't have the time, and 17% say that they feel incompetent. Lack of time results from a woman's double liability: home and work. Especially women with dependent children cannot find time for union activities because of their responsibilities toward their family and children out of working hours (Toksöz, 1994, p. 442). Likewise, according to a survey conducted in April 2012,[9] a total of 68.7% of women were not content with their working conditions. In all, 80.3% of women and 75.1% of men believe that women don't have the right to choose a trade union freely. (Akkaya, 2014).

According to the April 2011 records of Social Security Institution in Turkey, the unionization rate of the country was 8.94%. There are 10 million registered workers in Turkey, but only 922,000 of them were members of a trade union. It's observed that the workforce in the scope of a collective labor agreement decreased from 1.6 million in 1998 to 750,000–800,000 in 2010, and, accordingly, the unionization rate fell to 6%. However, it has to be emphasized that the situation is far more critical in the private sector. According to the 2011 records of the Ministry of Labor and Social Security in Turkey, in the private sector, there were only 370,000 workers who were under a collective labor agreement. It's reckoned that the unionization rate in the private sector was about 3.5% (Celik, 2014). Women can attain a directorial position only after regulating, first, the domestic life, and then the work life. Unfortunately, all over the world as well as in Turkey, the number of active male workers in union operations is much higher than that of women.

In 2019, the Ministry of Family, Labor And Social Security announced that there are 13,411,983 workers in Turkey, of which 1,859,038 were registered in unions. According to new communique *Numbers Of Workers In Business Lines and Number Of Members In Trade Unions* published in *Official Gazette*, unionization rate is 13.8%.[10] As can be seen from the table (Table 2.1), the number of women in the general administration of confederation is only one (three male, one female). Only 1% of women exist in unions affiliated to this confederation. Disciplinary and auditing boards also have the same pattern. The situation does not differ in free trade unions as seen in the other table (Table 2.2). The reasons for these situations will be discussed in the methodology section.

Method and analysis

The main question of the research is the women's image within union organizations. Discriminative practices that women have to face in organizations find their roots in gender perception, which are being loaded to both genders by society – patterns based on social structures stretch out to working life. That's why the study aims to reveal how trade unions as male-dominated structures see women. All statistical data exposed until today in the body of literature prove that in male-dominated union structure,

Table 2.1 Number of men and women in charge in mandatory organs of labor and employers confederations-2019

Confederation	*President*			*Managing Board*			*Presidents Boards*			*Auditing Board*			*Disciplinary Board*		
	M	*F*	*Total*	*M*	*F*	*Total*	*M*	*F*	*Total*	*M*	*F*	*Total*	*M*	*F*	*Total*
DİSK	0	1	1	6	1	7	28	2	2	3	0	3	5	0	5
HAK-İS	1	0	1	6	0	6	25	0	0	3	0	3	3 (noble) 1 (replacement)	2 (replacement)	4
TÜRK-İS	1	0	1	5	0	5	75	0	0	5	0	5	4	0	4
TİSK	1	0	1	26	1	27	18	0	0	3	0	3	5	0	3
Total	3	1	4	43	2	45	146	2	148	14	0	10	17	2	19
Ratio Women / Men			0,25			0,04			0,01			0			0,10

Source: This table was prepared by the author.

Table 2.2 Number of employees in charge of mandatory organs of confederations of state employee trade unions, by gender, 2019

Confederation	*President*			*Managing Board*			*Auditing Board*			*Disciplinary Board*		
	M	*F*	*Total*	*M*	*F*	*Total*	*M*	*F*	*Total*	*M*	*F*	*Total*
Public Workers Unions Confederation of Turkey (KAMU-SEN)	1	0	1	12	0	12	10 (data belong to 2013; new data not announced in the website)	0	10	10 (data belong to 2013; new data not announced in the website)	0	10
Conferedation of Public Employees Trade Unions (KESK)	1	1	2	4	3	7	3	2	5	3	2	5
Conferedation of Public Servants Trade Unions (MEMUR-SEN)	1	0	1	7	0	7	5	0	5	5	0	5
Conference of Independent Public Official Unions (BASK)	1	0	1	10	0	10	3(data belong to 2013; new data not announced in the website)	0	3	3(data belong to 2013; new data not announced in the website)	0	3
United Public Business Confederation (Birleşik Kamu-Sen)	1	0	1	7	0	7	3	0	3	2	1	3
HAK-SEN	1	0	1	9	1	10	5(data belong to 2013; new data not announced in the website)	0	5	5(data belong to 2013; new data not announced in the website)	0	5
Confederation of Progressive Trade Unions of Turkey (DİSK)	0	1	1	6	1	7	4	1	5	5	0	5
Total	6	2	8	55	5	60	33	3	36	33	3	36
Ratio Women / Men		11/132=%8										

Source: This table was prepaid by the authors (11 women/ 132 executive).

women's presence is limited. Questioning how academicians, who are working on unions and administrators of union organizations, interpret this situation would reflect the point of viewfrom both inside and outside.

As a result of reasons mentioned earlier, the study has been conducted from a point of view that would embrace women from a female point of view (emic/from inside), and also by a point of view that would select them as the baseline in trade unions. To collect data, structured interviews were conducted. Research model has been built on deep inspection of real opinions of surveyed people. While preparing interview questions, attention has been given to the views of researchers who study and question women's presence in a male-dominant cultural structure. While selecting the participants, priority was given to academicians who were women with work experience on trade unions. Three of them agreed to take part in the study. Then, we tried to reach out to persons working in a union, and five agreed to give an interview. The research area has become wide, including both academicians and unionists, but the number of respondents were only eight. It must be emphasized here that the unionist connection has remained limited to DISK, EGITIM-SEN, KRISTAL-IS, and PETROL-IS.

The research method used is the 'qualitative research,' and the respondents' names will be kept confidential. Instead of mentioning names, we'll be giving them numbers (Respondent 1, Respondent 2, etc.) when conveying their opinions. However, to reflect the participants' point of view better, we have to reveal who are the academicians and who are the unionists: five respoendents (Respondents 1, 3, 4, 6, and 8) are trade unionists, one respondent (Respondent 2) is an academician, and the other two (Respondent 5 and 7) are both academician and unionist. Their answers may become distinct by their gender too; for that reason, we had better indicate that only three of eight respondents are men.

Interviews with respondents were recorded with voice recorders and then put on paper. Research's validity and reliability were controlled by the comparison of results. The result of comparison by validity and reliability using the formula of Miles and Huberman (1994) (Reliability = consensus/ total consensus + total dissensus) was high at 90%. So, it's possible to claim that the study has an interpretative reality. The most important point that we have to emphasize is that the study is based on the qualitative research method and cannot be generalized because of its limited sample approach. In the meanwhile, facts such as no more than one data-gathering technique was adopted, the interview time was limited, and the use of voice recording devices could possibly deter the respondents from expressing themselves without hesitationshould be taken into consideration.

Findings

The aforementioned process – that the interview questions were structured and and the recorded interviews were first transcribed and then put onto paper – allowed us to determine the themes and the subthemes by content analysis method. Structured interview questions were effective for determining the themes, and the subthemes were structured according to the answers. So, starting from this point, we can introduce the themes and subthemes as listed in the following table:

To explain what the evidence indicates, the data in the table need to be descussed in detail accompanied by the discussions in the literature (Table 2.3).

Limited participation

To make their presence in work-life felt and represented, women have to take part in the trade union movements. But the number of women in union administration is very low compared to men. Harassment of companies against union activities is also very thought-provoking. There are many reasons for limited participation, which should be interpreted together with subthemes below and by interviews.

Male-dominant society and organizational structures

Turkish society has a patriarchal structure. Specific to Turkey, the patriarchal family structure is based on inegalitarian cultural roots, and roles and rules based on sex draw a picture edited by an underdeveloped capitalist economy (Eyuboglu et al., 2000). Male dominance in organizational structures continues its existence, thanks to male dominance in the social structure. And this situation is reflected in trade union activities too. Union

Table 2.3 Themes and subthemes

Themes	*Subthemes*
Limited participation	– Male-dominant society and organizational structures – Gender apartheid in terms of profession – Difficult working conditions and family-work conflict
Education	– Education tools
Meeting / not-meeting the demands	– Ignoring – Integrating / not integrating into managerial decisions
Glass ceiling	– Personal reasons – Organizational reasons
What to do	– Solidarity and collective struggle – Awareness – Budget – Social policies and regulations – Positive discrimination

activities followed the same pattern and became male-dominant (patriarchal) movement too (Toksoz, 2007, p. 90). This is a point on which all of the respondents agree.

> Respondent 7: 'Reasons like male perception about women's place in society, general problem of getting organized in the institutions where they work, male dominant manner of trade unions, profession based division of labor force, carrying the responsibilities like household and childcare alone on their shoulders, general mentality of society, are all obstacles in the way between women and trade union activities. Apart from these, there are also side effects – not properly established democracy within unions, union staff consisting of men, and general perception of trade unions as men-specific constitutions all are also problems for women.'
>
> Respondent 8: 'Turkey's patriarchal society is one of the reasons that make it harder for women to join into trade unions and this kind of organizations. Country's labor markets formed in a gender discriminating structure and the traditional divisions of labor; these are also some of the other reasons why women don't take part in trade unions and their management. Since trade unions have been patriarchal structures since day one and have never occupied themselves with the organization of women, women who don't feel themselves welcomed, prefer not to take part in trade union activities.'

Reasons for limited participation shouldn't be considered separately from social rights and legal regulations. We should remember that all the themes and subthemes we discuss here are integrated factors. That's why it would be more realistic to approach the themes in a holistic manner. Social rights and legal regulations also include subjects like eldercare or nursery for working mothers' children. This point that our respondents specially underlined is a continuation of women's gender, which had been constructed on a 'care' basis. This process, called ethics of care (EoC), contains traditional roles of women like taking responsibility, nurturing, showing compassion, and catering for others (elders and children) (Tronto, 1993, p. 2,130; Wood, 1994, p. 43). Therefore, women should perform their duties first in a private area (home) that they are identified with, and then in the public sphere (working life) (Ferree, 1990; Fletcher, 2005). This situation, which is supported by the social structure, affects women both in working life and in home life. Respondent 3 put it this way:

> Respondent 3: 'The facts that women's development is unwanted because of society's mentality and that women can't get healthy working conditions in employment, affect their social progress negatively. In addition to these, having extra responsibilities like housework, childcare, and eldercare inhibit women from being in trade union struggle.'

Society's prejudices can push women into corners where they have to work undeclared, accept low wages, work without a chance to get to management level; also, they do not get the opportunity to educate themselves and thus can't find a job later. Men dominancy in a world of organizations which is built on power, control, and possession categorizes women as emotional, unreasonable, passionate, and hokey, thus restricting their authority. In male-dominant organizations, women are still being considered unqualified, unproductive, and worthless (Olsson and Walker, 2004). This picture must be interpreted from the viewpoint of trade unions too. It's true that some social changes which the respondents mention have affected women's presence in their work life and hence their participation in trade unions negatively. Respondent 3, who is a trade unionist, explains this beautifully and holistically:

> 'The era between the years 1960–80 was the period when women gained power within the trade union and class struggles. Military, political, and economic pressure interventions after 1980 affected mostly women. During this process, women had been intimidated, left out of employment and trade unions, and their labor subordinated. Women suffering from effects of political tension in the country had difficulties to re-join to the employment also in the later years. One of those difficulties, which also sit **at the top of the problems of today's women,** was social ideologies. The second factor that disables the visibility of women is the market situation. By the implemented export-oriented economic policies after 1980, employment in agriculture decreased, but employment in industry in return didn't increase enough. Meanwhile, qualified women started to work in the developing service sector. But unqualified ones had to take illicit jobs because of conditions formed by the economic situation of the country.'

Gender discrimination in terms of the profession

Many aforementioned reasons prevent women from taking part in trade union activities, from being visible in unions, and frpm reaching up to management levels to have a say. The male-dominant social structure is a vicious circle based on discrimination, which, in turn, affects the work life too (Bielby and Baron, 1986, p. 759). The fact that women had to balance home and work life because of their role in society pushes women to professions that reflect their roles as mothers and wives, like a teacher, a nurse, or a secretary (Koray, 1993, pp. 27–34).

It's observed that the society of Turkey has a patriarchal structure in both socioeconomic and sociocultural aspects. Patriarchy is a system that produces certain patriarchal values and gender roles and is learned by socialization experience (Kazami, 2004, p. 251). In this circle, naturally, the one who is expected to be in work life is the man, and the one who is likely to stay at home is the woman. A woman's labor is evaluated within the context of her ability to do the tasks given in her private sphere. That's why it's possible to say that women are pushed to take jobs which generally suit to and are no obstacles for their responsibilities in the private area. These professions called *pink jobs* or *distaff jobs* block women's ways to the so-called 'man's' jobs and the so-called 'manly' manager positions by hindering their appearance in certain areas (Elmaci, 1996, pp. 79–123; Fletcher, 2005; Ilkaracan, 1998, pp. 173–192; Koray, 2000, p. 211; Oktik, 2003, pp. 75–92).

In this context, studies conducted in Turkey show that a separation between women's and men's jobs is quite common, and this system continues. Traditionally, facts like women having more responsibilities at home, father being the owner of monetary resources, and financial power being given the owner of the power resources are still valid (Arat, 1996, p. 46). If we look closer at the working life, which is a part of the society, we can say in parallel with the previous statement that leadership and management based on power are seen as man's job. On the other hand, women are being canalized to professions that are considered to suit them, like a nurse or a teacher, and so they do not get a chance to work in a management position ever. And looking at this study, we can claim that trade unionism is considered a man's job. Respondent 4 express this situation:

> Respondent 4: 'There are also obstacles caused by cultural norms related to gender roles, mindset patterns... Trade unionism can be seen rather as a man's activity. On the other hand, when we look at the language, culture, and places of trade unions, it's possible to see an area identified with rather men. It may not be easy for women to take place and get a sense of belonging in the dominant male structure of trade unions.'

The participants give the impression of still-existing gender apartheid. Because women are identified with the private sphere and housework is considered as their primary responsibility, work life is considered as secondary and a problematic area for women; thus, they are being canalized to professions which are called distaff works so that they can fulfill their responsibilities primarily at home. In this research, difficultness of working conditions is indicated as the reason for lack of female participation in trade unions. Now we'll try to explain the other subthemes considering that it cannot be separate from the aforementioned above.

Difficultness of working conditions and family-work conflict

As mentioned earlier, women's primary responsibilities are toward their home, and that's why taking part in trade union activities or management level is hard work. The number of women who are taking work life is gradually increasing, though it's observed that the family structure of societies doesn't change in direct proportion to it (Bond et al., 1998; Brewster and Padavic, 2000; Gerson, 1998). At the same time, women's ever-increasing responsibilities both at home and at work increase the probability of family-work conflict (Barnett and Rivers, 1996; Moen and Yu, 2000). So women find themselves doing two full-time jobs. This workload causes mostly stress, tension, and dissatisfaction with both works (Moen, 1992). When we approach the subject from the viewpoint of trade unions, Respondent 1 explains why and how the working conditions are being described as difficult:

> Respondent 1: 'The reason why women's participation rate in trade unions is low and why their representatives in management levels are so few is the difficultness of working conditions – not their unwillingness. As a head of the region with 20-year-experience in the 21st century, I can describe the working woman so: working women with two employers, two labors and four shifts (husband, work, home, and children) are tired and unhappy. If they take part in trade union activities, a number of their shifts will be increasing – not decreasing. And these circumstances make it for women harder to be active in a trade union.'

While women are facing the dilemma of 'either career or children' (either/or), men think that they have suitable conditions to harmonize them all – career, marriage, and children. In one sense, this situation shows that, for men, getting married and having children increase the satisfaction and works positively for their career path, but for women, getting married and having children are hindrances on their way to administrative levels and affect the work satisfaction negatively (quote from Friedman and Greenhaus, 2000). It makes us think that if the responsibilities at home are shared, women could advance their career more easily (Bond et al., 1998; Moen, 1992; Schneer and Reitman, 2002).

As seen, for women, the heavy workload at home affects their presence in work life and trade unions in a negative way. Furthermore, it's emphasized that, due to this, the risk of family-work conflict could increase. Family-work conflict, together with factors such as work outcome (e.g., work satisfaction, organizational commitment, intention of leaving) and family outcome (e.g., marriage, family satisfaction), influences the individual's physical and psychological health (e.g., depression, disorders) negatively (Greenhaus and Powell, 2006; Judge et al., 2006; Stoddard and Madsen, 2007). Increase in family-work conflict could impair the quality of life and ruin the family relationships of the workers (MacDermid, 2005). Until this point in the study, we have listed the reasons for lack of female participation in trade unions, using the opinions of our respondents as a base. Findings backed-up with literature help us to develop a point of view on the matter.

Education

If we want to talk about education in Turkey, we must primarily discuss the educational background of women in this society. As repeatedly said, women's place is considered to be at home. The mindset, which believes that women's place is only home, keeps girls away from education, especially in rural areas. Even within work life, women may need permission from their husband to work (Kardam and Toksoz, 2004). The professional success of women without education except for compulsory schooling is being afflicted with that fact. Since mandatory training doesn't bring any professional qualification or know-how, women without knowledge except compulsory schooling could only find job that were low-skilled or as pauper labor force, thus remaining dependent on their fathers and husbands (Serter, 1994). A vast majority of working women in this country work as unpaid family workers without insurance and social security. In rural areas, all that women get from their labor just enough to survive on and to provide bride price for father (Kocacik and Gokkaya, 2005; Ozer and Bicerli, 2003; Toksoz and Sayilan, 1998; TUSIAD, 2002). Because the number of women with higher education is lower than the number of men with higher education, the following question needs to be asked: What kind of educational activities offer trade unions for women? On this matter, the following subthemes are determined based on the opinions of respondents.

Educational tools

Following the interviews, we see that the education is limited to subjects such as creating awareness of gender, establishing commissions to raise awareness of trade unions, enhancing knowledge about domestic matters which are considered as women's primary responsibilities, and reproductive health. This situation is expressed by Respondent 7 as:

> 'Child health, women's health are two of those education programs. That creates a sexist feeling, and this perception turns into an attitude which prevents women from getting there where they wish to in trade unions.'

As seen from the interview, educational tools consist of those that are related to health issues. Identification of women from the domestic area has an impact even on education themes; later, we'll discuss this topic that apparently and inevitably creates the 'glass ceiling' factor. Apart from this, we must value the importance given to education by some trade unions that helps create awareness and gender equality, and shouldn't ignore the fact that it could bear fruit if the education is provided by other unions too. Now, after educational tools, we'll try to evaluate the respondents' opinions on our next subtheme 'necessity of education' together with the literature.

Meeting/not meeting the demands

Unions' ability to meet their female members' requirements must be considered as an essential matter. The most important subject to be questioned here is the reason why trade unions don't support female workers who face difficult situation at work. Because of the conditions based on gender differences, women's characteristic attitude, problems, and demands are being ignored (Urhan, 2009, pp. 84–91). While demanding social rights from the state for women labor, the trade union itself must stop ignoring its female members. Subthemes determined taking into consideration respondents' answers are described in the following paragraphs.

Ignoring

To understand women's demands, it's primarily necessary to be aware of what they go through. This will be discussed later under the theme of what to do. Here we'll be questioning the perception of 'trade unions' mostly ignoring approach to women's demands. Respondents explain this situation so:

> Respondent 2: 'Since the unions are men dominant structures, they have a manly thought system. To detect women's problems, some people from unions must be able to think like a woman and see things from a woman's perspective. When we look at union management, we see that female representation merely consists of numbers. Since there are so few women in management level, they can't bring women's problems to the forefront. Trade unions generally ignore these anyway. Women, whose demands continue to be ignored, give up after a while expressing their claims.'
>
> Respondent 4: 'To meet the demands of its female members, unions must have awareness and sensitivity about the fact that they could have characteristic demands.'
>
> Respondent 8: 'Trade unions are not meeting the demands of women because it's not one of their priorities. They don't have units which are solely concerned with women's problems and claims. Some unions have similar kind of units, but the relevant persons are either no experts or can't exercise due care because of workload.'

It is a crucial problem that women or their issues are ignored. When women realize their demands don't get attention, they are then unwilling to express their claims. That's why, to get more female participation, unions should stop ignoring these demands.

Including / not including in managerial decisions

To have more women taking part in unions, their problems must be tackled carefully at decision stages, and they must be involved in decision-making.

To have women to have a say in union decisions, their numbers, both in union and at the management level, must be increased. This topic will be discussed later, together with glass ceiling and what to do themes.

> Respondent 6: 'It must be explained to women that they should join in trade unions, take an active role there, and get involved in decisions – women must take part in the union movement.'
>
> Respondent 7: 'Women have many problems about working conditions. They explain these problems and their demands to unions. Having unionist women at management level is at the top of these demands. But their demands on this matter are not being taken into consideration. At this not-being–taken-in-consideration, we see the lacking visibility of demands as another reason for uncovered demands.'

Glass ceiling

Limited participation of women in unions prevents them from reaching up to management level. Achioeving an executive position, which is a power status indicator for men, is still harder for women. It's not different in unions, which are a part of men-dominant structure. None of the unions and confederations has a woman as its leader. On managing boards, KESK has 1 (16.6%), HAK-SEN has 1 (12.5%), TISK has 2 (8%), and BASK also has 2 (22.2%) women member (KA-DER, Women Statistics, 2012–2013).

As it's emphasized in feminist literature, women and men have different point of views and considerations. Men focus on individualizing and place importance on success and win; on the other hand, women care about communication and interaction and focus on relationships (Gilligan, 1982). This difference mostly is the cause of the thought that women are less qualified in work life than men. And when we talk about unionization as a part of historical continuation, it's even advocated that men react more aggressively to injustice and can approach as a warrior; on the other hand, women have a conflict-avoiding nature and tend to content themselves with what they get (Yang et al., 2000). In this regard, glass ceiling is described as '*invisible and artificial walls which are being built by organizational and social prejudices and hinder women from reaching up to executive levels regardless of their competence and achievements*' (Wirth, 2001, pp. 4–5). There are two main reasons why a glass ceiling occurs: personal reasons and organizational reasons. Now, we'll try to explain these on the basis of the respondents' opinions.

Personal reasons

Individual reasons include the situation of women who are caught between their workload in private sphere, that is, in domestic area, and their responsibilities in work life, and experience family-work conflict as a result of gender patterns. Women, seasoned to stay within the boundaries which were drawn for them by others, avoid being a manager and taking responsibility. Factors which are explained in feminist literature and emphasize the difference in women compared to men, can sometimes come their way as obstacles. Qualifications of a manager are described by some as *self-confidence, leadership abilities, ambition, being objective, and aggressive use of force*. Besides, it's believed that important managerial characteristics like *emotional stability, consistency, and analytical ability* are likely traits found in men rather than in women (Cullen, 1990). As seen, in addition to the obstacles imposed by society, a woman herself believes that it's not proper for her to take place at a managerial level, and hence adds personal reasons to the already existing men-dominant structure. Respondent 6 supports this, saying:

> Respondent 6: 'The right to work has a structure that prioritizes men, and this situation creates a trust issue from unionists' perspective about women labor. Because women would go back to her home in case of marriage, birth, or a possible change in family welfare. So, a lot of union activity made for women would be "in vain," that's why they'd better always remain only members. Therefore, women stay in the levels of management with limited authority. For stepping out of this restricted area, more know-how, ability, and effort needed than men would require. Or, even if they take part in upper levels of decision-making mechanism, their realm of authority has a character of an operational controller rather than a decision-maker. That's undoubtedly a result of perception under the influence of gender roles. Because it's believed that women are away from a certain, long-running social identity that can see the general structure and perceive its political projection. Besides, there's a process-logic that works so as if the things being done in the public sphere had no connection with the private sphere, and set it back. Since the things being done in private area are considered as women's responsibility, and women indigenize this, they stay away from existing in a public sphere which limits her presence and responsibilities in the private sphere.'

Home (private area), where a woman is limited due to gender, puts pressure on her and can create obstacles to prevent her from getting at the managerial position. Apart from that, male-dominant structure of society, of course, reflects itself and gives organizations a form of a men-dominant structure. That's why it's possible to claim that the organizational reasons that we'll mention in the following paragraph are rooted in male-dominance.

Organizational reasons

As mentioned earlier, the domestic responsibilities of the in-house-positioned women prevent their career advancemenst, and the fear of being unable to balance work-family life plays an active role in them not finding a job and heading to management positions. The malestream dominating business life generates androcentric gender customs and forces women partaking in the business world to apply these customs. For this reason, women executives seem to be less qualified than men. This kind of sex-oriented prejudices creates psychological obstacles in the selection, placement, and promotions of women executives (Fullagar et al., 2003, pp. 93–107). When we approach the subject from the viewpoint of Turkish unions, it can be seen that it's not so different. Respondent 1 puts it this way:

> 'Look, the leaders of the union organizations in the world, they are all women now. The women unionists elected by millions of members have a voice in the world trade union movement. Presidents of The International Trade Union Confederation (ITUC) and The European Trade Union Confederation (ETUC) are women. Leaders and secretaries general of the unions with millions of members are still women. Turkey falls extremely behind in this respect. There are not many women in the management of most unions. Women have no name in the union world. Union organizations are men organizations.'

Union malestream makes it difficult for them to accept women for the upper management positions, which is an indicator of men's power status. Both male-dominant social structure and indoor liabilities, as well as many such factors, cause women to feel reluctant to try to reach the levels of management. Therefore, attention should be given to both organizational structure and individual elements while discussing glass ceiling factor (Powell, 1993; Sinclair, 1998; Tzeng, 2006; Wajcman, 1999). This is a point supported by the respondents as well.

> Respondent 2: 'Sex discrimination is determinant, to step up to the higher places women need to have the essential education level, qualification, and merit based on the previous experience in the board. Women run as a candidate for such positions after they complete their personal development and acquire necessary managerial qualities. However, cooperation among men, or interpersonal relations between men employees, the fact that such decisions are made outside the workplaces and same political relations are determinative such as membership in the same party, in the same community they all are the barriers in front of women. Consequently, being out of these situations, women are precluded for subjective reasons even though they fulfill the required conditions objectively. Men to men solidarity networks are very common in Turkey. This is the current state, especially for the industry sector employees. This situation in point results in that men doesn't want to work under women executives.'

> Respondent 6: 'Power and hierarchy also shape men and so that solidarity continues in the union because power exists and needs to exist in a hierarchical structure according to the sense of manhood. Men don't want to come under the rule of women. They choose other men even though women are competent.'

Although the existence of women in working life now appears as a reality, there are still difficulties in the interiorization of their presence in organizational life and their perception as executives (Maier, 1997). Existence of women within an organization and in the line management necessitates some organizational changes such as power-sharing, communication, empowerment, and change in private-public differentiation (Ferguson, 1990, p. 154).

Actions to be taken

After we questioned women's position within unions, we asked the respondents what the government and the unions should do. The replies given to that question reveal that there are lots of things to be done. The following is an attempt to detail what they are.

Solidarity and common struggle

There are a lot of things to be done concerning women position in the society. Numerous institutions have to act together to ensure that. Respondent expresses it this way:

> Respondent 1: 'Male-dominant view makes itself perceptible in all fields of life. In any case, women shouldn't think that they would become entitled to acquire rights without a fight. Integration to unions doesn't only require being a member, with respect to that; women should try hard deliberatively to have a place in union management. Woman or man, they are all the same as laborers. On the contrary, women have more rights and more losses. Joint struggle requires solidarity. Acting alone wouldn't bring any improvement to any individuals or institutions with regards to gaining advantages.'

What has been told by the respondent is only a small part of what has to be done. Apart from these, it needs to establish awareness about the issues women face within society and unions.

Awareness

In our era, management of differences appears to be an important factor from the perspective of organizations. Organization environment requires many people from different aspects (race, gender, religion, age, socioeconomic background, nationality) work in the same organization. For all these variables, the term *diversity* is used. The ability of organizations to manage diversities, using the applications that have the potential of eliminating personal prejudices, would help minimize the negative attitudes such as the discrimination toward minority groups, sexual harassment, and mobbing in working life, because in organizational life, *social gender roles* and *gender differences in career development* are considered to be the key determinants in the management of diversities and the success of the organization (Grunow, 2006; Kanter, 1977). For this, awareness for these diversities has to be established. This is a point that all of the respondents agree to:

> Respondent 6: 'The expectations of the unions from the government occur based on more general considerations: struggle against unemployment, job security, social security, recording the informal labor, wages, improving working conditions and such. These are, of course, absolute musts, and they also cover women's labor force, yet the situation of women because of their social status requires several other demands. In addition to kindergartens, the unions must have some other demands on matters like the elimination of violence against women, protection of maternal and infant health. The unions either have no such demands at all or they happen to be flippant.'
>
> Respondent 7: 'A cultural and mental change has to occur, the unions have to make a difference in terms of their women members, they have to take women's fields of activity and demands into consideration, there also has to be a quota application in the organizations with women members in order to increase women representation, and the unions should also bear in mind the social factors that women are in.'

As is seen, first of all, public awareness must be raised to create awareness. The organizations with perception that play a part in the society can also have that awareness. If awareness cannot be created in a community, then that society's institutions with that consciousness will have to strive to maintain it. Therefore, it is important to create awareness in unions with regards to women employees. Another critical point is that the unions need to spare a specific budget to help attain these goals.

Sparing budget

It is a requirement for unions to plan a budget in order to maintain common struggle and solidarity, create awareness, and be able to fight for specific rights concerning the aforementioned issues related to women. Respondent 8 put it this way:

> 'Unions have important responsibilities in this matter. They must place importance on the organizing of working women and have the budget for the women related works.'

Within that budget, union training should also be included. As emphasized earlier, one of the reasons for limited women participation in union activities might be caused by insufficient training abd by focusing only on a specific field. Accordingly, unions should be more mindful about training. Respondent 6 emphasized the same point.

> 'The union trainings need to be considered important. These training have to transform into a structure which strengthens class consciousness.'

Unions have to make some demands of the government to ensure that women in work life can get special rights and assurances. Social policy and adjustments that are included in the actions to be taken make up another subtheme.

Social policy and adjustments

Other than unionization, the other subject, including social rights, is social securities. It is highly essential for wageworkers to have social protection against risks such as incapacities, old age, work accident, occupational disease, maternity, and unemployment. However, due to the high level of unemployment in the society we live in, most people accept to work uninsured and underpaid.

The facts that women join working life later as compared to men – they take up part-time jobs, they take a break from work because of reasons like marriage and having children – cause them to fall behind men in terms of payments made during retirement period and in benefiting from other social rights (Akpinar, 2005, p. 18). The obligation by the law for the companies with more than 100 women workers to establish a nursery room and a kindergarten might make them reluctant to employ women workers. Problems like kindergarten are points underlined by all the respondents.

> Respondent 2: 'Kindergarten is a severe problem, especially in the unions where women workers are organized; at that point, legislative regulations are not implemented. There is a number limit for the employers, women's movement, and unionist women have been demanding for a long time the number limit to be turned into the total number of workers independent of women workers. According to the law, a nursery has to be established if there are more than 100 women workers and a kindergarten if more than 150 women work. The employers keep the number of employees low, or they don't keep it low but prefer to pay whatever its penal sanction is.'

In Turkey, the low participation of women in union activities involves implementations like social rights in work life, union organization, social security, and power to strike. New production methods and restructuring of the labor market deepened the minor and weak position of women in working life. Ignoring women as labor force and the continuous approach to women as auxiliary workforce compelled women lead to characteristically unqualified, irregular, small commodity production and to home-based wage working type of practices (Urhan, 2009, pp. 84–89). The fact that women are more exposed to part-time working conditions might necessitate for them to work in the sectors where unionization rate is low. As a result of many aforementioned reasons that force women to accept unpleasant and precarious working conditions and limiting their areas such as exporting them out of work life during crisis, make it difficult for them to get close to the unions (Secer, 2009, p. 30). And respondent 3 especially underlines that point:

> Respondent 3: 'There are some encountered samples of discrimination such as certain occupations and professions are not socially approved as suitable for women, they aren't treated fairly in labor distribution, women are first to be discharged during economic crisis periods, and employers keep the wages low especially in the shadow sector. Because occupations and professions in the labor market are separated as "woman's work" and "man's work" and accepted so by the society, women concentrate only in traditional women's professions, give in to work in lower status and lower paid jobs. These jobs imply periodical and temporary working and social insecurity.'

Positive discrimination

Positive discrimination includes all the policies, strategies, methods, and applications developed to enable the people who are in a disadvantageous position within society to reach equality with others (Akbas and Sen, 2013). Within the borders of the European Union, wages equality and work-life equality have been adopted to ensure the equality of opportunity between women and men (Sural, 2002, p. 50). Especially in some countries, the quota policies which were implemented to make women reach the managerial levels bore positive outcomes in favor of women, thus toning down the regnant male dominance. Even in the research we conducted, all the respondents find the quota and positive discrimination favorable.

> Respondent 1: 'One of the ways to let union organizations out of "male organization" outlook is that a quota must be imposed on the union regulations. There are no women in three labor confederations, three public employee confederations excluding X as president and not even in the head office management. There must be a quota in trade unions. It's already late to defend positive discrimination.'
>
> Respondent 7: 'I think that positive discrimination is something which needs to be applied in all participatory institutions. It's debatable

> that positive discrimination might be anti-democratic in the places where people have equal chances opportunities, however, I believe that many invisible obstacles would be eliminated by means of quota application in a place where there are social obstacles, mental barriers, and at times legal hurdles and quota application will be an assurance for women increased the number of women nominations.'

These data can present us with a general framework about existence of women in unions. The final remarks based on that will be discussed in 'Conclusion.'

Conclusion

The women's status in the union movement has been the main research question of this study. For this answer-targeted study, the statistical data related to the number of women members of unions and confederations and the names of women placed in decision-making mechanisms of unions set light to the research to a certain extent. As a matter of fact, based on the result of the statistical figures and the findings obtained from the study, it has been determined that women are not sufficiently represented in the unions; in other words, women have no name in union organizations. It is seen that it's not an unexpected outcome when we look at the field studies on women. However, this outcome established ground to search the following question: What are the reasons why women don't (can't) have a place in union organizations?

Unions established on masculine experiences are re-fabricated within the structure and processes of male dominance thus lead to the marginalization of women. Besides, casting/ distribution of roles imposed on women and men by gender mainstreaming works against women in their choices of profession. Schoolteaching, nursing, and banking in the service sector, like textiles in the industry sector, are regarded as suitable professions in the sense that women can fulfill their home- and family-oriented traditional gender role thoroughly. The patriarchalism designs relationships and structures in working life with sex-oriented discrimination, both vertically – seeing management as a man thing – and horizontally – relatively trivializing the professions deemed appropriate for women. Likewise, unions got their share of that design as well. Concordantly, sex-oriented occupational discrimination is one of the causes of why the number of women members in the unions is lower than the number of men members.

Women cannot attend adequately or don't want to attend training given at union organizations because of their workload caused by social gender roles. Furthermore, the quality and content of the given training have to serve the purpose of solving women's problems.

The union organizations established with male experiences do not understand the female-specific problems, and thus they do not engage in the solution-oriented activities for the issues of their women members. As for women employees, they are not eager enough to join union operations where their problems are ignored and they cannot express themselves. In this regard, partaking of women experiences in line management will ensure the visibility of the women by minimizing gender inequality.

In the patriarchal settlements, management and leadership qualities are masculine characteristics, and management function is under the control of male hegemony. The reason for the fact that women cannot participate in the decision-making mechanism is not legal, but cultural. Cultural elements, attitudes, and values shaped by dominant male structure restrain women from taking part in administration. The thought that managerial occupation is not one of the socially imposed roles of women has been internalized even by women themselves. In the male-dominated organizations, the case that women don't relinquish their other functions (wife and mother roles), in other words, the thought that they shouldn't do so, is a considerable factor which causes women not to (not to be able to) participate in management processes.

Consequently, unions should primarily develop solution-oriented policies for the problems of women employees, and as regards to women, it is required to create a belief/mindset that the problems of women can be solved again through their efforts.

Notes

1 www.bask.org.tr/
2 http://disk.org.tr/organlar/denetleme-kurulu/
3 http://egitimsen.org.tr/
4 www.hakis.org.tr/index-eng.php
5 http://ka-der.org.tr/en/
6 www.kristalis.org.tr/yeni/?page_id=10616
7 www.petrol-is.org.tr/english
8 www.turkis.org.tr/default.asp?lng=2
9 Survey made using face-to-face interview method in houses; total 2,748 respondent workers (1,239 women and 1,239 men) aged over 16 years from 172 district and villages, 156 towns, 36 cities of 7 geographical areas in Turkey.
10 Ministry Of Family, Labor And Social Security, Trade unions, and collective bargaining agreements numbered 6356, Official Gazette Numbered: 30672, Jan 31st, 2019 www.ailevecalisma.gov.tr/media/3391/2019-ocak.pdf

References

Akbas, K. and I. G. Sen. (2013), "Turkiye'de Kadina Yonelik Pozitif Ayrimcilik: Kavram, Uygulama ve Toplumsal Algilar," *Anadolu Universitesi Sosyal Bilimler Dergisi*, Vol. 13, Hukuk Fakultesi Ozel Sayisi, pp. 165–189.

Akkaya, M. (2014), Rakamlarla Türkiye'nin İşçi Gerçeği (The Reality of Workers in Turkey by Figures), http://petrol-is.org.tr/haber/rakamlarla-turkiyenin-isci-gercegi-1-5883, Date accessed: 03.11.2014.

Akpinar, T. (2005), "AB Isgucu piyasasinda cinsiyet ayrimciliginin boyutlari ve ortadan kaldirmaya yonelik cabalar," *Ankara Universitesi SBF Dergisi*, Vol. 60 No. 4, pp. 1–21.

Arat, N. (1996), "Turkiye'de kadinlarin calisma yasaminda karsilastiklari zorluklarin sosyo- kulturel nedenleri." *Turkiye'de Kadin Olmak*. (Ed. Necla Arat). Istanbul: Say Yayinlari, p. 46.

Barnett, R. and C. Rivers. (1996), *She works/he works: how two-income families are happier, healthier, and better off*. San Francisco: Harper.

Bielby, W. T. and J. N. Baron. (1986), "Men and women at work: sex segregation and statistical discrimination," *American Journal of Sociology*, Vol. 91 No. 4, pp. 759–799.

Bond, J.T., E. Galinsky and J. Swanberg. (1998), *The 1997 national study of the changing workforce*. New York: Families and Work Institute.

Brewster, K. L. and I. Padavic. (2000), "Change in gender-ideology, 1977–1996: the contributions of intra-cohort change and population turnover," *Journal of Marriage & the Family*, Vol. 62 No. 2, pp. 477–487.

Celik, A. (2014), "AKP'nin On Yilinda Sendikalar ve Sendikasizlastirma (Trade Unions and Deunionization within a Decade of AKP (Justice and Development Party))," http://tr.boell.org/tr/2014/06/16/akpnin-yilinda-sendikalar-ve-sendikasizlastirma, Date accessed: 03.11.2014.

Cullen, D. (1990), "Career barriers: do we need more research?" *Journal of Business Ethics*, Vol. 9, pp. 353–359.

Elmaci, N. (1996), "Poligami; cok esli evlilikler." *Turkiye'de kadin olmak*. (Ed. N. Arat). Istanbul: Say Yayinlari, pp. 79–125.

Eyuboglu A., S. Ozar and H. T. Tanriover. (2000), *Kentlerde kadinlarin is yasamina katilim sorunlarinin sosyo-ekonomik ve kulturel boyutlari*. Ankara: T.C. Basbakanlik Kadinin Statusu ve Sorunlari Genel Mudurlugu.

Ferguson, J. (1990), *The anti-politics machine "development" depoliticization and bureaucratic power in Lesotho*. New York: Cambridge University Press.

Ferree, M. M. (1990), "Beyond separate spheres: feminism and family research." *Journal of Marriage and the Family*, Vol. 52, pp. 866–884.

Fletcher, J. K. (2005), "Gender perspectives on work and personal life research." *Work, family, and well-being*. (Eds. S. M. Bianchi, L. M. Casper and R. B. King). Mahwah, NJ: Lawrence Erlbaum Associates, Inc., pp. 83–95.

Friedman, S. D. and J. H. Greenhaus. (2000), *Work and family—allies or enemies? What happens when business professionals confront life choices*. New York: Oxford University Press.

Fullagar, C.J., M. Sverke, H.C. Sumer and R. Slick. (2003), "Managerial sex-role stereotyping: a cross-cultural analysis," *International Journal of Cross Cultural Management*, Vol. 3 No. 1, pp. 93–107.

Gerson, K. (1998), "Gender and the future of the family: implications for the post-industrial workplace." *Challenges for work and family in the twenty-first century*. (Eds. D. Vannoy and P. J. Dubeck). New York: Aldine de Gruyter, pp. 11–22.

Gilligan, C. (1982), *In a different voice*. Cambridge, MA: Harvard University Press.

Greenhaus, J. H. and G. N. Powell. (2006), "When work and family are allies: a theory of work-family enrichment," *The Academy of Management Review*, Vol. 31 No. 1, pp. 72–92.

Grunow, D. (2006), *Convergence, and diversity in male and female careers: does context matter in an era of globalization?: a comparison of gendered employment mobility patterns in West Germany and Denmark*. Opladen: B. Budrich.

Ilkaracan, I. (1998), "Dogu Anadoluda kadin ve aile." *75. Yilinda kadin ve erkekler*. (Ed. A. B. Hacımirzaoğlu). İstanbul: Turk Tarih Vakfi Yayinlari, pp. 173–192.

Judge, T. A., R. Ilies and B. A. Scott. (2006), "Work-family conflict and emotions: effects at work and at home." *Personnel Psychology*, Vol. 59 No. 4, pp. 779–814.

KADER Women Statistics. http://cms2.ka-der.org.tr/images/file/635106274588385879.pdf, Date accessed 01.07.2014.

Kanter, R. M. (1977), *Men and women of the corporation*. New York: Basic Books Inc.

Kardam, F. and G. Toksoz. (2004), "Gender-based discrimination at work in Turkey: a cross-sectoral overview," *Ankara Universitesi Sosyal Bilgiler Fakultesi Dergisi*, Vol. 59 No. 4, pp. 151–172.

Kazami, F. (2004), "Toplumsal cinsiyet, Islam ve politika". (Translated by D. Özpolat). *Ankara Universitesi Dergisi*, Vol. 53 No. 1, pp. 251–268.

Kocacik F. and V. B. Gokkaya. (2005), "Turkiye'de calisan kadinlar ve sorunlari," *Cumhuriyet Universitesi Iktisadi ve Idari Bilimler Dergisi*, Vol. 6 No. 1, pp. 195–219.

Koray, M. (1991), *Calisma Yasami Penceresinden Kadin Gercekleri (The Realities of Women through the Window of Work Life)*. İzmir: Tuses vakfi.

Koray, M. (1993), *Turkiye'de kadinlar, Turkiye'nin sorunlari dizisi 4*. Istanbul: Yeni Yüzyıl.

Koray, M. (2000), *Sosyal politika*. Bursa: Ezgi Kitabevi yayinlari.

MacDermid, S. M. (2005), "(Re)Considering conflict between work and family." *Work and life integration: organizational, cultural, and individual perspectives*. (Eds. E. E. Kossek ve and S. J. Lambert). Mahwah, NJ: Erlbaum, pp. 19–40.

Maier, M. (1997), "Gender equity, organizational transformation, and Challenger," *Journal of Business Ethics*, Vol. 16 No. 9, pp. 943–962.

Miles, M. B. and A. M. Huberman. (1994), *Qualitative data analysis: an expanded sourcebook*. 2nd ed. Thousand Oaks, CA: SAGE Publications.

Ministry of Family, Labor and Social Security, Trade unions and collective bargaining agreements numbered 6356, Official Gazette Numbered: 30672, Jan 31st, 2019, www.ailevecalisma.gov.tr/media/3391/2019-ocak.pdf, Date accessed: 23.06.2019.

Moen, P. (1992), *Women's two roles: a contemporary dilemma*. New York: Auburn House.

Moen, P. and Y. Yu (2000), "Effective work/life strategies: working couples, work conditions, gender, and life quality," *Social Problems*, Vol. 47, pp. 291–326.

Oktik, N. (2003), "Koy, kasaba ve kentte kadin olmak: Mugla bolgesinde kadinin degisen konumu". *Kadin yasantilari*. (Ed. A. Yaraman). Istanbul: Baglam Yayincilik, p. 78.

Olsson, S. and R. Walker. (2004), "The women and the boys: patterns of identification and differentiation in senior women executives' representations of career identity," *Women in Management Review*, Vol. 19 No. 5, pp. 244–251.

Ozer, M. and K. Bicerli. (2003), "Turkiye'de kadin isgucunun panel veri analizi," *Anadolu Universitesi Sosyal Bilimler Dergisi*, Vol. 3 No. 1, pp. 55–85.

Powell, G. (1993), *Women and men in management*. Newbury Park, CA: SAGE Publications.

Schneer J.A. and F. Reitman (2002), "Managerial life without a wife: family structure and managerial career success," *Journal of Business Ethics*, Vol. 37, pp. 25–38.

Secer, B. (2009), "Kadinlarin sendikalara yonelik tutumlari ile cinsiyet ayrimciligi algilarinin sendika uyesi olma istegine etkisi," *Calisma ve Toplum*, Vol. 4, pp. 27–60.

Serter, N. (1994), *Turkiye'nin toplumsal yapisi*. Istanbul: Filiz Kitabevi.

Sinclair, A. (1998), *Doing leadership differently- gender, power, and sexuality in a changing business culture*. Melbourne: Melbourne University Press.

Stoddard, M. and S. R. Madsen. (2007), "Toward an understanding of the link between work-family enrichment and individual health," *Journal of Behavioral and Applied Management*, Vol. 9, pp. 2–15.

Sural, N. (2002), *Avrupa Toplulugunun Calisma Yasaminda Kadin-Erkek Esitligine Dair Duzenlemeleri ve Turkiye*. Ankara: T.C. Basbakanlik Kadinin Statusu ve Sorunlari Genel Mudurlugu.

Toksoz, G. (1994), "Kadin Calisanlar ve Sendikal Katilim (Women Employees and Union Participation)," *Anakara Universitesi SBF Dergisi*, Vol. 49 No. 3, pp. 439–454. www.politics.ankara.edu.tr/dergi/pdf/49/3/34_gulay_toksoz.pdf, Date accessed: 03.11.2014.

Toksoz, G. (2007), *Turkiye'de kadin istihdami durumu raporu*. Ankara: ILO.

Toksoz, G. and F. Sayılan. (1998), "Sendikalarin Egitim Programlari ve Kadin Calisanlar," *Ankara Universitesi SBF Dergisi*, Vol. 53 No. 1, pp. 297–306, file:///C:/Documents%20and%20Settings/Administrator/Belgelerim/Downloads/5000053717-5000071809-1-PB.pdf, Data accessed: 17.12.2012.

Tronto, J. (1993), *Moral boundaries*. New York: Routledge.

TUSIAD. (2002), *Turkiye'de isgucu piyasasi ve issizlik*. Yayın No: TÜSİAD-T/2002/12- 354, Ankara: TUSIAD.

Tzeng, R. (2006), "Gender issues and family concerns for women with international careers: female expatriates in Western multinational corporations in Taiwan," *Women in Management Review*, Vol. 21 No. 5, pp. 376–392.

Urhan, B. (2009), "Gorunmezlerin gorunur olma mucadeleleri: calısan kadin orgutlenmeleri," *Calisma ve Toplum*, Vol. 2, pp. 83–110.

Wajcman, J. (1999), *Woman and man in corporate management*. Cambridge: Allen & Unwin.

Wirth, L. (2001), "Breaking women in management: closer break through the glass ceiling." *Women gender and work*. (Ed. M. Fehherlof Louti). Geneva: International Labour Office, p. 18.

Wood, J. T. (1994), *Who cares? Women care and culture*. Carbondale: Southern Illinois University Press.

Yang, Y., C. C. Chen, J. Choi and Y. Zou. (2000), "Sources of work-family conflict: a sino-U.S. comparison of the effects of work and family Demands," *The Academy of Management Journal*, Vol. 43 No. 1, pp. 113–123.

www.tuik.gov.tr/PreHaberBultenleri.do?id=16056, date accessed: 03.11.2018.

www.csgb.gov.tr/csgbPortal/ShowProperty/WLP%20Repository/csgb/dosyalar/istatistikler/CalismaHayati-2013, date accessed: 06.11.2018.

www.csgb.gov.tr/csgbPortal/ShowProperty/WLP%20Repository/csgb/dosyalar/istatistikler/CalismaHayati-2013, date accessed: 06.11.2018.

www.bask.org.tr/

http://disk.org.tr/organlar/denetleme-kurulu/

http://egitimsen.org.tr/
www.hakis.org.tr/index-eng.php
http://ka-der.org.tr/en/
www.kristalis.org.tr/yeni/?page_id=10616
www.petrol-is.org.tr/english
www.turkis.org.tr/default.asp?lng=2

3 Women in business and management

Case study of Kosovo

Artë Kastrati and Samire Sahiti

Introduction

Women, as part of the society, play a significant role in a country's development. This means women should be involved in all critical processes occurring in the country, especially in procedures related to the business activities and management. The primary research questions about this paper are as follows:

- What are the reasons for women's hesitation to participate in business and management?
- Which factors are affecting the success of women in business and management?

Historically, the participation of women in these two critical spheres was lower than it should be for a country to attain a higher growth rate. Based on previous surveys, it is argued that the participation of women, in general, is essential for the country because women are contributing in numerous spheres such as education, health, security, politics, economics, and medicine. However, to be more developed and integrated, it is essential for the country to support women participating in activities which are considered to have a direct impact on social and economic development. Kosovo, as one of the developing countries, was facing challenges in the gender aspect. The role of women in business and management, as well as in other essential spheres, was lower during all the past years. A few years ago, some changes had been made in the social and economic inclusion of the women, related to managerial positions and entrepreneurship. However, more work needs to be done to improve women's place in society and consequently to improve country's development.

Historical evidence

In the past centuries, women were deprived of their rights in society, especially before the 21st century. Some substantial changes made during the past years have improved the role of women in society. Some of these changes that we considered as the most important and relevant to be part of this paper are presented in the following section, by giving the most important events over the years.

1848 – The first women's rights convention is held in Seneca Falls, New York. This was a significant step toward the improvement of gender equality and development of the role and the rights of women in society, and ultimately proceeding to the next steps and initiatives.

1850 – The first National Women's Rights Convention took place in Worcester, Massachusetts. This was also an essential step because it lifted the society to an equal one.

1893 – Colorado is the first state to adopt an amendment granting women the right to vote. Since the initiative was taken during this year, the role of women in society improved more regarding decision-making positions. Also, in the following years, women's place in society started growing in other aspects as well.

1896 – The National Association of Colored Women is formed, bringing together more than 100 black women's clubs.

1903 – The National Women's Trade Union League (WTUL) is established to advocate for improved wages and working conditions for women. The most critical step of women's movement related to the topic of this paper is considered to be the establishment of this League because this led to increased participation of women in labor market; this was reinforced more after 17 years when another crucial step was taken.

1920 – The Women's Bureau of the Department of Labor is formed to collect information about women in the workforce and safeguard healthy working conditions for women (Fact monster, 2016).

Women in decision-making positions

The society was characterized by lower participation of women in all spheres for a long time, including education, economics, politics, health, social, and numerous other aspects and activities which have a crucial impact on the economic and social development of a country. Therefore, it was necessary to start working on improving the decision-making positions for women worldwide. Women have made inroads into decision-making positions in many spheres of life, and, although they still represent only 21% of board members of the most prominent listed companies, this constitutes a significant (9% points) improvement over the last five years (European Union, 2015). One of the most critical improvements regarding decision-making positions has been made in politics field, by enabling women to be elected as congresswoman with electoral gender quota law. It is important to mention that the gender quota is at 30% in Kosovo (The Assembly of the Republic of Kosovo). This quota was enforced to facilitate the position of women in the parliament, and consequently in most spheres which are considered to be more attractive and suitable for them.

Women's international and local organizations/institutions

Women from all over the world are facing obstacles that preclude them from expressing their capacity to do the best for business and management. Therefore, since the beginning and the organization of the institutional life, strong support was needed from institutions and organizations to improve the gender equality. We have summarized some of the many organizations and institutions which are established, and are functioning either at international level or the local level (Kosovo).

- *Women for Women International* – With more than 20 years of on-the-ground experience working with women in countries affected by conflict, Women for Women International understands that a comprehensive program addressing the social and economic empowerment of marginalized women is the most effective approach (Women for Women International, 2016).
- *The International Center for Research on Women (ICRW)* – This is a global research institute, which identifies women's contributions as well as the obstacles that prevent them from being economically healthy and able to participate in society sufficiently to engage in community fully. (International Center for Research on Women, 2016)
- *Women Aid International* – Founded over ten years ago as a humanitarian aid and development agency, Women Aid's mission is to provide relief and assistance to women and children suffering from distress caused by wars, disasters, or poverty; to empower women through education, training, and provision of credit; and to campaign against violations of women's human rights (Women Aid International, 2000).
- *The Association for Women's Rights in Development (AWID)* – This is an international, feminist membership organization committed to achieving gender equality, sustainable development, and women's human rights (Association for Women's Rights in Development, 2016).
- *The Association for Women in Communications* – This is a professional organization that champions the advancement of women across all communications disciplines by recognizing excellence, promoting leadership, and positioning its members at the forefront of the evolving communications era (The Association for Women in Communications, 2016).
- *The International Labor Organization* – It identifies the necessary measures to improve women's position and consequently implements the changes required in this aspect. In the range of Kosovar institutions and organizations which are supporting women in business and management, this Institution was established specifically to strengthen gender equality in Kosovo.
- *The Agency for Gender Equality* – This was created by the Prime Minister's Office and works toward providing support to all women, including organizing activities that would reinforce the role of

women and preparing documents which raise awareness among people about the importance of women's inclusion in all spheres of the daily basis.

Based on the responsibilities of this Agency, the *Kosovo Program for Gender Equality* has been prepared and published. This is a strategic document for integration of gender equality in policies and public programs of the Government of the Republic of Kosovo. Except for the Agency for Gender Equality, other institutions of government including ministries, municipalities, agencies, and so forth have their existing offices (sectors) which take care of policies, documents, and similar activities to achieve the gender equality within these relevant institutions.

- *The Kosovo Women's Network (KWN) mission* – This mission is to support, protect, and promote the rights and the interests of women and girls throughout Kosovo, regardless of their political beliefs, religion, age, level of education, sexual orientation, and ability. KWN fulfills its mission through the exchange of experience and information, partnership and networking, research, advocacy, and service (Kosovo Women's Network, 2016).
- The mission of the *Kosovar Gender Studies Center (KGSC)* – This is is to integrate gender-sensitive analysis, programs, and policies in all sectors of Kosovar society by increasing gender awareness and a focus on gender issues, developing gender studies, and ensuring the inclusion of gender-sensitive strategies through research, policy development, advocacy, and lobbying (Kosovar Gender Studies Center, 2015).

In addition to the organizations and institutions for women, the Republic of Kosovo had also prepared and approved the Law on Gender Equality which was enforced in 2015. This law determines the general and specific measures to ensure and protect the equal rights of men and women and defines the institutions responsible for it and their competencies (Law on Gender Equality, 2015).

Gender budgeting

When we talk about the supporting measures of the institutions and organizations toward the integration of women in Kosovo in institutional life, it is important to mention that gender budgeting plays a significant role in improving women's position in that aspect.

Gender Responsive Budgeting was launched at an event organized by the United States Agency for International Development (USAID) in partnership with the KWN. The initiative will institutionalize Gender Responsive Budgeting (GRB) within the Ministry of Trade and Industry and the Ministry of Environment and Spatial Planning (USAID Kosovo, 2016).

Furthermore, the Ministry of Finance, with the help of the Women's Network of Kosovo, in the First Budgetary Circular for the implementation of the budget of 2017, has made clear requirements for gender-responsive budgeting to comply with their obligations under the Law on Gender Equality. Under the current format of the budget process, conditions set by circulars are focused on information about gender distribution of budgetary inputs, wages, and employment; goods and services; as well as other economic categories of expenditure (Ministry of Finance, 2016).

Challenges of women in business and management – institutional support

The challenges that women face every day differ from circumstances in which they occur, but the most sensitive areas which affect women's lives are the business and management. Kosovo institutions have consistently increased their support toward women's integration in the abovementioned fields by taking specific activities with the aim of encouraging women to be more involved in business events. One of those institutions is KIESA (Kosovo Investment and Enterprise Support Agency) which organizes some activities for women who are leading businesses. Some of these activities are as follows:

- *The most successful women in business* – It is an annual event of MTI / KIESA co-organized together with the Kosovo Women's Chamber of Commerce – G7. It aims to encourage successful women entrepreneurs, who have managed to become competitive in the local and foreign market. (Kosovo Investment and Enterprise Support Agency, 2016) Besides, the first prize for the most successful businesswomen, some other awards are given to the most successful businesswomen in some business activities such as; production, services, trade and the award for the most creative businesswomen.
- *"Women's Entrepreneurial Leadership" conference* – It's a conference which discusses essential topics as the role of women in leadership and entrepreneurship. The meeting presents successful examples of women leaders and entrepreneurs. (Kosovo Investment and Enterprise Support Agency, 2016) This enables the businesswomen to discuss and exchange experiences with the participants of the conference. This conference provides considerable room for women to discuss their matters with the leaders of the Kosovo Institutions as well as find solutions for their issues.
- "Women *in Business" trade fair* – The fair aims to promote women in business and create new opportunities in networking and new markets. It's a traditional event organized by Kosovo Investment and Enterprise Support Agency. The fair gathers about 50 businesses that are owned or managed by women. (Kosovo Investment and Enterprise Support

Agency, 2016) This is also an opportunity for women to introduce and promote their products and consequently seek for greater cooperation with other businesses and other relevant institutions.

The other indicator that proves the support by the institutional mechanisms for women in Kosovo is the fact that The Women's Economic Forum is part of the National Council for Economic Development (NCED). At the 115th meeting of the government of the Republic of Kosovo, the Women's Economic Forum has become an equal member with full rights in the National Council for Economic Development (NCED). The Women's Economic Forum is made up of organizations that are engaged in empowering involvement of women contribution in the economy. (Ministry of Trade and Industry, Republic of Kosovo, 2016)

Results

With the purpose of getting real and significant data, we did a questionnaire for women in business and management. So, we have identified some of the women that are involved in these positions and have sent it to them through email and physically as well. This questionnaire contains 15 questions which are classified into two categories: general questions and specific questions. The first part is about public problems, and in the second part are including questions about our research, with the main propose to make our paper useful and significant for policy-makers. We have formulated some problems that can be found at the end of the article like an appendix, and we will elaborate them in this part (Figures 3.1 and 3.2).

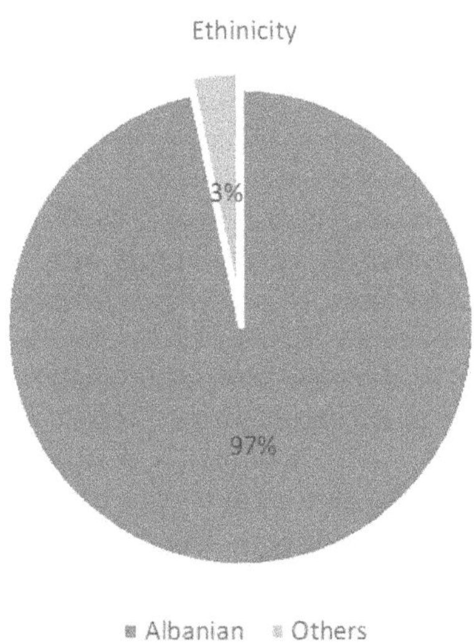

Figure 3.1 Age group.

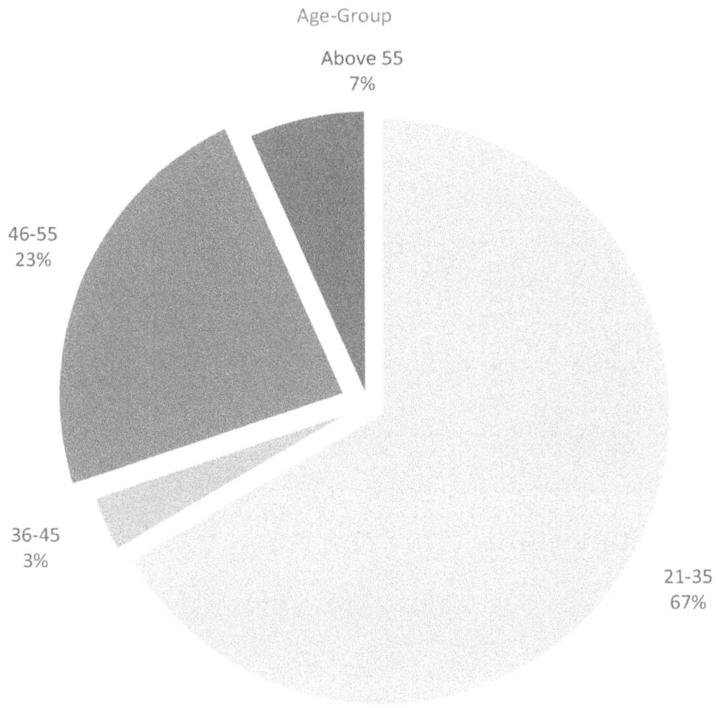

Figure 3.2 Ethnicity.

According to the response of the questionnaire, most of the women were Albanian, and only 3% of them were others, minorities specifically, Ashkali that live and work in Kosovo. We did this to see both Albanians and minorities' women if they have the same challenges and difficulties in business and management. We would like to mention that this is a tiny percentage of minorities, but it is in correlation with Albanian's women challenges, and it means we can conclude that both of them have almost the same challenges and difficulties, which will be elaborated below in the paper. Another important fact about women in business and management positions is women's age. Based on our results, most of them are between 21 and 35 years, and it is near 65%, which means this category of women has better conditions regarding education and advancement of their academic level. The second significant group is between 46 and 55 years, the results of which are around 23%. The other age-group is 36–45 years, and it is 3%, and for women above 55 years is 7%. So, we can conclude that older women have more difficulties, and they do not have many opportunities for access to business and management, as result of many factors like; the lack of education, the emancipation of woman, not enough support from family (Figure 3.3).

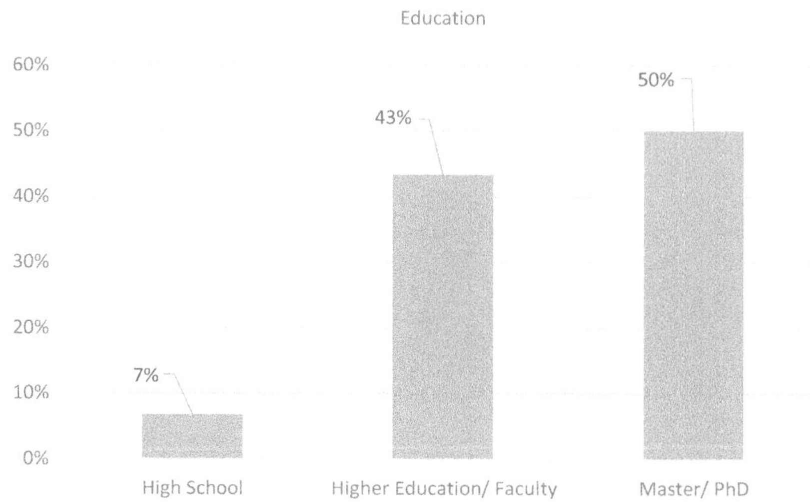

Figure 3.3 Level of education.

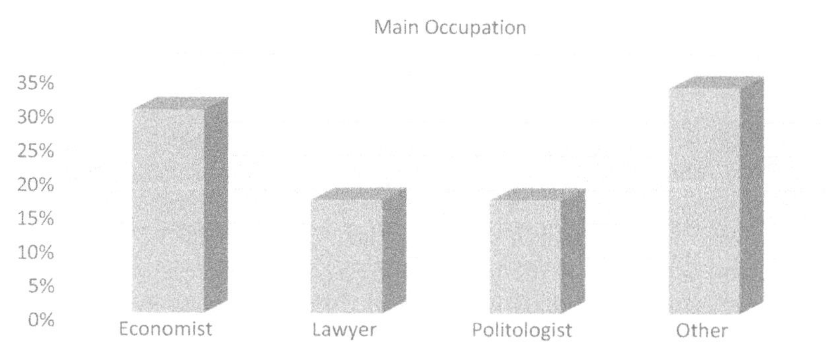

Figure 3.4 Primary occupation.

Despite the fact that we have not enough women in business or leadership positions, women in Kosovo are well-educated, and according to the response of the questionnaire, we managed to understand their level of education, and came to the conclusion that it is a relatively good level of women's education. Based on this point, most of the women (50%) have a master degree or Ph.D., and 43% have higher education/ faculty completed, and only 7% have a high school diploma.

As seen in the above (Figure 3.4) on the question related to the women's occupation, the results show that most of them were in other professions including; psychologist, sociologist, etc. Then the other large group of their primary job is Economist, Politologist, and a few of them are lawyers which means that the purpose of this question was to obtain information from most of the professions and to achieve the results as close to the reality of women in business and management respectively (Figure 3.5).

Regarding the women's professions, we have also formulated a more detailed question to understand in which sectors they are engaged. The results of this question show that

63% of women respondents are currently working in the public industry,
27% are working in the private sector,

and always based on our questionnaire, the smallest percentage is for women that are involved in others sector, e.g., NGOs, and it is 10% (Figure 3.6).

To see the involvement and position of women in public sector, private sector or at NGOs, we have formulated another question about their current situation, and from the women surveyed, most of them (80%) are in decision-making positions, and the rest of 20% are entrepreneurial.

To see more closely why women are hesitating to participate in business and management, we did this question, with some alternatives that are presented in the above (Figure 3.7). According to the responses of women in that question, we have achieved the following results; 35% of our social norms, 24% are from patriarchal family. Also, women think

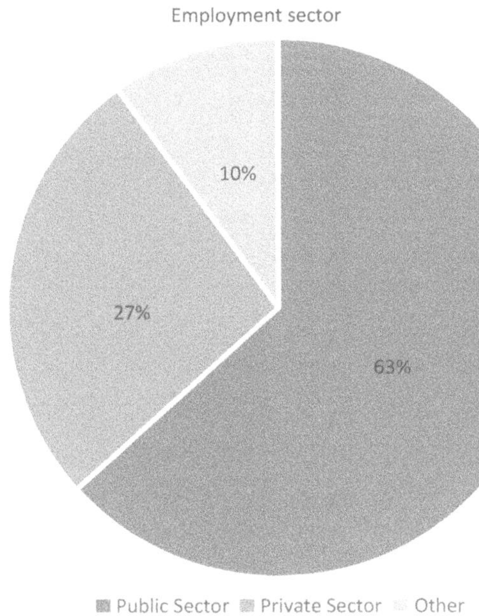

Figure 3.5 Sector.

their biggest hesitation to participate in business and management derives as a result of limited participation in the competitive labor, which is 41%. Women in Kosovo face multifaceted obstacles due to among other things the strong traditional and patriarchal social norms. Often, these norms limit women to own and inherit property and land, and it is estimated that women hold only 8% of the features in Kosovo. Women's independence is limited due to the inheritance issues and limited access to financial resources (Figure 3.8).

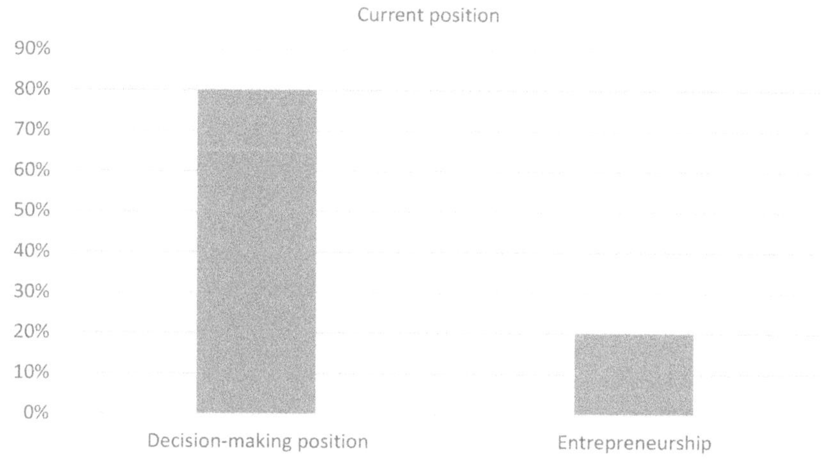

Figure 3.6 Current position.

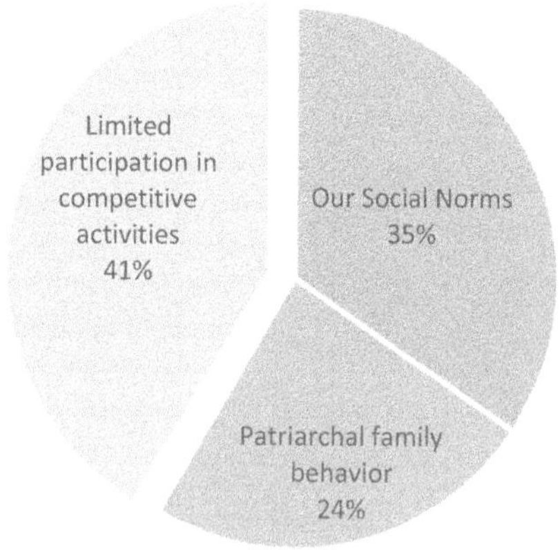

Figure 3.7 Explanation of the hesitation of women to participate in business activities and management in Kosovo.

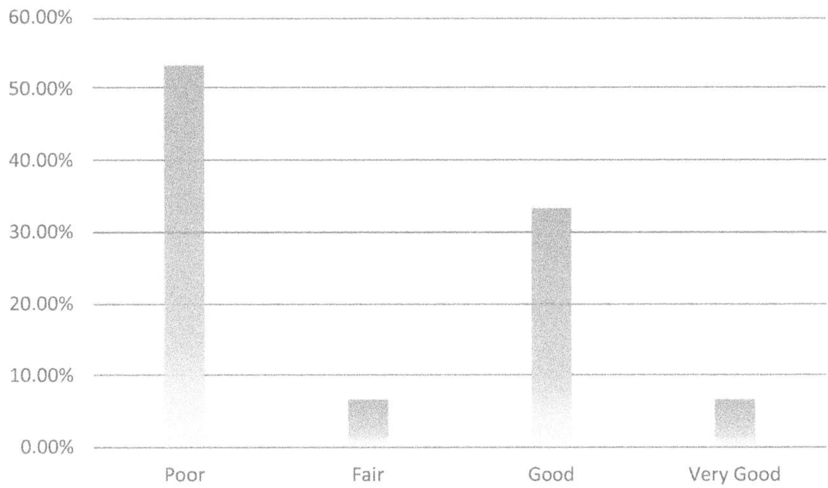

Figure 3.8 Institutional support for the role of women in society.

Except for the question why women hesitate to participate in business and management, we have designed another problem, because we consider that more factors negatively affect women's participation in these activities. In other words, the problem is; which are the factors affecting the success of women in business and management in Kosovo?

We have received different answers for this question, and the results are as follows; 53.3% think it is poor, 6.7% believe that it is fair, 33.3% think that is good, and 6.7% think it is perfect. Then we can conclude that the lack of institutional support in our society is another important factor which has an impact on women's hesitation in business and management (Figure 3.9).

We are aware that starting a business and succeeding on it is more challenging. The procedure to obtain the Business Registration, Fiscal Number, and Value Added Tax (VAT) number has been merged into a single procedure. One stop shops have been established in 26 municipalities and are now routinely issuing business registration and economic numbers (and if requested VAT registration) in a single procedure.[1] (World Bank, 2016). But women who have achieved success in business and decision-making in Kosovo say that some factors have a significant impact to reach the success in that field. Therefore, the answers by women's for our research are as follows; it should exist a simplification of procedures for establishing a business, make it easier the access to credit, and it should exist a guide for women to education in specific profiles. Specifically, the results by their answers are:

6.7% simplification of bureaucratic procedures,
easier access to credit is 33%, and
for education and specific orientation are around 60%.

However, there are not the only hesitations facing women's empowerment in Kosovo. Also, they have presented other important institutional barriers that, if addressed, can lead to a greater systematic change.[2] (CIPE, 2012) Strengthening these economic and political institutions will ensure Kosovo's democracy delivers to all citizens, regardless of gender (Figure 3.10).

We have expressed interest in the opinion of women who are currently part of any business or in decision-making positions, and we asked them

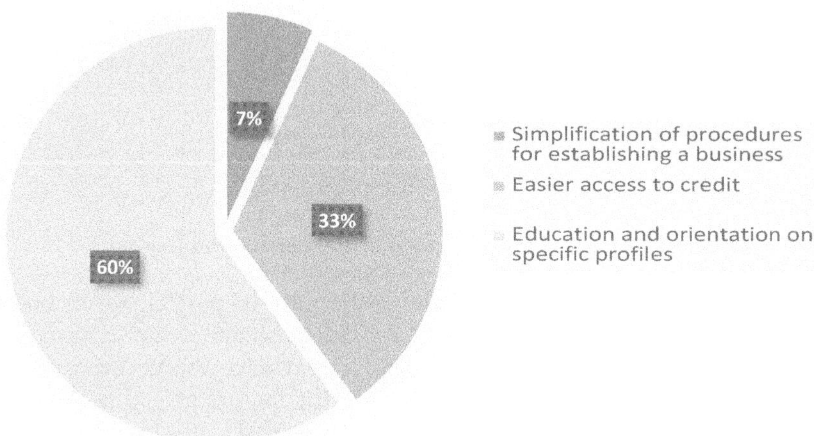

Figure 3.9 Factors affecting the success of women in business and management in Kosovo.

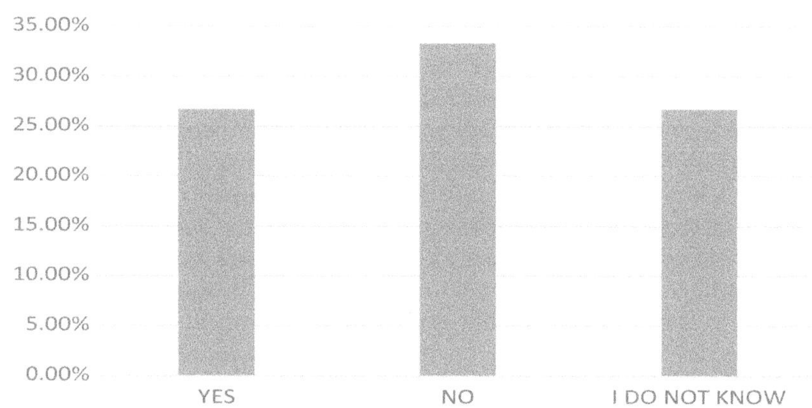

Figure 3.10 Opinion of responders if profiling of women in Kosovo is in the right direction.

whether they think the profiling of women in Kosovo in the right direction and their answers were;

26.7% believe profiling of women is in the right direction,
33.3% think it is not in the right direction, and
the rest that is 36.7 answered that they do not know whether or not is in the right direction.

According to the above question whether if the profiling women in Kosovo is in the right direction, most of the answers were for not and we asked them to give their opinion on where they think women in Kosovo should be focused, and we achieved these results (Figure 3.11):

- Entrepreneurship 50%,
- Management 26.7%,
- Education 13.3%,
- 10% political.

As it can be seen in the above (Figure 3.12), women in Kosovo are characterized by some occupations during the 2014–2015. Thus, the labor market is covered mostly by *women professionals (33%)* that mean women in Kosovo have improved their position in society in the last two years. *Service workers and shop and market sales workers* with 16.6% cover a significant part of the labor market, given that the service and sales sector has a wide range Kosovo's market. The other occupations such as *Technicians and associated professional* and *Craft and related trade workers* are characterized by a 10% of women's participation in those sectors. The

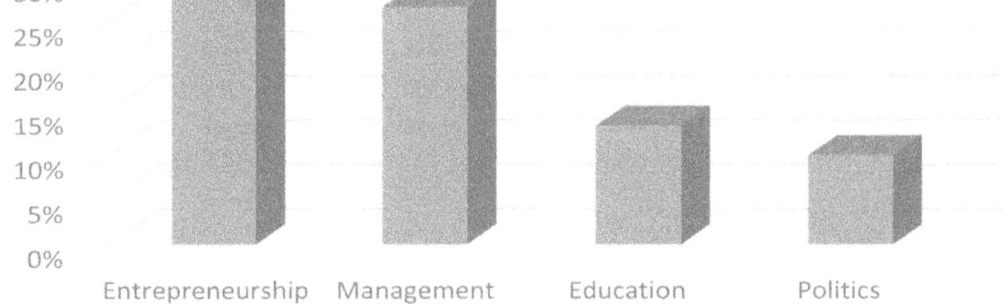

Figure 3.11 Opinion on which fields/areas is necessary to empower women.

Occupation	Occupation employment shares (%)
Legislators, senior officials and managers	4.8
Professionals	33.4
Technicians and associated professionals	10.9
Clerks	9.5
Service workers and shop and market sales workers	16.6
Skilled agricultural and fishery workers	0.1
Craft and related trade workers	10
Plant and machine operators and assemblers	0.7
* Elementary occupations	14.1

Figure 3.12 Occupation of the employed, female (aged 15 and above) 2014–2015.
Source: KAS (2016). Invasion employed female (aged 15 and above) 2014–2015.

Elementary rules also are described by a significant involvement of women, more concretely with 14%.

Conclusion

As a final point, we can arrive at some conclusions which are considered even essential or have an impact on the events that will be developed further. Overall, an outstanding finding is that women are not satisfactorily at the position in the society, and efforts have repeatedly been made for their support and contribution. Such a thing has had a result, but it is not reached the level of equitable with men. For this purpose, there are established various local and international organizations around the world and in Kosovo as well. The main aim of those organizations was to help women succeed and have a crucial role in society.

Women have made many achievements in education, so as a result, the management skills are increasingly rapidly. The other important conclusion of this paper is that the results of the questionnaire we have managed to identify the problems and challenges faced by women, the absence of institutional support have been a factor or stumbling why women have not managed to engage in business. As they do not have their support from family, lack of property rights are also factors that have influenced the current situation, that means women do not have "the right" to be part of a business. Another important thing that we can draw is that over 50% of respondents stated that they are not taken their pleasure with the support of the institutions of Kosovo, which remains a significant challenge for women in business and management. Meanwhile, the new initiatives taken by the relevant institutions are expected to impact on improving the women's position in these two critical fields.

In the end, the women always had significant influence in the world and supporting them with no doubts; it would be the most significant thing that a country could do because they would lead up to a large developed economy in a state. For Kosovo, as a developing country, it is essential to support women in business and management to make the state more sustainable and developed.

Recommendations

The data presented in this paper and the response of women on our questionnaire gave us a brief overview of the situation in which women are now and consequently led us to some recommendations. First of all, in that questionnaire, we have asked women on the way of how they would support women if they had this opportunity. We decided to make those responsible as recommendations because women are directly affected by them, and no one could know better than them about the challenges, and how much and in what way they need support.

- Women should primarily have moral support in our society, by family and friends;
- They should be supported through training and should have access to supporters' donations;
- Organizing of study visit abroad for women, and take the best practice from them;
- Ensuring equal opportunities for both men and women, and increasing the number of women in decision-making positions;
- Identifying the areas where they have the capacity and can achieve success, providing grants and creation of new jobs to bring positive results for the country's economic development; supporting young women to create start-up businesses, creation of a database to reinforce professional skills of women.

Based on the question if profiling of women in Kosovo is in the right direction, their recommendations are as follows: Women should be profiled where they can contribute greater for their family, and for society, and above all where they find themselves better in which position they fit well. They also recommend that women should engage in self-initiative behavior and they should be more involved in the public sector. However, women think that the problem is in the weakness of education system and as such, this problem affects whole society but in particular women and girls due to patriarchal rates which have only reinforced the education system. Therefore, solving the problem starts in this field. Furthermore, they think, women should have support from the government to create the best conditions for the opening a business or offering specific training.

Notes

1 World Bank (2016). Doing Business in Kosovo. Retrieved from: www.doingbusiness.org/data/exploreeconomies/kosovo#starting-a-business [28.11.2016].
2 CIPE (2012). Women's Empowerment in Kosovo. Retrieved from: www.cipe.org/blog/2012/04/19/womens-empowerment-in-kosovo/#.WFpUtxorLIU [28.11.2016].

References

The Association for Women in Communications. (2016).

CIPE (2012). *Women's Empowerment in Kosovo; Infoplease Article.* Fact Monster. 2000–2013.

European Union. (2015). *Strategic Engagement for Gender Equality.* Brussels, Belgium. doi:10.2838/454429.

International Center for Research on Women. (2016).

Kosovar Gender Studies Center. (2015).

Kosovo Agency of Statistics. (2016). *Occupation of the employed female.* Prishtinë: Kosovë. Association for Women's Rights in Development.

Kosovo Investment and Enterprise Support Agency, KIESA, Republic of Kosovo. (2016).

Kosovo Women's Network. (2016). *Mission.*

Law on Gender Equality. (2015). *The Assembly of the Republic of Kosovo*, Law No. 05/L -020, Article 1, Paragraph 2.

Ministry of Finance. (2016). *News.*

Ministry of Trade and Industry. (2016). *News.*

Sandbox Networks, Inc., Publishing as Fact Monster. 28 November 2016.

USAID Kosovo. (2016). *News & Information.*

Women Aid International. (2000).

Women for Women International. (2016).

World Bank. (2016). *Doing Business in Kosovo.*

Appendix 1

Questionnaire About Women's Position In Business And Management

October 2016

This questionnaire aims to collect data for realizing of the research paper about the Women's Position in Business and Management in Kosovo. This paper will be presented at the Conference: "7th International Conference of the Balkan Women and Business", which will be held at the University of Prizren. So, we kindly ask for your help to have research with statistical importance and completed with real information. Your answers will be completely confidential and compliant with international standards of research, and your personal information will not be published in any way. (**PLEASE:** Click on the answer that best describes you and fill in the required information)

Comment: Questions noted with (*) are optional!		
General questions:		
1 Your age-group?	□ 21–35 years □ 36–45 years □ 46–55 years □ >55 years	
2 Your Ethnicity?*	□ Albanian □ Serbian □ Bosnian	□ Turkish □ Ashkali Other: ________
3 What is your main occupation?	□ Economist □ Lawyer □ Political Scientist	□ Doctor Other: ________
4 What is the level of education that you have completed?	□ High school □ Higher education/ not graduated	□ Higher education/ graduated □ Master/PhD

Following questions require your opinions about women's position in society	
5 Which sector are you engaged in?	□ Public Sector □ Private Sector □ Other: ________
6 What is your current position?	□ Decision-making position □ Entrepreneurial
7 Your challenges to reach this position?*	Explain:
8 How do you see the women's place in Kosovar society?	□ It is not at the right level □ It is at the right level Other: ________
9 How do you explain the hesitation of women to participate in business and management in Kosovo?	□ Our social norms □ Patriarchal family behavior □ Limited participation in competitiveness Other: ________
10 Institutional support for the role of women in society?	□ Poor □ Fair □ Good □ Very good
11 Which are the factors affecting the success of women in business and management in Kosovo?	□ Simplification of procedures for establishing a new business □ Easier access to credit □ Education and orientation on specific profiles Other ________
12 If you would have the opportunity to support women, in which field you would support them?*	Explain:
13 In which field you think need to empower women?	□ Entrepreneurship □ Management □ Health □ Education □ Politics Other: ________
14 Do you think profiling of women in Kosovo is in the right direction?	□ Yes □ No □ I do not know
15 If not what would you suggest?	Explain:

Thank you for your help in responding these questions. If you have any questions, please do not hesitate to contact us on the following information: arte.kastrati@gmail.com and samirasahiti@gmail.com.
Your comments for us:

Date: __/__/__

Part II

Women entrepreneurship

Country cases

4 Modateca social FCAP

Apprehending entrepreneurship

Izabele Barros, Doutoranda Ana Rita Valverde Peroba, Maria do Livramento Aguiar, and Nayade Kennedy Sales dos Santos

Introduction

The state of Pernambuco is in the tenth place on the country's economy, having a GDP of 2.5% (gross domestic product) in accordance with the IBGE (*Instituto Brasileiro de Geografia e Estatística*) research of 2010 (*Contas Regionais do Brasil*). The economy of the state of Pernambuco increased to 4.2% between 2002 and 2010, presenting a rate above the national average (4%) for the period (IBGE, 2010).

In the economic market, textile and clothing (T&C) industry/fashion has a significant place in the state economy. The research project Modateca Social FCAP works on the conceptualization of social network that demonstrates its contemporary importance to services in the public politics that point out to the importance of social business. The purpose is to qualify women in social vulnerability situation, creating a bridge for the full performance citizenship. The results obtained along the years demonstrate that it is possible through the concept of social business to promote business opportunities that stimulate the social and human development.

The social undertaking's priority is not the maximization of the financial income for the satisfaction of personal or purely economic interests. The goal of social enterprise is the reduction of social sore spots and environmental degradation. Thus, the social business also contributes to the social transformation of the region that has reach out, stimulates fair trade, has a healthy commerce that is profitable, and is thus able to provide financial stability to its members. This kind of business aims at empowering people who are disadvantaged economically and also has the potential to be applicable on a large scale to different localities, thus reaching to a large number of people. However, the inclusion of communities in situation of social risk to the process of human dimensions is beyond trial and good faith. We should not only work toward strengthening social affairs, but also inspire the cooperativism (system of production, consumption, and credit with collaboration of several actors working for a common aim) with companies involved in the process, in order to make them social correspondent agents. The responsibility of building and achieving social, professional, cultural, and ethical skills, and training the people in communities for inclusion in society as a productive force is not easy. To achieve both of these, actions focused on social aspects that are able to establish cultural and social development programs and involvement of various social actors in favor of social dialogue mechanisms are necessary. This enables promoting the repairing and improvement of the social systems.

Several actions in Pernambuco state try to achieve the capitalist strength to reach objectives that go besides the economic growth. The Project Modateca Social FCAP is an initiative that concentrates its efforts in assuaging the social problems through improvement of women's work capabilities in situation of social vulnerability. This article proposes to present the bases of conceptualization that permeate the project as well as its acting and partial results obtained in the year of 2015.

From program Modateca to project Modateca social FCAP: promoting synergy between society and university

Inaugurated in 2010, the University Modateca Extension Program (combination of the word fashion and specialized library in textiles and relatives) of the University of Pernambuco (UPE), was conceived to carry out the interaction between campus activities and outside world (society). The program gives opportunity to the pupils (graduation students) to put in practice the studies carried out in the university, consolidating an education not only for the work's world, but even for life, and oriented to benefit the public with actions based on critical reflections and developed studies.

The project Modateca Social FCAP (PMS FCAP) is part of the umbrella's program to extend the social axis. The communities that present situation of social risk are invited to participate on and over several types of actions. The integration of the communities is manifold, through workshops that are conducted for the development of fashion products and craft works, notions of design, entrepreneurship, sales skills, visual merchandising, window displays, and business management. The PMS FCAP is based on the concept of 'social business' which aims to reach sustainability through procedures articulated in the necessary social, economic, and environmental dimensions for the evolution of communities, as well as of their families, strengthening the familiar nucleus and reaching to community as a whole.

These actions were implemented in 2011, into hinterland of Pernambuco, the pole of the industrial development, that turned to textile chain production and clothing commerce and craftwork. Since 2012, the program spread out to Metropolitan Region of the Recife (RMR, capital of the state), where the partnership began with the Consulate of Germany, and then spread to four communities through the ONGs: *Lar Transitório de Christie* (AELTC), located at city of Olinda – PE; *Casa Menina Mulher* (CMM), located at city of Recife – PE; *Aldeias Infantis*, Recife – PE; *Instituto de Desenvolvimento Social e Cultural* (IDESC), which acts in the Region Administrative-politically of the city of Recife (RPA6).

From the time when it started to the year of 2014, it developed its activities that were linked to the UPE campus Caruaru (rural region), and, from 2015, the activities got linked to UPE campus Benfica/FCAP in the capital of the state, Recife. Along its trajectory, approximately 180 persons including children, young, and the elderly persons have already been impacted, but it is mainly the women who benefited. People who benefited included around eight teachers, four undergraduate UPE scholarship holders to each year, and over 25 volunteers, besides several extern collaborators, academics, students of other educational institutions, and professionals.

The nucleus of the proposal rests in the belief of viability to familiar groups qualification of susceptible communities creating a bridge for the opportunity to commercialize products developed in workshops. These products are created keeping in mind the quality and the fashion trends priced at a rate that is able to compete in the market. These products are developed on the concept of EcoFashion that intends to make citizens conscious about the transforming impact of these products and the careful, conscious consumption of them, keeping in mind its effect on the future generations and the environment.

The weaving of PMS FCAP internalizes the conceptualization of social net and reflects its contemporarily relevance to the continuation of the public politics that points to the importance of social business. For Latour (1994:12), 'the nets are at the same time real like the nature, narrated like collective speech as society.' Being so, the PMS FCAP presents the interconnections and interdependences of each stage of the work that is constituted in the practical and theoretical experience. It makes possible for the public to avail a bigger opportunity relating to work while stimulating social and including businesses that appoint models of entrepreneurship through which the activities developed by an institution produce impacts and social transformation. In this way, the holistic system of apprenticeship is used, which is in agreement with Yus (2002) based on the genesis of interconnection, globalization, and inter-relations (relations between linear thought and intuition, mind and body) – in other words, the mixture of all the experience survived between the community and the whole group of collaborators of the PMS FCAP.

Knowing the dimensions of acting of PMS FCAP

From 2015, the developed activities dispose the welcome of beneficial women, sensitizing conversations, technical visits, and courses offered for increase qualification in the axles of fashion, environmental education, entrepreneurship, and business management. A total of 45 women were selected in 2015. The selection was conducted in partnership with the following NGOs: CMM, IDESC, and the Lar de Frei Francisco (CFF), entity connected with the Institute Dom Hélder Câmara (IDHeC).

Capacity-building sessions happen in the physical space of Modateca that includes 02 rooms located in FCAP\UPE building, a place where the planned activities are implemented by the external collaborators, pupils, volunteers, and teachers of UPE. In parallel to these classrooms, productive processes are carried out in the NGOs. The development of products grows stronger by association, cooperativism, and entrepreneurship, producing an increase in social affairs and thus enabling the future insertion of women into society as productive strength for the construction of a more just and sustainable world. It's worth pointing out that the experience acquired by guiding teachers, scholars, and volunteers in previous versions of the project (2012, 2013, and 2014) ensured an expertise in realization the trainings.

Several important institutions support PMS FCAP: the Consulate of Germany, the Vicunha Textile Industry, the State Secretariat of Environmental and Sustainability (SEMAS), the Secretariat of Economic development of State of Pernambuco(SDEC), the Pro-Rectory of Extension and Culture UPE, The enterprise J7 Promo, the Institute of Administration and Technology UPE (ADM&TEC), the Brasilian Service of Support to the Micro and Small Business (SEBRAE), the enterprise Provanza Recife, and the FB Industrial assemblies. The diversity of public and private institutions that are partners of the project and contribute financially and economically by the consolidation of the project in the State of Pernambuco, were vital for the results achieved over the years, making extensionists actions viable and sustainable.

Methodology

PMS FCAP works with research: search mode that brings together a practice to academic research. A four-step cycle is as follows: (1) planning: annual immersion meeting in which the team defines goals, analyzes results achieved in the previous year, and performs mapping of new partnerships and elaboration schedule of activities; (2) implementation: after sensitization and selection of benefits with NGOs begins the theoretical and practical training; (3) monitoring/record: questionnaires and interviews are applied throughout the semester for the standardization of the monitoring indicators; (4) evaluation: the final phase is the conference goals and analysis of indicators.

The group takes four classes/hours per week at Modateca. It consists of lectures, practical issues, and training. There are lectures on visual basic elements and strategies for using visual techniques, making it clearer '[...] the psychological and physiological implications of creative composition [...].' The participants are introduced to a new way of understanding the elements that handle the application of creative techniques and the way the diverse options and possibilities of use of these elements can be worked. In short, the participants are introduced to the world of design by applying directly to the proposal from the communications Professor Donis a. Dondis, where the theory and the process, definitions and comprehension exercises are combined for understanding Design methodology (1997:2).

As a proposal of action-research that Thiollent (1998) explains is a kind of social investigation to solve a collective problem in which researches and the target public are involved together, participating and cooperating to construct a solution. In PMS FCAP, research material of qualitative and quantitative nature are collected using questionnaires and interviews that serve as a basis for the preparation of academic studies and that, if transformed into material for scientific publications, result in improvements of the project itself.

In the context of fashion expertise, knowledge is generated through methods and techniques of design, customization, technological concepts, laboratory of creativity, construction of fashion identity, and trends research, provided these skills are used in the production system. The methodology used in workshops related to creation and fashion customization deals with various handcraft techniques such as embroidery, painting, and fuxico,[1] among others, as well as manual art crafts which primarily use discarded materials (inputs), scraps of fabric, and trims from donated materials and from waste related to manufactured apparel, sometimes due to non-conformity during production, rejected material, or spare material. This eliminates the possibility of abandoning these materials in the environment resulting in further damage and instead strengthening environmental impact reduction bias approached conceptually in the project. This highlights that learning transfer skills of PMS FCAP add value to handcraft skills already acquired by each participant before the project. Therefore, identifying creative processes developed in each NGO is crucial, as it helps maintains the principle of local development by sustainable actions.

On the axis of business management there are lectures on social entrepreneurship concepts, business management, pricing, as well as on the techniques of marketing, communication essential to the establishment, and development of future business. The thematic axes include 180 class/hour consisting of theoretical and practical approaches. At the moment, the project is in phase (2): theoretical and practical training. All the hours of training are permeated by playful actions aimed at encouraging empowerment of the union, collaborativism, and strengthening of self-esteem of each woman. This complementary care of personal empowerment aims at transformation of each individual, which consequently will reflect in the strengthening of their families.

By the end of 2015, these 45 women were directly impacted and approximately 100 people were indirectly benefited through educator who will also be qualified in group.

Knowing women benefited by the PMS FCAP 2015

The PMS FCAP tries to understand the environment in which women who have benefited live, and with it, the whole universe of features to which they belong. In order to outline goals for the qualifications and assist personal and professional development of each participant of the PMS FCAP, systematic follow-ups are carried out throughout the course. The introductory questionnaire (APPENDIX) brought responses from 27 women. The questions sought to understand not only the particular universe of participants, but also the expectation of the same in relation to the training offered.

Majority of women already are trained in other areas of craftworks, including work with fuxico and painting on canvas (Table 4.1 and Figure 4.1). The technicality of fuxico was transformed in the skill base of the PMS FCAP. This technique involves drawing skills, cutting, sewing, color perception, and improvement of creativity.

The process connects women to their cultural universe, awakening them to the everyday surrounding and, based on this observation, helping them

Table 4.1 Most activities undertaken by participants

Activity	*Amount People*
Fuxico	10
Fabric painting	10
Seam	8
Crochet	7
Embroidery	4
Drawing	4
Dolls	2
Macramê	2
Modeling	2
Painting on canvas	2
Clay	1
Others	5

Source: Authors.

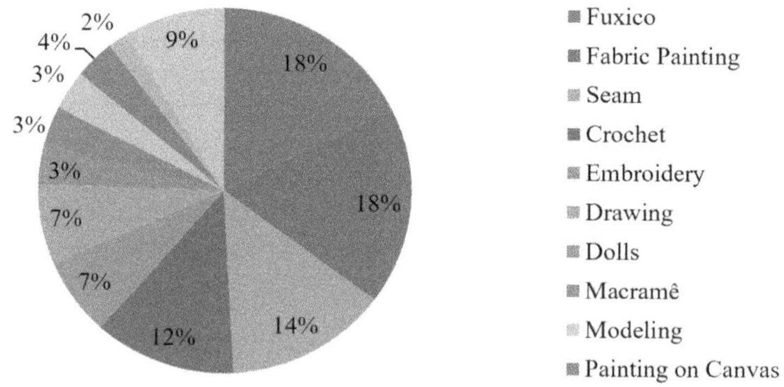

Figure 4.1 Relationship skills and previous knowledge.

Note: *Macramê* is a technique of machines that weave threads without the using intertwining varied knots and drawings, creating a sort of trimming done from thick line or string.
Source: Authors.

build unique products that are part of their life history. For this, various activities are realized during the training course in order to specialize in their area of expertise and introduce new ways and opportunities.

The survey shows that nearly half the participants do not sell the products developed currently (Table 4.2), but 92% responded that they wish to expose their products with objective of generating income after completion of the training (Table 4.3). This shows how much the PMS FCAP already is important in the lives of beneficiaries, as it gives them as opportunity for improvement in the quality of life through the possibility of generating income. This involves financial characteristics, besides an increase in self-esteem of each one of them, generating a positive return that includes the future clients, the beneficiaries, the educators, and the community as a whole (Figures 4.2 and 4.3).

Table 4.2 Time to market products currently developed

Time Marketing	*Amount People*
Not commercialize	11
Less than 1 year	5
1 to 2 years	2
2 to 5 years	6
Over 5 years	3

Source: Authors.

Table 4.3 Marketing expectation of products with techniques developed in the training course PMS FCAP

Marketing Expectation	*Amount People*
Yes	25
No	1
No reply	1

Source: Authors.

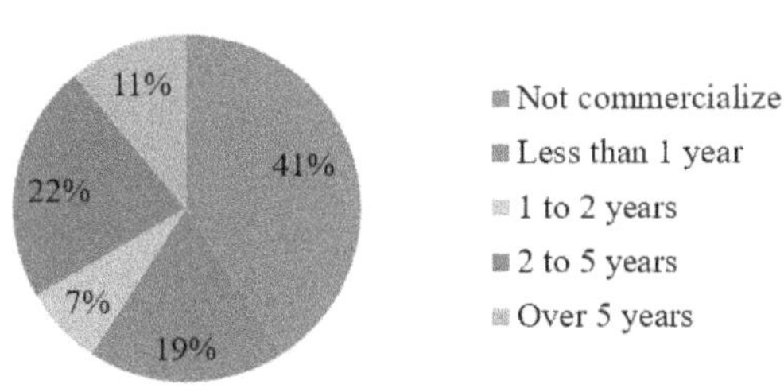

Figure 4.2 Time of participation in commercial activity.
Source: Authors.

Figure 4.3 also suggests a peculiarity trend that needs to be investigated – although a vast majority (41%) of the interviewees do not sell products developed using the techniques and skills they possess, 92% of them dedicate part of their time for learning activities with the objective of commercial purposes. This indicates that they have some background to practice commercialization, but don't activate this ability. This factor could significantly alter the gains of families served, as seen in Table 4.4 and Figure 4.4.

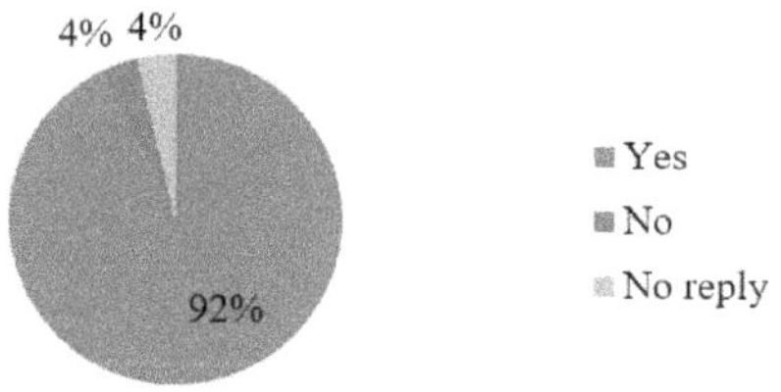

Figure 4.3 Marketing expectation of products at the end of training.
Source: Authors.

Table 4.4 Financial and monthly average percent monthly income

Financial Source	*Average Values*	*Percentage of Income*
Salary	R$ 366,59	40,46%
Government aid	R$ 138,74	15,31%
Extra income of family members	R$ 400,70	44,23%

Source: Authors.

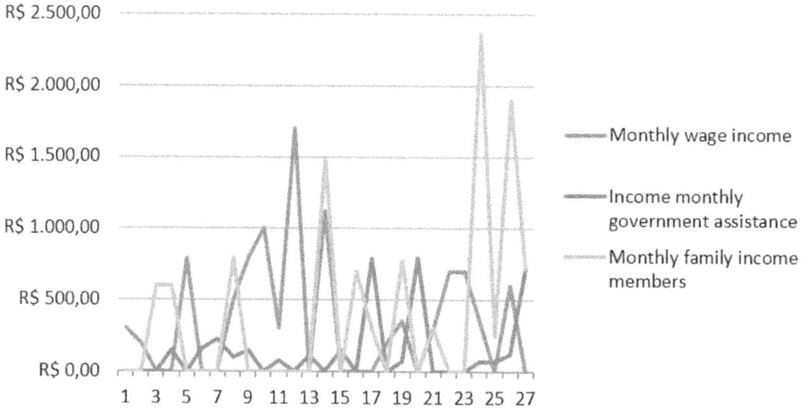

Figure 4.4 Source of income.
Source: Authors.

Table 4.5 Average age, number of children, number of dependent children, and total inhabitants of the house

Average Age of Participants	*41*
Average number sons	2
Average number dependent children	2
Average number of residents of the house	4

Source: Authors.

The vast majority of families have all children who are still dependent but, at the same time, they get financial aid (*Table 4.4*). It is also possible to note that the average age of the members participating in the project is 41 years and that the average number of children per woman is 2; it's identical to average amount of dependent children. However, approximately four people live in the same house, (Table 4.5), which facilitates the increase in monthly income, making it possible for the junction of the incomes of family members get through, on average, personal income.

As one can see, groups are formed by families. According to IBGE (2012), private homes are places where the relationship between occupants is dictated by ties of kinship, domestic dependency, or living standards. Of these, urban households are located in city areas, which are internal areas of the urban perimeter of a city or town as defined by municipal law.

The value of the nominal average monthly income of private households with permanent situation of the urban domicile in the city of Recife is $ 3,755.53 (IBGE). This is a deficit of more than 1,700 *reais* (R$ 1,700.00) in the income of the wealthiest families among the group interviewed.

This analysis makes possible the interpretation of social risk which are involved in this project. For Janczura (2012), risk and social vulnerability are distinct concepts, but intrinsically related. The risk comes from the fragile conditions of the contemporary technological society, while the vulnerability "[...] identifies the condition of individuals in that society" (author's translation). This is key to the perception that there is still much to be done in order to eradicate poverty in Brazil, mainly in the north and northeast regions of the country. The project also will be evaluated every six months, studying what comes up from the subjects involved, through polls, in addition to oral assessment of the direct participants in relation to the performance of the project and its aspects.

Educational aspects

As stated by Morin, education must contribute to awareness of oneself as a citizen, invoking his responsibility as an individual and society, restoring the essence of the human condition (2011:18). Effectively, as advocated by Morin (2011:13) and confirmed at the International Conference on the seventh knowledge necessary for the education of the present, "[...] complex thinking, with ecological concern, able to contextualize and reconnect different knowledges or dimensions of life" (author's translation) is of the utmost importance for the future of mankind. The contextualization of objects developed is what makes them relevant and valued. Teach and learn how to interpret ideas visually, moods, or even the environment, giving a feature, in the case of pieces created by handling consciously a specific message, which propagates culture is the role of education for design. In the words of anthropologist, sociologist, French philosopher Edgar Morin, this is only fully possible "[...] human being by culture and in culture" (2011:47).

The word culture has changed its meaning throughout the history of mankind, but its meaning is first to cultivate, plow the Earth, and take care of field and the cattle. In short, (the) culture is part of the symbolic contribution of societies, and it gains its meaning for those who recognize it (1999:239). It supports the way in which people relate to one another and produce their goods, becoming "Foundation of social dynamics" (1999:244, author's translation). The articulation of artistic and cultural experiences in communities where women attend (ed) and live with the pedagogical approach used in (the) training(s), makes learning process easier. Education with this approach becomes strategic to the cultural, social, and economic development of the country (Brasil 2015).

Design aspects

It is believed that by mastering a technique, anyone is capable of producing an infinite variety of creative solutions to visual communication problems as far as the development of a personal style is concerned (1997:3). The statement of the participants, not only to recipients, readers, customers, and also creators of these Visual messages that today, more than at any other time in human history, we are all bombarded daily, provides the participants use the opportunity to understand the process of formation of these messages and change the look to a more critical proposal building empowerment, by releasing these women. In the words of Ambrose and Harris: "a solid understanding of the principles of the creative project is of extreme importance to produce effective designs and attractive, a base from which creativity can emerge" (2011).

The implementation of the extension project PMS FCAP generates an approach that results in mutual growth for UPE and for communities in search for a more egalitarian society, which is an essential tool design because it is through social search design the local culture is appreciated. Conceptually, Abbonizio (2009) proposes that this interaction between the design and the communities is called 'collaboration' design. For this collaboration to occur properly, it is necessary to switch the view of the designer as problem solver, to the view of the designer as a participant of a changing process of an educational and active practice. Therefore, objects that in their creation are treated as a productive planning, which cover not only the commercial aspects but also focus on sustainability of the ideals, have an inherent value that plays real transformations of human realities.

Social aspects

Technically, what differentiates the various areas of visual language and its applications is the utility and aesthetics. "The point designates the Design and the manufacture of objects, materials and demonstrations that respond to basic needs" (Dondis, 1997:7–8). The participants of the training began their steps into the world and were "differentiated" for work related to kitchen, babies, house that are purely decorative or used as a record of place; sometimes these women, often still girls, to fulfill certain needs and essential in everyday life to learn the techniques, tools, and materials to sew, cut, and weave. Those that stand out are those that end up turning this basic need in trade and way of life. The family and the community start recognizing the talent and requesting orders, which lead to the beginning of a generation of income.

The creation of artifacts, the utility products project development, brings together since intrinsic assumptions to any human being, to facilitate a task or achieve, by instruments, perform a task, to build a socio-ethical environment fairer and healthier through the design process (Peroba, 2008:19). The passage from the stage of mere breeders of "recipes" learned to "creators" through the externalization of own expressions, is not easy or quick to vast majority. Many, even with training, do not develop this aspect of their skills. "The most cited difference between the utility and the purely artistic is the level of motivation that leads to the production of the beautiful" (Dondis, 1997:8). That means, believe in themselves and their capability is the first step in the development of products that build an identity, carry value, and communicate with other people.

John Heskett already recognizes the intrinsic relationship between the crafts and the work of design, with aesthetic features and the commercial activity. This tripod that supports the craftsmanship was spread too thin over time in various communities and hence just a few members carry notions of techniques used for generations. The resumption of the importance of the typical modus operandi of the craftsman in developing countries, especially in times of crisis, demonstrates the validity and relevance of re-signification and enhancement of this process these days (1998:90). The creation of products and processes is a productive activity which develops as the human and social capital. This contributes directly to the notion of social welfare. "The Social Design becomes an activity that leads to economic growth and development of the site where the project is carried out" (Peroba apud Margolin, 2008:41). For Dondis, "the human visual experience is fundamental in the learning process so that we can understand the environment and react to it" (1997:7). This brings us to the issue of social vulnerability of the families of these women admitted in the PMS FCAP. According to Janczura (2012:303)

> One of the risk factors to the psychological and social development is the low socioeconomic level. In poor families, operate as high risk factors, in addition to the low socioeconomic status, parental compensation, low educational level, large families and the absence of a parent.

Therefore, the communities attended and the target audience of the PMS FCAP almost entirety are affected by these five risk factors. Understanding this complex socio-political-economic environment and the tensions involved into these families is fundamental for the preparation of a design program that encompasses the social aspects. Moreover, the awareness about the responsible use of resources makes the benefited public reflect about the materials, tools, use, recovery, reuse, and disposal. It also leads them to be aware about these resources, environment, ecology, and sustainability.

Sustainable aspects

The concept of sustainable development (SD) guides the people to develop in a sustainable environment, thus ensuring a better future. Many authors such as Neves (2003:319) highlight sustainable development:

> [...] designates a normative approach of integrated strategic planning and management and participatory development, seeking the satisfaction of basic needs of the population, their participation in decision-making about development strategies, solidarity with future generations and ecological prudence. Contemplating both the social justice, political autonomy, economic efficiency and ecological prudence.

As you can (come to conclusion or conclude) (tell) by the current prominence in the media, the themes related to the SD are far-reaching and of general interest; globalization boosts the information and makes the communication happen very quickly, resulting in an increasingly dynamic and informed world. Jesus (2003) collaborates, saying that local development means a process that mobilizes individuals and institutions with a view (to) transforming the local economy and society, with the prospect of greater opportunities (*for) into employment and income for the people of the place and geographical region. This author considers local development as a way out of the crisis because it makes changes that enable or contribute to local development, enabling an effort located in the territory to which he adds the concentration between leaders, institutions, companies, and inhabitants of a particular place enabling the potential and local resources. Also, from this perspective, we have Callou (2007) defending local development as a strategy to resolve, through a dynamic of "consultation" of the territories, the problems of social exclusion by a collective effort of the various social actors in these territories.

During the practical activities in the productive workshops held in NGO's (non-governmental organization), the principle of reuse of textiles and of EcoModa presents itself as a purposeful, multidisciplinary, and dialogic tool in pursuit of sustainability. In the dimension of sustainability, the PMS FCAP is supported by Reigota's suggestion (1994:12): work environmental education that is community-oriented, encouraging the individual to participate actively in the resolution of the problems in context of specific realities.

Because of the lack of qualified workforce and the need for a sustainable development in the globalized world, there is a need for people with entrepreneurial training, broad vision, and those who can make innovative contributions to the business. Although innovation is important for success on the market, this still does not represent a long-term strategic goal for all companies (Aranda, 2009). The definition of the professional role depends, widely, on the perception of the skills and competences and their relationship to the demands of the professions in the labor market, which is the stimulus to entrepreneurship basic to PMS FCAP.

As Leite (2002) explains, being an entrepreneur means having capacity to initiate, imagination to conceive ideas, flexibility to adapt them, creativity to turn them into a business opportunity, motivation to think conceptually, and the ability to view and understand the changes as an opportunity, taking seriously the management of business.

By expanding the concept of social entrepreneurship objective, we achieve positive results within a society, establishing measures and strategies that generate a positive environmental and social return. By joining the business community actions, we generate profit and improve communities and reduce social and economic inequalities from(the) creation of sustainable social business which are at core of the PMS FCAP. The actions proposed by the PMS FCAP aimed at the benefit of women, seeking a fairer form of life in which social differences are reduced and the environment is preserved, these being the social entrepreneurship fundamental precepts.

Results obtained and expected

The project that has been developing since 2011, and during this period, 180 women have qualified. For the year 2015, innovates adding beyond knowledge about fashion, craft and design the concept of Social Affairs through the vision of entrepreneurship, management and marketing of enterprises. The impact of the action will come to an end in 2015, with 225 women directly and 325 indirectly affected. The trainings and actions carried out by the project will benefit the public directly, generating impact and improvement to the social segments: residents of subhuman housing (slums) attended by NGO partners.

In addition, the PMS FCAP stimulates the creative economy, social entrepreneurship, and (the) generation of employment and income, demonstrating that the social dialogue mechanism in which various social actors come together in support of sustainable development is feasible and necessary for the transformation and growth of the fair due to inclusion of the communities in situations of social risk to the process of human dimensions. The expectation is that at the end of the biennium 2014/15, the embryo of a network of fashion design crafts will be operationalized with the deployment of a selling point.

Conclusion

The participation of women in the economy is a great challenge of the 21st century. According to Arrancha González, general director of the International Trade Centre, each $1.00 invested by a woman turns into $7.00 in the economy. They invest 90% of what they receive in the community where they live, that is, the social development and inclusion of entire communities in the process of citizenship through the hands of women. The paradigm shifts pointed out by this reality are immense (Flach & Bezerra, 2015:18). The PMS FCAP acts as social vector plotting within interpersonal relations communities. From the mother cell of these – the woman – urging them to spread their affections and creativity in the community in which they live, for small production and natural objects that are useful, loaded with history, are beautiful and loaded with possibilities. Changing the condition mainly look for these objects, and the perception of huge value transformer in techniques and handicrafts, passed by family, neighbors and the commodities of a driving force of the economy: sustainable development.

Finally, it is important to note that the partial results of the extensionists project PMS FCAP demonstrated that the concept of "social entrepreneurship" worked out in the various actions, and articulated with the social, economic, and environmental dimensions is impactful and necessary for social transformation: this type of society is no longer considered utopian, but presents itself as a way of reality and salvation.

Note

1 This technique works with rounded small pieces of fabric sewed by hand with needle and thread on the fringe remember a flower's form. The name is a slang that means gossiping.

References

Abbonizio, M. A. de O. (2009). Aproximação teórica das intervenções de design no artesanato com os princípios pedagógicos de Paulo Freire: caminhos para uma prática emancipatória. 2009. 136 f. Dissertação (Curso de Pós-Graduação em Design) – Universidade Federal do Paraná, Curitiba.

Ambrose, G. and Harris, P. (2011). *Fundamentos de Design Criativo*. Porto Alegre: Bookman.

Aranda, M. (2009). Retrieved from: www.lume.ufrgs.br/handle/10183/15689 Acesso em 18 de julho 2015.

Brasil. (2015). Cultura e Arte como Base para a Educação Integral. Retrieved from: www.cultura.gov.br/educacao-e-cultura Acesso em 26 de julho de 2015.

Callou, Â. B. F. (2007). *Extensão Rural: polissemia e memória*. Recife: Bagaço.

Cuche, D. (1999). *A Noção de Cultura nas Ciências Sociais*. Trad. Ribeiro, V. São Paulo: EDUSC.

Dondis, Donis A. (1997). *Sintaxe da Linguagem Visual*. São Paulo: Martins Fontes.

Flach, N. and Bezerra, P. (2015). Entrevista. Dinheiro. Ano 17 nº 919. 10 jun. páginas 18–20.

Heskett, J. (1998). *Desenho Industrial*. Rio de Janeiro. 2 Ed. Trad. Fábio Fernandes. São Paulo: José Olympio.

IBGE (Instituto Brasileiro de Geografia e Estatística). (2010). *Contas Regionais do Brasil 2010–2013*. Numero 38. ISSN 1415-9813

IBGE. (2012). *Cidades, Recife, Síntese das informações*. Retrieved from: https://cidades.ibge.gov.br/brasil/pe/recife/panorama

Janczura, R. (2012). Risco ou Vulnerabilidade Social? *Porto Alegre: Textos & Contextos*, v. 11, n. 2, p. 301–308, ago./dez.

Jesus, P. de. (2003). Desenvolvimento Local. In: *A outra economia* Antônio David Cattani (Org.). Porto Alegre.

Latour, B. (1994). *Jamais fomos modernos*. Rio de Janeiro: editora 34.

Leite, E. F. (2002). *O Fenômeno do Empreendedorismo Criando Riquezas*. 3 ed. Recife: Bagaço. 560.

Morin, E. (2011). *Os Sete Saberes Necessários à educação do Futuro*. 2 ed. Trad. Catarina Eleonora F. da Silva e Jeanne Sawaya. Brasília: Cortez, UNESCO.

Neves, M. (2003). *Consumo Consciente: um guia para cidadãos e empresas socialmente responsáveis*. Rio de Janeiro: E- Papers Serviços Editoriais.

Peroba, A. R. V. (2008). Design Social: Um Caminho para o Designer de Moda? (*Master's thesis in Design*, Universidade Anhembi Morumbi). Retrieved from: http://tede.anhembi.br/tedesimplificado//tde_busca/arquivo.php?codArquivo=255 Acessado em: 20 julho de 2015.

Reigota, (1994). *M. O que é educação ambiental*. São Paulo: Brasiliense.

Thiollent, M. (1998). *Metodologia da pesquisa-ação*. São Paulo: Cortez e Autores Associados.

Yus, R. (2002). *Educação Integral: uma educação holística para o século XXI*. Porto Alegre: Artmed. http://www.cidades.ibge.gov.br/xtras/temas.php?lang=&codmun=261160&idtema=16&search=pernambuco|recife|sintese-das-informacoes> Acesso em 17 de junho 2015.

Appendix 1
Initial Inquiry

Modateca Social FCAP: Apprehending Entrepreneurship

Name:
Address:
Birth date: Institution
Number of children (sons and daughters): marital status
Please answer questions in as much detail as possible

1 What courses have you already taken?
( ) Arts
( ) Embroidery
( ) Screen print
( ) Paint
( ) Pattern
( ) Bijoux making
( ) Draw
( ) Clay
( ) Others ______________________
( ) Sewing
( ) Masks
( ) Tricot
( ) Puppets/dolls
( ) Crochet
( ) Estamparia

2 Which activities do you do nowadays?
( ) Screen painting
( ) Knitting
( ) Mask making
( ) Textile painting
( ) Crochet
( ) Dolls
( ) Draw
( ) Bordado

( ) Fuxico
( ) Sewing
( ) Pattern
( ) Others ______________________
( ) Knotting
( ) Clay

3 How many years do you work with this?
( ) None
( ) Less than 1 year
( ) 1 to 2 years
( ) More than 3 years
( ) More than 5 years

4 How long have you marketed your products / services?
( ) Never
( ) Less than 1 year
( ) 1 to 2 years
( ) 2 to 5 years
( ) More than 5 years

5 What is your monthly income?
Salary R$ ____________
Government income R$ ____________
Others R$ ____________

6 Do you expect to commercialize the products at the end of the project?
( ) Yes
( ) No

7 How many people live with you?

8 How many children depend on your income?

9 What is your interest in participating in the Modateca Social FCAP project? Talk about your expectations with the course: what do you expect will change in your life after the course, if you believe that you will work regularly with the activities you learn in the project and any other information that you think is important.

5 Challenges faced by female entrepreneurs[1]

Dafina D. Abdullahu

Introduction

Women can participate in business, but not in leadership position, is considered a problematic area needing special attention. Nowadays the role of women in business is increasing. This is due to the fact that women are now more educated than ever before. Today, we have a large number of women participating in different governing structure, education, business, and in almost all spheres of life; this serves as model for a new generation. This made us realize that women have the power to choose and to define themselves, not only when it comes to a family or household and the organization, but also in choosing their career path. Kosovo government decision no. 5/131, dated February 1, 2005, established the *Office for Gender Equality* as a special body of the *Government of Kosovo* in accordance with article 5.1 of UNMIK Regulation no. 2004/18, dated June 7, 2004, on the promulgation of the *Law on Gender Equality* adopted by the Assembly of Kosovo (Law no. 2004/2), with the decision of the Government of Kosovo no. 03/2006, dated July 12, 2006, Office of Gender Equality, from 1 September 2006, the Agency for Gender Equality[2] (Newsletter, 2014), and Office of the Prime Minister (Republic of Kosovo Office of the Prime Minister Agency for Gender Equality, 2018).

When it comes to gender equality in Kosovo, it mainly means to advance the position of women in society, especially in public life and in decision-making positions. Law on Gender Equality (Law on Gender Equality, 2018) defines the conditions and opportunities for gender equality through policies that support overall development and improvement, especially the position of women, so that they are valued and can enjoy authority in the family and society.

Kosovar society has continuously made efforts to achieve gender equality, in particular the advancement of women in society and public life. After the last war in Kosovo, efforts for the emancipation of women not only increased but also assessed their contribution to society and advanced their position. A considerable number of different organizations, including NGOs, local and international, through various programs and projects, have contributed to the advancement of women toward achieving gender equality. Kosovo institutions have consistently taken a number of actions to ensure equal opportunity and treatment without discrimination, including gender differences. In some cases, affirmative action measures were taken that lead to the achievement of gender equality such as the assignment of gender quotas or similar. To reflect the current situation in the field of gender equality and efforts made by public and private institutions, the following report provides an analysis of the legislation in power in Kosovo, which promotes and encourages the achievement of gender equality in Kosovo, in particular the promotion of participation of women in the workplace and in leadership positions and decision-making.

The weak economy, cultural practices, discrimination in the labor market, and even property rights and inheritance constitute some of the obstacles in improving the situation. According to the latest data from the Agency of Statistics, women have a high degree of absenteeism in the labor market, with 81.9% of them not being active (Economia, 2018).

Review of the literature

Women play an important role in guiding small businesses especially. Due to the numerous skills and training that they have undergone to achieve a balance between professional and personal life, they perform more and give excellent results. According to Kofi Annan, 'Gender Equality is more than a goal in Itself. It is a precondition for meeting the challenge of Therapeutic Poverty, Promoting sustainable development and building good governance' (Garfinkle, 2018).

According to Caliper (2005), women leaders are more assertive and persuasive, have a stronger need to get things done, and are more willing to take risks than men leaders. Women leaders are also found to be more empathetic and flexible, as well as stronger in interpersonal skills than their men counterparts (Maseko, 2013).

Mandipaka (2014) stated that the main obstacles that women face in business are related to education and work. Literature confirms that skills training and business education have a positive effect on enterprise performance (Akanji, 2006; Cheston & Kuhn, 2002; Kuzilwa, 2005).

Shane (2003) acknowledged that the exploitation of entrepreneurial opportunity depends on the entrepreneur's level of education, skills or knowledge acquired through work experience, social network, and credit.

Ibru (2009) stated that many women entrepreneurs lack training and education both in developed and developing countries, and hence the need for training especially in developing economies must be highlighted (Mandipaka, 2014).

The importance and role of women leaders in Kosovo

Kosovar women are considered to possess an inherent untapped talent for potential business from a significant number of local and international organizations. However, the use of this potential has remained far below the levels of expectation. Official data on the structure of our businesses show that gender differences are significant in relation to ownership. Women in Kosovo today generally tend to be the owners of smaller businesses that operate with capital many times lower than male business owners, establish the functional businesses in sectors predominantly less in value, and face social, cultural, and environmental barriers. To increase the participation of women in business and change the current nomenclature gender of businesses, a multidimensional approach is the necessity of the day. This multidimensional approach requires intensive involvement of institutions, agencies, and business associations. Such an approach requires a more friendly and favorable business environment, an easier access to capital, and a more fair society. Moreover, change in our attitudes toward women by showing faith in them, giving them opportunity to prove themselves, and by protecting pathways to female entrepreneurship initiatives are all prerequisites for an environment that creates value. Women in Kosovo have a lot to give to Kosovo's economy (Abdixhiku, 2012). There are many sectors (example, trace textiles and food processing) where Kosovar women give the country not only domestic but also potential comparative advantage in the region. Kosovo needs to build on these advantages. Based on this, we can conclude that large gender differences exist in the labor market, where, among other things, we will mention:

- Nearly one in five (18.1%) women of working age are active in the labor market, compared with about three-fifths (56.7%) of working-age men.
- Among persons in the labor force, unemployment is higher for women than for men (36.6% compared with 31.8%).
- The employment rate among working-age women is only 11.5%, compared with 38.7% for men.
- This very low degree of unemployment among women stems from the combination of very low participation in the labor force and high unemployment.
- Family responsibilities were the main reason for non-activity of women in the labor market; 38.5% of female respondents gave this reason.
- Women were employed mainly in the sectors of education and health (40% of employed women).
- Men were mainly employed in the manufacturing, trade, and construction (employing more than 40% of employed men) sectors.
- Men tend to work longer hours than women; 29.5% of men work more than 48 hours a week compared with 10.6% of women. A greater proportion of employed women (26.4%) worked less than 40 hours compared with 13.2% of men (Statistical Agency of Kosovo, 2016).

The challenges facing the Kosovar women today

Regarding the challenges women face nowadays, there are many in Kosovo, first being the mentality that exists in the society. However, only a few challenges are listed, as there are ways and mechanisms for changing the reports of representation of women in society, and the change of mentality requires a longer time. Society needs to build a new mentality on the role and status of which are part gravem komplemtentare society as men. Therefore, women face greater unemployment than men. Today, more women than ever before are very keen to be educated as it alone provides the opportunity to progress in life and to confront it difficulties.

It is generally known that leadership is male-dominated; however, women are trying to enter leadership positions and adopt men's style. Both, male and female have different style of leadership. Therefore, we need to analyze the main reasons that more men are holding leader positions while females face barriers to the leadership and management positions. Research is based on theory about leaders, leadership, and management, as well as male and female leadership style. Qualitative method was chosen for this research. Relevant information from articles, journals, books, the Internet, and web sites has been discussed. It is common knowledge that female want to reach the position of top management, but they face some obstacles to achieve that goal. Also, it is obvious that men have leadership positions in many spheres. However, research is mostly about differences in leadership and management between females and males (Kadyrkulova, 2007–2008).

Female leadership qualities:

1 openness,
2 flexibility,
3 empathy,
4 relational strengths,
5 inclusiveness, and
6 preference for collaboration (Cocchio, 2009).

Research results

The main work was intended to identify the participation of women in leadership positions in various companies. Therefore, we surveyed 25 companies whose results have shown only a very small participation of women in leadership positions. Therefore, all results will be presented through the following graphics (Figures 5.1–5.8):

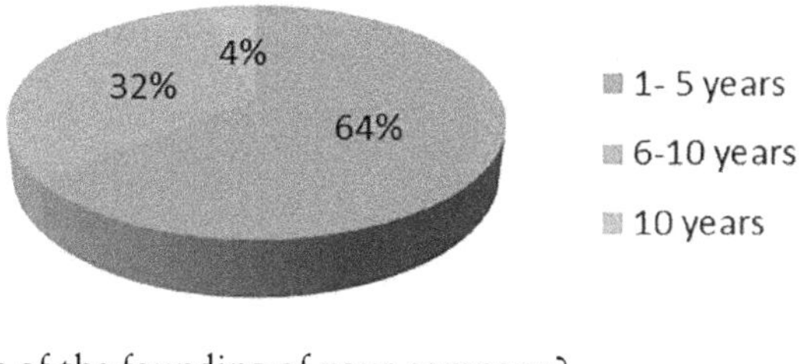

Figure 5.1 Years of the founding of your company?

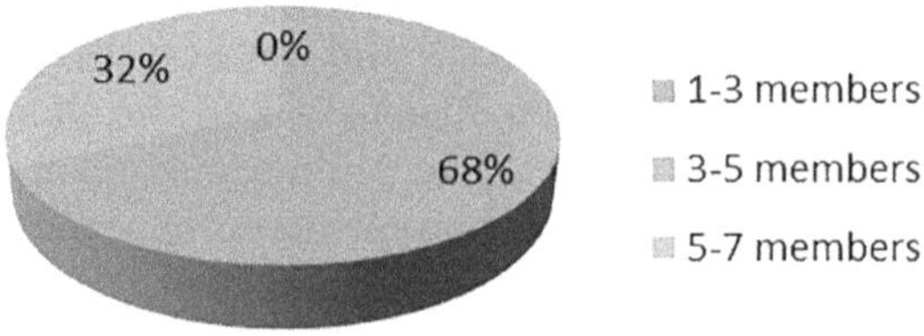

Figure 5.2 How many board members does your company have?

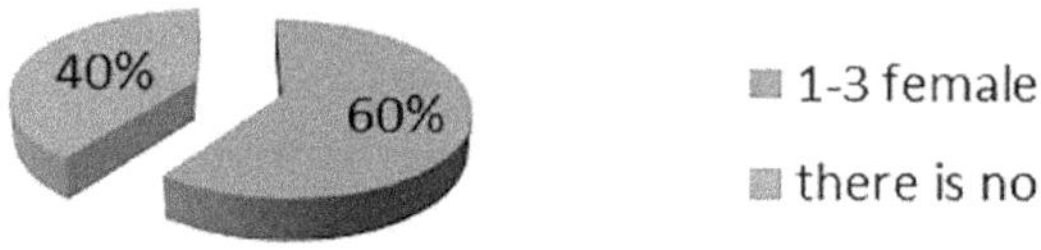

Figure 5.3 What is women board participation?

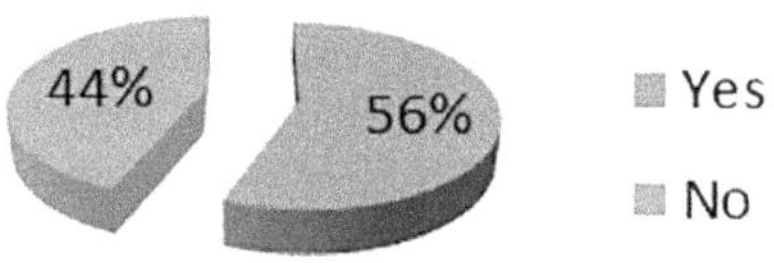

Figure 5.4 Does it affect women in decision-making?

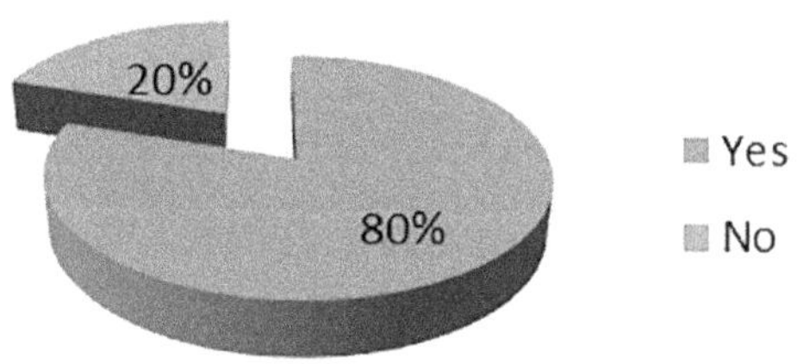

Figure 5.5 Does the company's performance enhance by the presence of women?

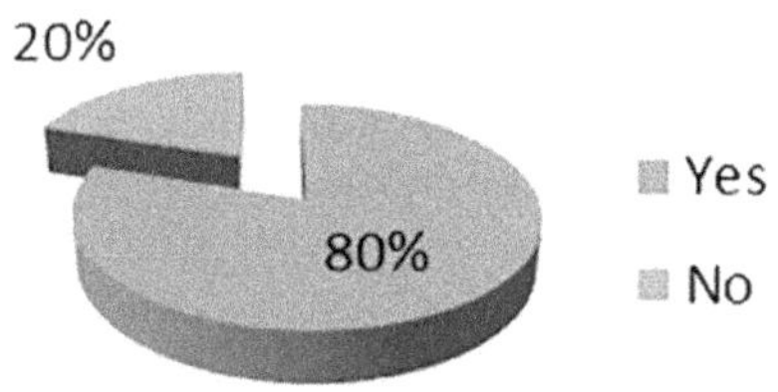

Figure 5.6 Is the salary of women same as that of men in the same position?

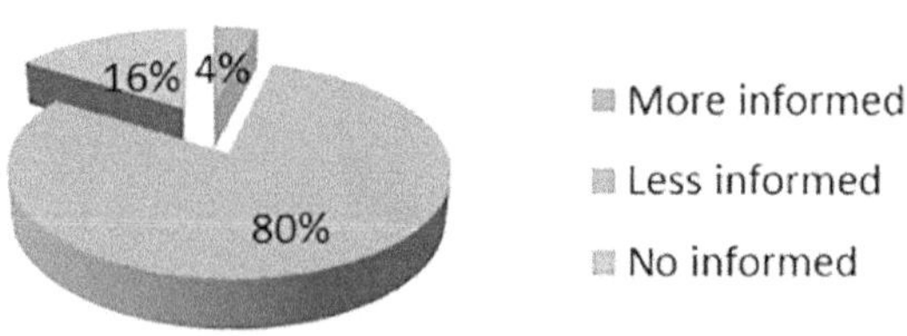

Figure 5.7 Do women get influenced by other people when making decisions?

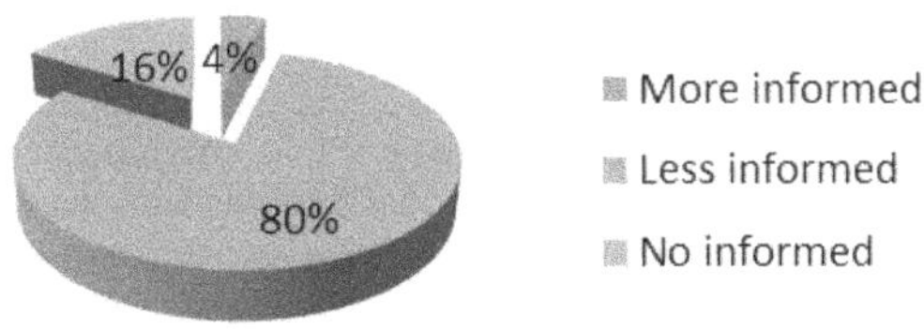

Figure 5.8 Are women informed about their rights?

Testing of hypotheses

Hypothesis 1

H_0 – Females have no impact on decision-making in companies that they work in
H_A – Females have an impact on decision-making in companies that they work in

This hypothesis is confirmed by non-parametric chi-squared test (Hi square). As seen earlier, the value calculated by SPSS-Pearson chi-squared is $X^2 = 5{:}11$. Once Asymp.Sig.[3] $p = 0.000 < 0.078$, H0 hypothesis is rejected (Tables 5.1–5.3). So the alternative hypothesis is accepted, which means that females impact decision-making in companies that they work in.

Hypothesis 2

H_0 – years of establishment of the company have no impact on the rate of growth of the females employed
H_A – years of establishment of the company have impact on the rate of growth of the females employed

This hypothesis is confirmed by non-parametric chi-squared test (Hi square) (Tables 5.4 and 5.5). As seen above, the value calculated by SPSS Pearson's chi-squared = 0871 X^2. Once Asymp.Sig. $p = 0.000 < 0.667$ or 67.7%, H0 hypothesis is rejected. So the alternative hypothesis is accepted, which means that the founding years of the company have no impact on the growth of the females employed.

Conclusions

From the study we can see that the concern remains that we have a low number of women employees, especially in leadership positions. Therefore, the government should develop policies aiming at raising awareness and increasing the role of women in active labor market, given that the labor market in Kosovo is unfavorable considering the fact that unemployment is quite large and dominates the female gender. Women should have as many equal opportunities in terms of their professional orientation. There is an

Table 5.1 Case-processing summary

	Cases					
	Valid		*Missing*		*Total*	
	N	*Percent*	N	*Percent*	N	*Percent*
As it affects women in decision-making	25	100.0%	0	0.0%	25	100.0%

Table 5.2 Chi-square tests

	Value	*df*	*Asymp. Sig. (2-sided)*	*Monte Carlo Sig. (2-sided)*			*Monte Carlo Sig. (1-sided)*		
				Sig.	*95% Confidence Interval*		*Sig.*	*95% Confidence Interval*	
					Lower Bound	*Upper Bound*		*Lower Bound*	*Upper Bound*
Pearson chi-square	5.114[a]	2	.078	.050[b]	.045	.054			
Likelihood ratio	6.129	2	.047	.050[b]	.045	.054			
Fisher's exact test	4.520			.050[b]	.045	.054			
Linear-by-linear association	.486[c]	1	.485	.599[b]	.589	.608	.443[b]	.433	.453
N of Valid Cases	25								

a Four cells (66.7%) have expected count less than 5. The minimum expected count is.40.
b Based on 10,000 sampled tables with starting seed 926214481.
c The standardized statistic is .697.

Table 5.3 Symmetric measures

		Value	*Approx. Sig.*	*Monte Carlo Sig.*		
				Sig.	*95% Confidence Interval*	
					Lower Bound	*Upper Bound*
Nominal by nominal	Phi	.452	.078	.050[c]	.045	.054
	Cramer's V	.452	.078	.050[c]	.045	.054
N of valid cases	25					

a Not assuming the null hypothesis.
b Using the asymptotic standard error assuming the null hypothesis.
c Based on 10,000 sampled tables with starting seed 926214481.

Table 5.4 Chi-square tests

	Value	*df*	*Asymp. Sig. (2-sided)*
Pearson Chi-square	.781[a]	2	.677
Likelihood ratio	.997	2	.607
Linear-by-linear association	.750	1	.386
N of valid cases	25		

a Four cells (66.7%) have expected count less than 5. The minimum expected count is .20.

Table 5.5 Symmetric measures

		Value	*Approx. Sig.*
Nominal by nominal	Phi	.177	.677
	Cramer's V	.177	.677
N of valid cases	25		

a Not assuming the null hypothesis.
b Using the asymptotic standard error assuming the null hypothesis.

increasing need to increase the number and impact of women in leadership positions and decision-making. Recommendations:

- The equal treatment without discrimination
- To be informed about the rights that belong
- To increase the participation of women in the labor market
- To give more support from local institutions in order to promote decision-making skills
- To have as much training which informs that women should be part of the labor market
- To have the highest level of educated women.

Notes

1 This study was presented in 7th International Women and Business Congress, November 9–11, 2016, Prizren Ukshin Hoti University.
2 Agency for Gender Equality is important for the functioning of democratic institutions and has a mandate to develop, implement, propose, coordinate, and monitor national and international public policies on gender equality and is responsible for the promotion, protection, and advancement.
3 The abbreviation Asymp. Sig. (2-Sided) stands for the term asymptotic.

References

Abdixhiku, L. (2012). *Roli Gruas Në Ekonominë Kosovare*. http://abdixhiku.blogspot.com/2012/03/roli-gruas-ne-ekonomine-kosovare.html,March8th,2012 (Accessed on February 4th, 2018).

Akanji, O. O. (2006). Microfinance As a Strategy for Poverty Reduction. *Central Bank of Nigeria Economic and Financial Review*, 39 (4), 111–134.

Caliper. (2005). *Women Leaders Study: The Qualities that Distinguish Women Leaders*, http://www.caliperonline.com/brochures/WomenLeaderWhitePaper.pdf, (Accessed on May 13th, 2019)

Cheston, S., & Kuhn, L. (2002). *Empowering Women through Microfinance. A Case Study of Sinapi Aba Trust, Ghana*. USA: Opportunity International, http://www.chs.ubc.ca/srilanka/PDFs/Empowering%20women%20through%20microfinance.pdf, (Accessed on March 16th, 2019)

Cocchio, L. K. (2009). *Executive Leadership for Woman*. University of Alberta Edmonton, Alberta, March 11th, 2009.

Ekonomia, Zëri i Amerikës. (2018). Empowering Women Challenge for Kosovo, Fuqizimi i grave sfidë për Kosovën. www.ekonomia-ks.com/?page=1,5,392649 (Accessed on April 13th, 2018).

Garfinkle, Joel. (2018). *Male & Female Leadership: Difference between Male & Female Leadership*. http://careeradvancementblog.com/male-female-leadership (Accessed on March 15th, 2018).

Ibru, C. (2009). *Growing Microfinance through New Technologies*. Akure: Federal University of Technology.

Kadyrkulova, A. (2007–2008). Master Thesis: Female and Gender Leadership, Dr. Pr. Phillippe Daudi and Pr. Mikael Lundgren. Master's Program in Leadership and Management in International Context, Baltic Business School, University of Kalmar, Sweden, www.diva-portal.org/smash/get/diva2:238/fulltext02 (Accessed on May 15th, 2018).

Kuzilwa, J. (2005). The Role of Credit for Small Business Success: A Study of the National Entrepreneurship Development Fund in Tanzania. *The Journal of Entrepreneurship*, 14 (2), 131–161.

Law on Gender Equality. (2018). General Provisions, Article 1 Point 1.2. www.gazetazyrtare.com/e-gov/index.php?option=com_content&task= view&id=76&Itemid=28&lang=en (Accessed on March 15th, 2018).

Mandipaka, F. (2014). *"An Investigation of the Challenges Faced by Women Entrepreneurs in Developing Countries"*. University of Fort Hare December. www.mcser.org/journal/index.php/mjss/article/viewFile/5196/5013 (Accessed on May 15th, 2018).

Maseko, I. T. (2013). *A Comparative Study of Challenges Faced by Woman in Leadership: A Case of Foskor and the Department of Labour in Mhlathuze Municipality*.

Newsletter (2014). *Gender Equality Agency, Raporti i dytë Monitorues për Progresin e Implementimit të Planit të Veprimit për zbatimin e Rezolutës 1325, "Gratë, Paqja dhe Siguria"* 2013–2015, p. 3. http://abgj.rks-gov.net/Portals/0/Shqip_B9.pdf (Accessed on February 8th, 2018).

Republic of Kosovo Office of the Prime Minister Agency for Gender Equality. (2018). Newsletter 2014 Gender Equality Agency, p. 3. http://abgj.rks-gov.net/Portals/0/Shqip_B9.pdf (Accessed on March 15th, 2018).

Shane, S. (2003). *A General Theory of Entrepreneurship: The Individual-Opportunity Nexus*. Cheltenham: Edward Elgar.

Statistical Agency of Kosovo. (2016). Labour Force Survey in Kosovo, Rezultatet E Anketës Së Fuqisë Punëtore 2015 Në Kosovë Qershor 2016, June 2016. http://ask.rks-gov.net/media/1684/rezultatet-e-anketes-se-fuqise-punetore-2015-ne-kosove.pdf (Accessed on June 5th, 2018).

6 Women entrepreneurship – source for livelihood opportunities in rural areas of Kosovo and in Bulgaria

Diana Kopeva, Nikolay Shterev, Ekrem Gjokaj, and Kapllan Halimi

Introduction

Women entrepreneurs have a significant role in the modern economy. Over the past three decades, women business owners have been active at all levels: at the local and regional levels and on a global scale. The formation of private businesswomen in contemporary world, more specifically in Bulgaria and Kosovo, is slowly encountering many social, economic, and legal barriers. A woman, as a business figure, is faced with a particular set of social problems and prerequisites: conflicts of roles in public and private life, mass consciousness, the deformation in the direction of the patriarchate, and so forth.

Entrepreneurship in rural areas is object of growing interest among researchers, consultants, and "policy makers" in Bulgaria and Kosovo. Entrepreneurs are a natural engine of economic development in many countries. In the context of the evolving globalization and new economic paradigm, the question about women entrepreneurship is keeping its vitality and importance, especially when the focus is on the discussions of women entrepreneurs in rural areas.

Inevitable in the transition to a market economy, structural reorganization requires a revision of the conceptual and methodological approaches to the formation of female entrepreneurship. We are talking about creating favorable conditions for disclosure of creative potential of women. This is important not only for policy of women's employment for the future, but also to solve the current, sometimes very acute, problems of definition in career field. Moreover, among the unemployed population, the majority are still women.

The main purpose of this chapter is to identify, analyze, and compare the role of women and women entrepreneurship in rural areas of Kosovo and Bulgaria. Women entrepreneurship has been recognized, during the last decade, as an important untapped source of economic growth. Women entrepreneurs create new jobs for themselves and others, and by being different, they also provide society with different solutions to management, organization, and business problems as well as to the exploitation of entrepreneurial opportunities. Women play very important roles in both rural development and the sustainable development of the countries, in particular rural women whose economic well-being depends on rural/agriculture resources. Therefore, women make vital contribution to the improvement of family livelihoods through the utilization of rural resources. The chapter also aims to analyze the women entrepreneurship within the institutional policy and legal framework that governs rural management, as well as to assess the economic impact of women entrepreneurship on rural economy, in order to provide recommendations on how to mainstream women entrepreneurship in rural policies in Kosovo and Bulgaria more effectively.

Women entrepreneurship in Kosovo and Bulgaria: state, perspectives, opportunities

The world has been changing daily as the role of women in the economy and the society has been changed. Many possibilities that were closed for the women 20 or more years ago are now rediscovered in a different manner.

With these words we could explain how the understanding of the women entrepreneurs has been changing in Bulgaria and Kosovo for last two decades. Something that looked like impossible 20 years ago, that is, women entrepreneurship, now is something usual.

But, what is the common state and status quo of the women entrepreneurship in Bulgaria and Kosovo?

There are not many studies on women entrepreneurs and women entrepreneurship in Kosovo and Bulgaria as the gender division of the entrepreneurs is not encouraged. Nevertheless, most of the previous researches focused on the women's emancipation and women's rights, that is, on the **gender equity.**

Gender equality and women's empowerment at all levels are Kosovo's policy priorities and are an integral part of achieving socially, economically, and ecologically sustainable development in the country. Kosovo's current Development Policy Programme stresses that the eradication of poverty can only be achieved through sustainable development. Women's rights are not sufficiently respected in Kosovo, although institutional and legal frameworks in addition to the constitution exist, including the law on gender equality (Law No. 2004/2) that aims to preserve, treat, and establish gender equality as a fundamental value for the democratic development of Kosovo, providing gender equal opportunities for participation in the political, economic, social, cultural, and other fields of social life.

According to the United Nations Development Programme (UNDP) (2010), Kosovo scores 0.76 on the Gender Development Index, which is the lowest in Balkan. Poverty data on Kosovo point to a 'feminization' of poverty and a rise in the number of women among the poor population. The picture of women in the labor force clearly reveals that inequality continues to prevail, but it also reveals clearly that traditional patterns are undergoing fundamental change. Women are generally disadvantaged, and unemployment continues to be a big challenge for them. Only 12% of women who are part of the formal labor force, which accounts for only 28.4%, have a permanent full-time job. Among Kosovo's business owners, only 6% are women. Only 4% of women conduct formal activities in the field of agriculture (livestock and agriculture). Only 15% are involved in production activities (textile products, dairy products, vegetable preservation, bakeries, traditional carpets, wedding gowns, etc.). The majority of women are involved in service and trade activities, with 38% providing services and 43% involved in trade. Economy is one of such sectors where women are unsatisfactorily represented. One such indicator is the share of women in the labor market in Kosovo, which is assessed at the lowest rate in Europe, with only 35% of women actively participating in the market. For these reasons, the government and development agencies should provide special funds for women in the economy and employment – especially for women in rural areas and women entrepreneurs.

The absence of sex-disaggregated data and information on SME continues to present a challenge for the design of gender-sensitive monitoring and evaluation systems. This gap is problematic for policy planning because these types of data and information are necessary for the development of policies based on the heterogeneity of local communities, including gender roles, enjoyment of rights, concerns, and access to opportunities. Data focused on women and gender issues in SME would facilitate the development of targeted policies and frameworks to achieve gender-sensitive rural policies, strategies, and programs.

Based on these facts, women were promoted as small business owners who historically had only the ceremonial role – the need to incorporate female skills and the development of her position encouraged all shareholders to provide to clients businesses, products, or quality services with high quality and value. This came through a real engagement of women from within and outside the company, while adding the instinct of care from the women's perspective to their clients, managing the current market share and expanding it to the market share. To achieve this, women entrepreneurs need to be aware of how to deal with the challenges, and they need to be secure to stay motivated, working constantly and enthusiastically for a qualitative change.

The role of women in the SME is an important generator of the economic development of a particular country, and especially in Kosovo as a transitional country. But women's challenges in SME organizations in Kosovo are numerous, starting from the most fundamental definition of market share, dishonest competition based on women's ignorance, informal economy, and financial skills to create an environment of sustainable action. One of the most important challenges for women entrepreneurs is undoubtedly the ability to manage a business and care for the evolved family, and

Kosovar women are more career-oriented in a harsh and dynamic environment; they can track competitors using innovations and high-tech products as well as communication, reduce entry barriers in some markets as a result of e-business, and respond quickly to customer needs, which requires not only meeting functional and emotional needs but also fulfillment in terms of spirit of mind, soul, and heart (Syla, 2015). Knowledge generation on gender rights, roles, and responsibilities in entrepreneurship is important in overcoming the perception of agriculture as a 'male domain' and in facilitating women's participation in agriculture use and management. In Kosovo, gender disparities in rural SME are still largely related to social norms that reinforce agriculture as a 'male' profession and the notion that women cannot benefit from engagement in agriculture-related activities.

Other major constraints in terms of women's participation in agriculture and rural SME activities are their heavy labor responsibilities, including their unpaid labor within the household, and their limited knowledge about what and how to cultivate and about running an SME, especially in the more remote villages. In addition to being trained in recognizing rural SMEs, women need a market to sell their products. Agriculture product prices change frequently, and women are unsure about whether they can sell their products at the same prices as the previous day. The low price of agriculture local products is another factor that discourages women from being more active in rural SME-related activities. Women in general lack information about the different training and grant opportunities that are provided either by the municipality or international organizations. Providing door-to-door information or more media campaign dedicated for women could represent a step forward in raising awareness.

When women do start their own businesses, they often face the problem of sustainability of their businesses. Women also need to build their assertiveness skills in order to feel confident in their decision-making role in a traditionally male-dominated society. Nevertheless, women are legally equal to inherit the land. However, legislations and conventions often have little impact on widespread traditional practices of registering property in men's name and inheritance system that favors men. If existing conventions and legislations were indeed implemented, many of the problems women encounter would certainly be eliminated.

A main problem for women is the limited access to land, property rights, and inheritance (e.g., in Kosovo, only 8% of real estate is owned by women), causing problems in providing collateral at the financial markets. Land is mainly handed down in a male line of descent, and due to tradition, it's not uncommon for women to lose the land use rights at the death of their husband and also at the death of male descents in their father's family. The problem of property related to heritage and ownership makes it almost impossible or very difficult for women entrepreneurs to get credit (loans) from the banks, government, or development agencies.

Bank practices such as those that require a male co-signer also discourage women. In addition, many poor women, especially those with little education, have difficulties completing the complicated application forms required by lending agencies to have access to same loaning opportunities. In reality, several traditions in the Kosovar society work against gender equality. The society was and is characterized by patriarchal structures, especially in rural areas.

Organization for Economic Co-operation and Development (OECD) analyzes and reports the state of the women entrepreneurship all over the world. At the 2nd OECD conference of ministers responsible for SMEs in 2004 [1], the main conclusions of the report are summarized as follows:

- Women entrepreneurs have an important impact on the economy, both in their ability to create jobs for themselves and to create jobs for others.
- Women still represent a minority of those that start new firms, are self-employed, or are small business owner-managers.
- Governments still do not know what the actual economic impact of women's entrepreneurship is in most OECD member countries. Women entrepreneurship must be examined both at the individual level (i.e. the choice of becoming self-employed) and at the firm level (the performance of women-owned and women-managed firms).
- Some specific obstacles to women entrepreneurship were found: type of education, lack of role models in entrepreneurship, gendering of entrepreneurship, weak social status, competing demands on time, and access to finance

In the OECD 2004 Report, Bulgaria is evaluated highly as the women employers Bulgaria (33.5%) were among the highest in Europe, varying between 29% and 35% in 2000. The given data for Bulgaria are given in the table (Table 6.1):

The Global Entrepreneurship Research Association (GERA) does an annual report on the women entrepreneurship – Global Entrepreneurship Monitor (GEM) [2]. Basically, they divide countries by their economic development stage and analyze the figures according to the group inclusion. According to their methodology, Bulgaria and Kosovo are European

Table 6.1 Self-employment rate in Bulgaria

	1990		1995		2000		2001	
Men	191,200	65.28%	206,900	65.75%	280,200	66.49%	245,500	65.71%
Women	101,800	34.76%	107,700	34.22%	141,0000	33.46%	128,000	34.26%
Total	292,900		314,700		421,400		373,600	

Source: [1].

developing countries. Even though Kosovo has been observed from 2015, and Bulgaria from 2016, some of the results for the developing countries for 2012 that could be applied to Kosovo and Bulgaria as well are summarized as follows:

- The level of innovation of women's start-ups (Total Early-Stage Entrepreneurial Activity (TEA) rate) is not high, and they are **efficiency-driven ones.**
- The number of single-person business is higher in women entrepreneurial business compared to men inside this group.
- One-fourth of women entrepreneurs in Developing Europe project five additional employees in five years as a projected level of growth.
- Developing Europe showed the highest level of internationalization among observed women entrepreneurs.
- Women entrepreneurs in Developing Europe are typically young and highly educated. They are also wealthy, as nearly half of them are in the highest one-third household income bracket.

In the 2015, the GEM report [3] includes Kosovo as observed country. The overall results describing women entrepreneurship are as follows:

- Basically, women matter to economic development as they invest in their communities, educate their children, and pay back the benefits they receive by helping others.
- Improvements in education provide better career choices for women, whether it is work as an employee or the launch of high-impact entrepreneurial ventures.
- Women entrepreneurs participate heavily in the consumer-oriented sector, which is considered easier to enter, but more difficult to sustain because of low entry barriers and high competitiveness.
- Women in factor- and efficiency-driven economies (like Kosovo and Bulgaria) report less difference from innovation-driven economies on job aspirations, compared to other impact indicators.
- Low female entrepreneurial (TEA) rates and female-to-male ratios in innovation-driven Europe are consistent with many of the efficiency-driven European countries. This suggests that regional characteristics, rather than economic development level, are important factors contributing to the low level of entrepreneurial activity.
- In efficiency-driven Europe, established business rates among women are low, and women in almost two-thirds of economies have established business rates less than half of those of men.
- Efficiency-driven Europe has low female entrepreneurial rates, particularly compared to the average for economies at this development level. The average rate lies around 40% of the average for the factor and efficiency development levels.

- High levels of teamwork among women (as well as high levels relative to men) are seen in a number of economies such as Kosovo, Croatia, and Bosnia and Herzegovina.

The main results for Kosovo [3] are as follows (Figure 6.1):

- Activity rates among women in Kosovo are low, including intentions, TEA, and established business activity.
- Opportunity perceptions are twice the regional average, capability perceptions are 50% higher than average, and there is low fear of failure.
- Female entrepreneurs in Kosovo show low participation in business services, but job expectation, innovation, and international sales levels are among the highest in the factor- and efficiency-driven group.

The 2016 GEM Annual Report [4] includes Bulgarian profile (Figure 6.2). The main conclusions from the previous report are valid as the women inclusion into the entrepreneurial business is not so common phenomenon.

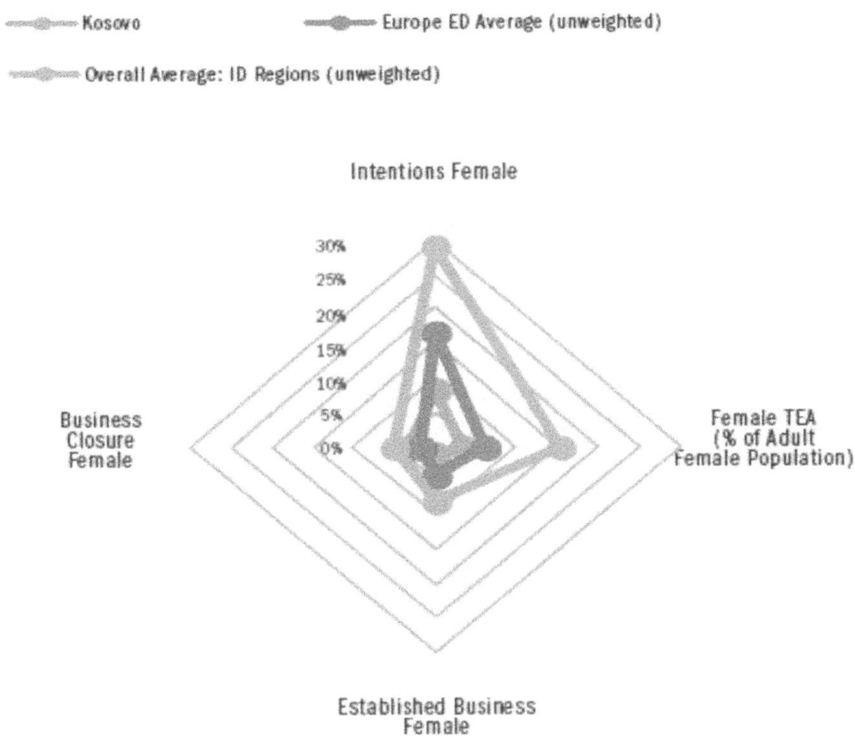

Figure 6.1 The profile of woman entrepreneurship rates in Kosovo in 2001.
Source: [3].

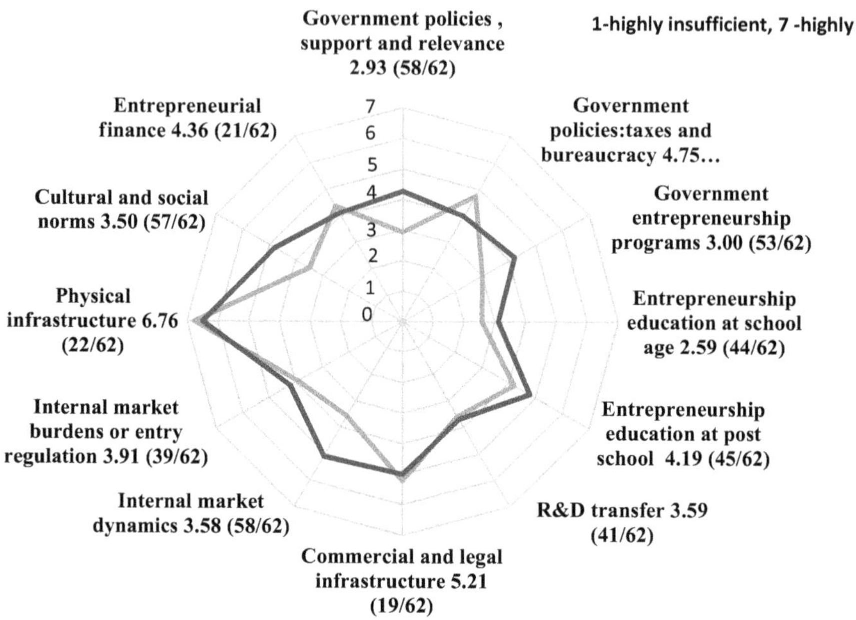

Figure 6.2 The Bulgarian 2016 profile of woman entrepreneurship rates.
Source: [4].

But the most interesting is that Bulgaria is not in a good women entrepreneurship profile and lags behind the average for all observed countries:

- Total Early-stage Entrepreneurial Activity (TEA rate) for 2015 is 3.5%, ranking Bulgaria at 59 place from 60 countries.
- Entrepreneurial Employee Activity (EEA rate) is 0.4%, ranking Bulgaria at 55 place from 60 countries
- Improvement-Driven Opportunity/Necessity Motive is 0.9%, ranking Bulgaria at 55 place from 60 countries
- Job expectations (6+ years) is 7.3%, ranking Bulgaria at 54 place from 60 countries
- Innovation that is applied in practice is implemented in 0.3% of women start-ups, ranking Bulgaria at 59 place from 60 countries.

The European Commission Country Fiche [5,6] for Bulgaria in 2014 verified the aforementioned statements about women entrepreneurship.

- In 2012, around 34% of all entrepreneurs in Bulgaria were women compared to 31% in the EU-28. The majority of these women entrepreneurs (71%) were solo entrepreneurs.
- Women entrepreneurs constituted about 8% of the women in the active labor force.

- Women entrepreneurs in Bulgaria were slightly older than men entrepreneurs. In 2012, the proportion in the age groups 25–49 years was slightly lower, and the group of 50–64 years was slightly higher.
- The average education level of women entrepreneurs was higher than that of men entrepreneurs. Compared to the total EU, women entrepreneurs in Bulgaria had a lower education level.

According to different research methodology presented earlier, we can analyze the state of women entrepreneurship in Kosovo and Bulgaria according to the official statistic data [7].

The main data for Bulgaria for the period 2000–2017 could be summarized as follows (Figures 6.3–6.5).

The main conclusions based on the (Figure 6.6) are as follows:

1. The self-employment rate in Bulgaria is almost stable for the period 2000–2017. The figures show that there are 345.3 thousand entrepreneurs, and 111.3 thousand (32.2%) of them are women at the beginning of 2000, and their number are almost the same: 336.5 thousand were entrepreneurs, and 111.9 thousands (33.3%) of them are women entrepreneurs in 2017.
2. The self-employment in the agribusiness in Bulgaria is quite different as there is a huge decrease in the agri-entrepreneurs for the period 2000–2017. The figures show that there are 130.5 thousand entrepreneurs in agribusiness, and 46.5 thousands (35.6%) of them are women at the beginning of 2000, and their number is almost twice decreased: 74.2

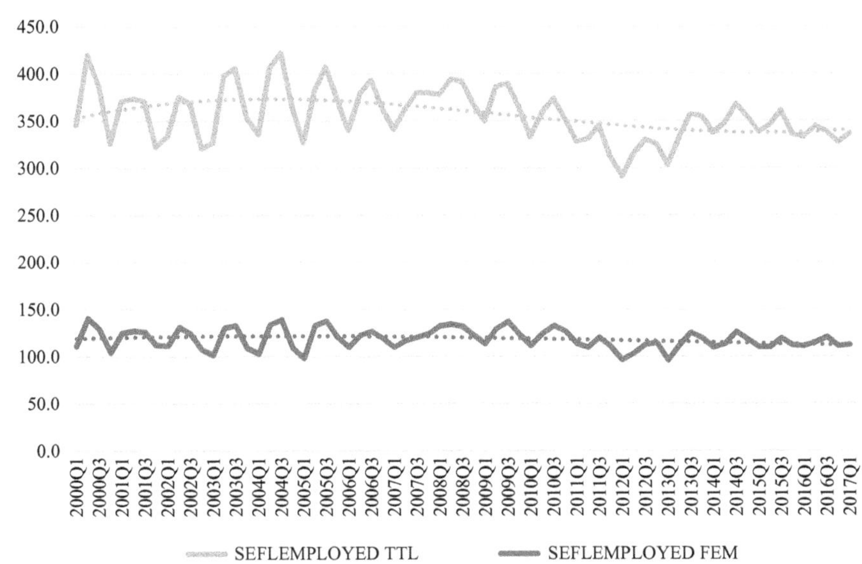

Figure 6.3 Kosovo: Self-employed total in all sectors of economy and self-employed women in total. FEM = Female/women.

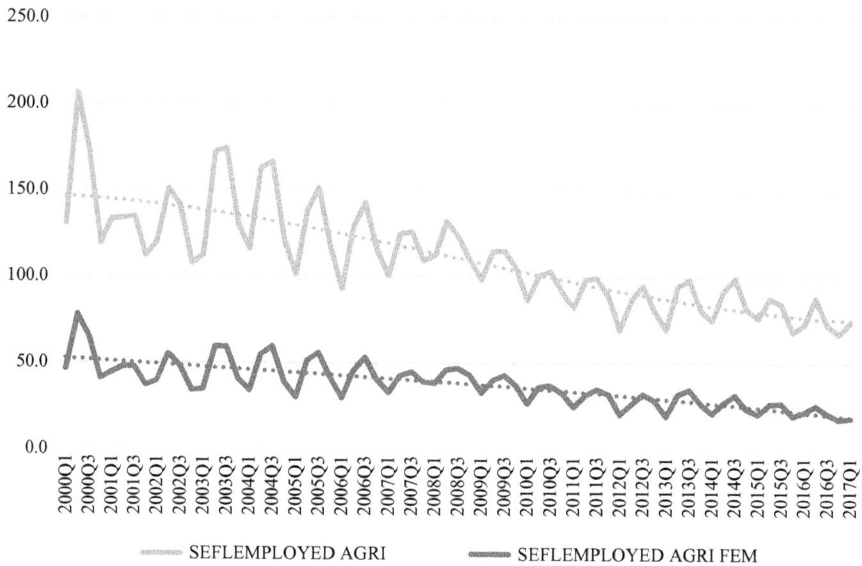

Figure 6.4 Kosovo: Self-employed total in agriculture of economy and self-employed women in agriculture. FEM = Female/women.

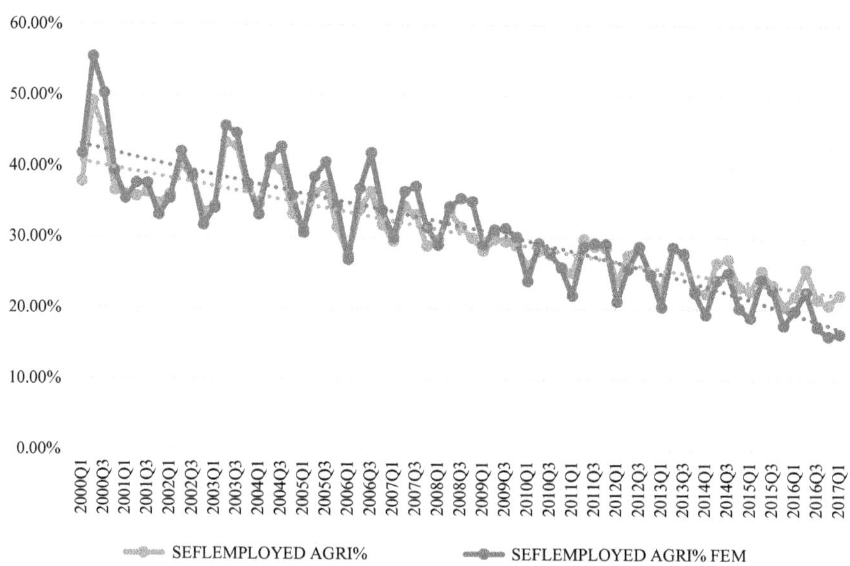

Figure 6.5 Kosovo: Self-employed women in all sectors of economy and self-employed women in agriculture. FEM = Female/women.

Source: [7].

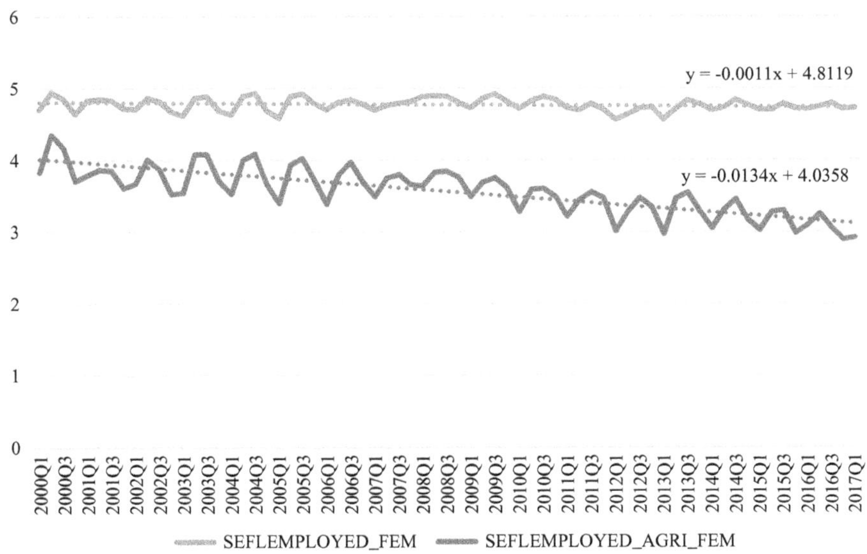

Figure 6.6 Kosovo: Self-employed total in agriculture sector (percent) and self-employed women in agriculture (percent). FEM = Female/women.

thousand are entrepreneurs, and 18.5 thousands (24.9%) of them are women entrepreneurs in 2017.

3 The change of agribusiness entrepreneurship attitudes could be presented by the percentage of self-employed in agribusiness. Their numbers decreased faster for women than for total population. The figures show that there are 38% of entrepreneurs, and 42% of women entrepreneurs are in agri-food sector in 2000, and their number decreases to 22% and 16%, respectively, in agri-food sector in 2017.

4 The trends are quite obvious when the log function of number of women entrepreneurs is presented. The number of women entrepreneurs in Bulgaria is stable (the time impact is –0.0011 per quarter period) as the log function of women entrepreneurs in agribusiness is strongly decreasing (the time impact is –0.0134 per quarter period).

5 Most of the self-employed are without any employees. The share of only one-man self-employment is greater for women, as 85.4% of women entrepreneurs and 98.3% of agribusiness women entrepreneurs do not manage any employees in 2000. The trend of decrease figures is positive, as the share of only one-man self-employment is 74% for women entrepreneurs and 97.0% for agribusiness women entrepreneurs. Nevertheless, the share of no-employee business is quite great, especially for women's self-employment in agribusiness in Bulgaria.

6 In comparison with the EU trends, the Bulgarian figures of women entrepreneurs are quite better, as 29% (32% for Bulgaria) of EU

entrepreneurs are women and 32% (36% for Bulgaria) of EU agri-entrepreneurs are women in 2000. Their number decrease as 32% (33% for Bulgaria) of women entrepreneurs are self-employed and 28% (25%) are involved in agribusiness self-employment.

The comparison between Bulgaria and Kosovo for the period 2000–2017 is summarized in Tables 6.2 and 6.3.

The main conclusions based on the Tables 6.2 and 6.3 are as follows:

There is a huge difference between Bulgaria and Kosovo in three dimensions:

a The women in Kosovo are almost twice more in the self-employment category at 13.9% (in 2017) as compared to women in Bulgaria at 7.9% (in 2017). Nevertheless, the women entrepreneurship rate decreases in Kosovo (2016–2017) by 5%, while the rate in Bulgaria decreases (2016–2017) by less than 1%.

b On the other hand, the rate of unpaid women labor force is seven times less in Bulgaria (1.0% in 2017) than in Kosovo (7.5% in 2017).

Compared to the Bulgarian figures, women entrepreneurship in agribusiness in Kosovo increases (Table 6.4).

Table 6.2 Self-employment rate in Bulgaria, 2000–2017

	2000			*2004*			*2007*		
	TTL	*Women*	*Men*	*TTL*	*Women*	*Men*	*TTL*	*Women*	*Men*
Employed persons	2,733.5	1,280.8	1,452.7	2,784.0	1,301.8	1,482.2	3,135.4	1,467.9	1,667.5
Employees	85.7%	89.2%	82.7%	86.0%	89.6%	82.8%	88.1%	91.0%	85.5%
Self-employed persons	12.6%	8.7%	16.1%	12.0%	7.9%	15.7%	10.9%	7.5%	13.8%
Contributing family workers	1.2%	1.7%	0.8%	1.6%	2.1%	1.1%	1.0%	1.5%	0.6%
	2010			*2013*			*2017*		
	TTL	*Women*	*Men*	*TTL*	*Women*	*Men*	*TTL*	*Women*	*Men*
Employed persons	3,030.9	1,408.4	1,622.5	2,855.0	1,360.6	1,494.4	3,036.7	1,412.0	1,624.7
Employees	88.0%	90.7%	85.8%	88.7%	91.1%	85.8%	88.2%	91.1%	85.7%
Self-employed persons	11.0%	7.9%	13.6%	10.6%	8.0%	13.8%	11.1%	7.9%	13.8%
Contributing family workers	1.0%	1.4%	0.6%	0.7%	0.8%	0.4%	0.7%	1.0%	0.5%

Source: [7].

Table 6.3 Self-employment rate in Kosovo

	Q1_2016			*Q2_2016*			*Q3_2016*		
	TTL	*Women*	*Men*	*TTL*	*Women*	*Men*	*TTL*	*Women*	*Men*
Employee	72.4	78.8	70.4	70.0	76.5	68.2	69.3	77.0	67.1
Self-employed with employees	6.2	3.2	7.1	7.0	3.6	8.0	7.5	3.3	8.7
Self-employed without employees	13.8	11.4	14.6	14.5	11.9	15.3	15.5	12.7	16.4
Unpaid family worker	7.6	6.5	7.9	8.4	8.1	8.5	7.6	7.1	7.8

	Q4_2016			*Q1_2017*		
	TTL	*Women*	*Men*	*TTL*	*Women*	*Men*
Employee	68.2	79.0	65.3	68.3	78.6	65.4
Self-employed with employees	7.8	2.9	9.2	7.9	2.9	9.3
Self-employed without employees	16.0	11.1	17.3	16.0	11.0	17.4
Unpaid family worker	7.9	7.0	8.2	7.8	7.5	7.9

Source: [8].

Table 6.4 Self-employment rate in agribusiness in Kosovo

	Q1_2016		*Q2_2016*		*Q3_2016*		*Q4_2016*		*Q1_2017*	
	TTL	*Women*	*TTL*	*Women*	*TTL*	*Women*	*TTL*	*Women*	*TTL*	*Women*
Economic activity by gender (000s)	7.8	0.6	14.8	1.7	16.8	2.2	17.4	2.2	17.5	2.9

Source: [8].

c Finally, women entrepreneurship in Bulgaria was researched through the National Entrepreneurial Census by the Bulgarian National Statistic Office in 2005 [10].

Two of the main tables are presented (Tables 6.5 and 6.6).

The main conclusions based on the Tables 6.7 and 6.8 are as follows:

- Women basically start a new start-up business (93.4%), while men's (one-tenth) start-up businesses are reactivation of existing ones.

Table 6.5 Start-up number in Bulgaria, 2002–2005

	Total	*Males*	*Females*
Number of units having survived from 2002 to 2005	18,648	11,046	7,602
Start-up type – new enterprise	17,139	10,034	7,105
Start-up type – reactivation after more than 2 years	1,615	1,083	532

Source: [10].

Table 6.6 Source of start-up number in Bulgaria, 2002–2005

	Total	*Males*	*Females*
Employee	11,059	6,559	4,500
Running another enterprise	2,273	1,732	541
Student	843	532	311
Unemployed and available to labor market	2,165	1,084	1,081
No gainful activity and not available to labor market	2,311	1,139	1,172
Start-up type – Total	18,648	11,046	7,602

Source: [10].

- In addition, the rate of women entrepreneurial business failure is twice less (7.9%) than the men's rate (15.7%).
- The women entrepreneurship is more like a labor opportunity –14.2% of start-ups come into existence because of women's unemployment, and 15.4% because of non-availability of women's job at the labor market. The rates for the men are quite less – 9.8% because of men's unemployment, and 10.3% because of non-availability of men's job at the labor market.

So, in conclusion, women self-employment (not just in Bulgaria nor Kosovo) represents a very important alternative for them in order to gain income. Therefore, women being or becoming self-employed is a career choice among other available options.

Even though it is hard to estimate the women's entrepreneurial economic impact, we can conclude that women play an important role in providing resources for themselves and their families. This is of social and economic importance to their respective economies. In addition, the entrepreneurial census in Bulgaria [10] gives two more perspectives (Figures 6.7 and 6.8).

Considering that most Bulgarian women entrepreneurs are above the age of 40 and they have the orientation to percept the start-up business as a job opportunity, it is reasonable that the most important motivation factors are as follows (Figures 6.9 and 6.10):

- prospect of making more money: 79%;

- avoiding unemployment: 74%;
- combining work and private life: 61%.

The less motivation factors are:

- self-employment in the family: 30%;
- to make a living from a hobby activity: 39%.

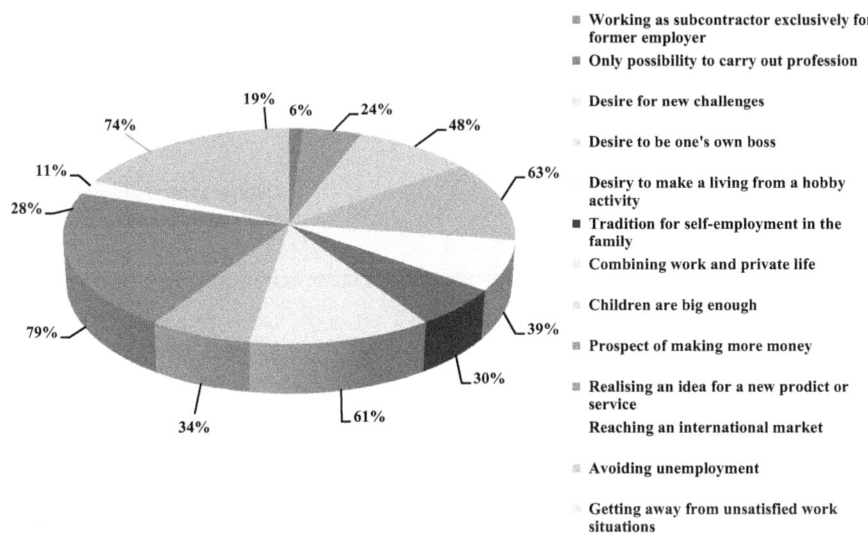

Figure 6.7 The motivation of women entrepreneurs in Bulgaria.

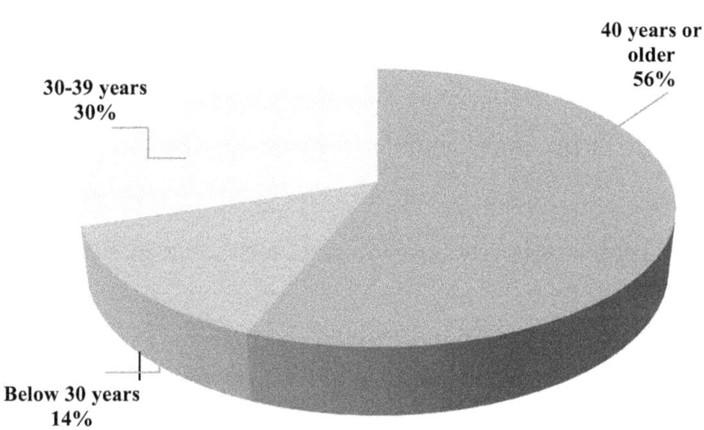

Figure 6.8 The motivation and age of women entrepreneurs in Bulgaria.
Source: [10].

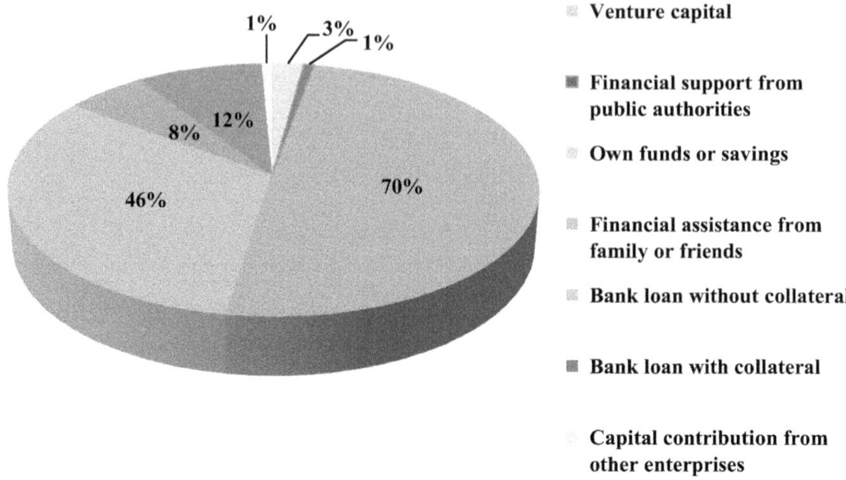

Figure 6.9 Funding opportunities for women entrepreneurship.

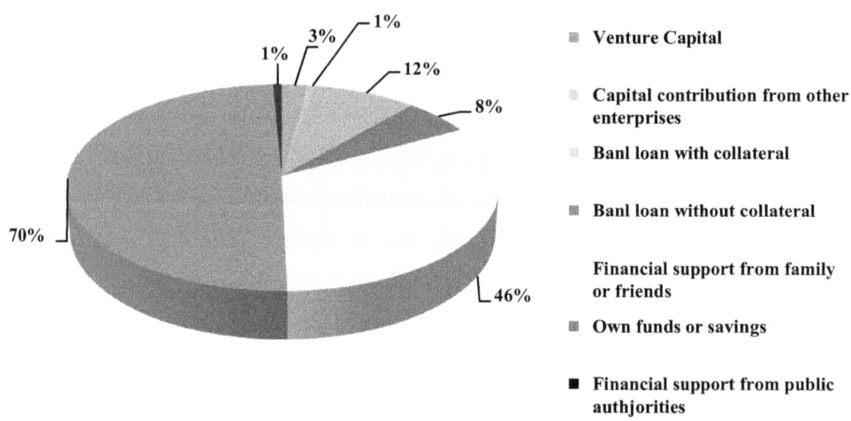

Figure 6.10 The financing and problems of women entrepreneurs in Bulgaria.
Source: [10].

The biggest problems for the growth of women's entrepreneurial business are as follows:

- to establish contacts with customers: 64%
- to deal with legal/governmental/administrative matters: 62%
- to get financing: 46%. This is a real problem, as 70% of women use their saving, 46% of them receive financial assistance from family, just 12% receive bank loans, and 1% receive funds for financing women entrepreneurs.

Therefore, we could state that the **Bulgarian policy measures do not encourage women entrepreneurship strongly enough.** This is more strongly affected in agribusiness sector where the number of entrepreneurs, especially women entrepreneurs, has decreased twice over the last 17 years.

Diversification of activities in rural areas

Role of entrepreneurship for development of rural areas in Kosovo

Improving the country is associated like never before with the business enterprise. Institutions and people advancing the country's progress now consider the enterprise as a key improvement intervention that can accelerate the simple improvement process. In addition, institutions and people seem to agree with the critical need to advance simple efforts: improvement offices see the provincial enterprise as a colossal labor potential; government officials consider it a key system to avoid domestic riots; farmers consider it as an instrument for increasing farm incomes; and women consider it as a business probability close to their homes, which gives self-rule, freedom, and a reduced demand for social assistance. For each of these meetings, in any case, the business enterprise remains a tool to enhance personal satisfaction for people, families, and groups and to support a healthy economy and well-being.

Entrepreneurial Presentation for Rural Advancement accepts business venture as the central task of financial development and improvement, without the various advancement elements being lost or lost. However, recognizing the business as a compulsory focal point independent of anyone else will not foster provincial improvement and the progress of rustic efforts. What is required most is a situation that enables the enterprise in the provincial territories. The presence of such a situation largely relies on arrangements that advance simple business ventures. The appropriateness of such approaches thus relies on a reasonable structure around the business enterprise, what it is, and from where it originates (Petrin, n.d.).

Role of entrepreneurship for development of rural areas in Bulgaria

The role of the women entrepreneurship for development in the rural areas of Bulgaria is a research topic of several research projects. By using one or more of the aforementioned methodologies, some economic, social, and demographic aspects of the women entrepreneurs in agribusiness sector in Bulgaria are found.

1 Georgi Gerganov and Radka Nenova (2012) use the Eurostat methodology in their analysis [9]. Some of their conclusions are as follows:
   - the registered farm households by Bulgarian women are 44% (2005) and 43% (2007). Their share is steady enough, and the structure of the women's households by the legal form is presented in Figures 6.11 and 6.12.
   - the number of women in farm households decreases not just because of the decreasing number of women-managed households (–28.8%) but because of the decreasing number as family workers (–49.4%) (Figure 6.13).
   - the establishment and management of farm households have been changed during the research period as the motivation has changed, from acquiring additional money (resp. in 2003) to the basic activity or unemployment opportunity (in 2010) (Figure 6.14)

2 By the demographic characteristics, the women entrepreneurs in agribusiness in Bulgaria are
   - unpaid farm household at the age that is over the average age >55 years.

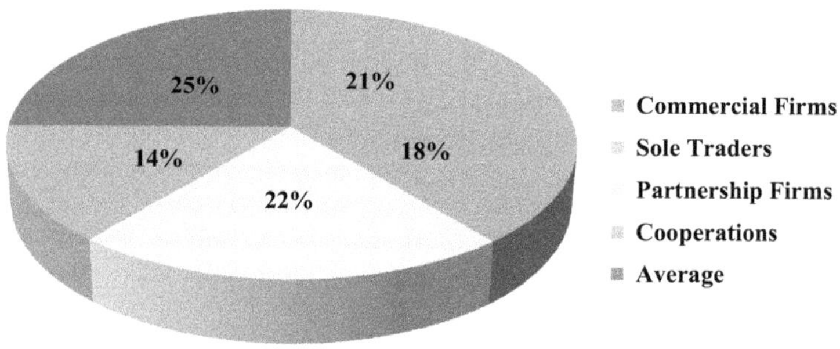

Figure 6.11 Structure of women entrepreneurs' households by legal form in Bulgaria in 2005.

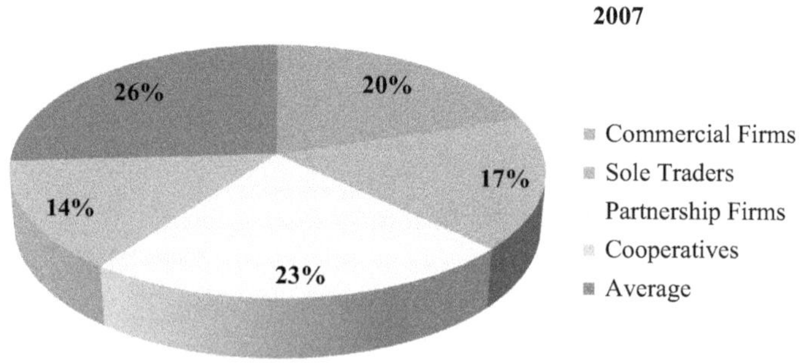

Figure 6.12 Structure of women entrepreneurs' households by legal form in Bulgaria in 2007.

Source: [9].

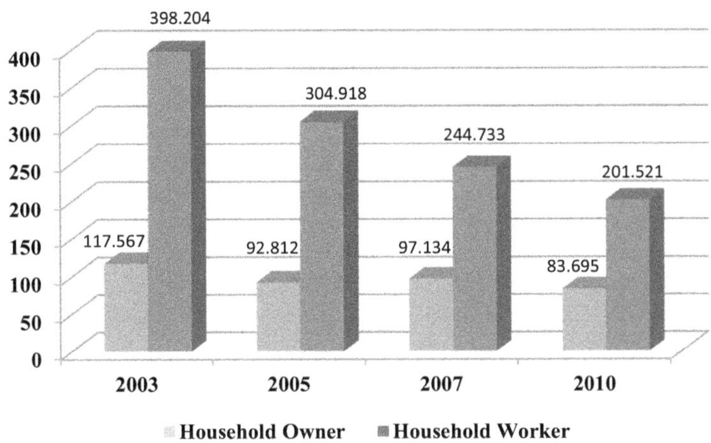

Figure 6.13 Number of women entrepreneurs' households in Bulgaria.
Source: [9].

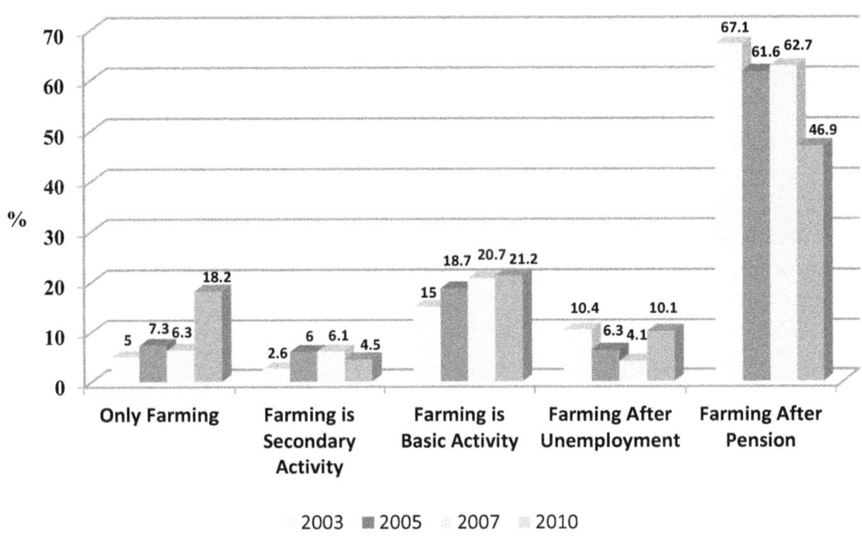

Figure 6.14 Structure of motivation for women entrepreneurs' households in Bulgaria.
Source: [9].

- managers or owners of the farm household as a secondary activity, and the motivation is additional money source at the average age of 35–55 years.
- managers or owners of farm household as a basic activity of unemployment opportunity at the age that is below the average of <35 years.

Institutional policy and legal framework that have an impact on women entrepreneurship in rural areas

The case of Kosovo

Kosovo's constitution guarantees correspondence of gender equality as a fundamental incentive for advancing the law in society. The Law on Gender Equality in Kosovo (Law 2004/2) was adopted to equalize the level the inequalities between men and women:

- Providing equal opportunities for both female and male participants in the political, economic, and sociocultural fields of society;
- Creating conditions and opportunities for gender equality through policies that support the overall development, with a specific focus on improving the status of women;
- Eliminating any barriers to achieving gender equality; and
- Setting the main principle of equal behavior and equal opportunities by applying specific measures that need to be undertaken to achieve equal rights.

The law creates conditions and opens the door to gender balance through strategies that help in overall advancement, particularly to improve the status of females in order for them to be qualified as experts in the eyes of the public and family. An Office for the Balance of Gender Equality with the oversight motivation of the implementation of the Law on Gender Equality was set up and the relevant gender budgeting program. For this reason, a clergy meeting was established to regulate issues related to sexual orientation. In addition, in all services, an officer of sexual orientation enterprises is responsible for implementing gender equality methodologies under the gender equality program.

MAFRD officials (Managing Financial Resources and Decisions) for gender issues are particularly responsive to the gender issues of females in the rural areas and female farmers, which also include the collection and observation of special aid measures, which are custom-prepared, think about visiting and transferring data. Establishing sustainable relationships to advancing gender issues in the gender workplace equality and escorting annual courses for the ladies as awareness raising and data cases are additional exercises supplemented by the gender justice officer MAFRD.

The MAFRD oversight expert, who is responsible for preparing the ARDP 2014–2020, has consulted with the human rights unit built within the MAFRD between the advancement of ARDP. The assignment of the human rights unit is to guide whether the ARDP is in line with the standards of sexual orientation of justice and hostile to the division.

The Constitution of the Republic of Kosovo has established human rights and group rights at the central review point. In accordance with worldwide and European standards, the Government of Kosovo embraced the Law on Separation 2004/3 and the Administrative Order on its Use (No. 4/2006). The aim of the law is to foresee and fight division, to increase practical honesty, and to apply the standard of equal treatment for all residents of Kosovo. The law depends on the accompanying standards:

- Equal treatment;
- Fair representation; and
- Good understanding and inter-ethnic tolerance.

The ARDP and its implementation in 2014–2020 has to do with most of the agreements set forth in the Anti-Separation Law and equivalent treatment standards. There should be no immediate or indirect victimization of any individual in the light of gender, age, masculine status, dialect, mental or physical incapacity, sexual intercourse, political alliance or belief, ethnicity, nationality, religion, race, or status. The implicit rules of the Supervisory Expert and the Organization for the Improvement of Agriculture, supplementing as the Paying Office, fully consider all hostile agreements on the separation established by the applicable law, which will also be reinforced by proper preparation for workers.

The primary finding from investigating Kosovo's legal, institutional, and its approach to sexual orientation correspondence is that it is fully aligned with universal adoption and arrangements. Moreover, the constitution states that global human rights traditions, including CEDAW and the European Tradition of Human Rights (ECHR), come foremost, even before national adoption. However, the use of laws from and to remain a test. Disclosure of Principles by Investigating a Legal, Institutional and Access System includes the following:

- The government's general sexual orientation agreement and methodologies are not all coordinated in the Timberland methodology.
- There is a lack of information and understanding by the provincial women (and by ordinary groups in general) on the rights of women over the land.
- There is a tendency of two farmers and government workers to distinguish only one individual from the family unit (usually male) as the landowner.
- Regardless of the legitimate structure created, the division of property within the family is essentially in the view of standard law.
- The inheritance rights of women's property covered in Kosovo (Kosovo Center for Gender Concentration, 2011) show that there are ongoing difficulties regarding the poor use of the Law on Inheritance and the continuation of the unwritten laws.

The case of Bulgaria

In Bulgaria, there are no particular policy funding schemes that are particularly suited to women entrepreneurs. Existing financing schemes are under European Operational Programs with a specific duration and specific requirements for the beneficiaries and the sectors in which they work.

Because of the given characteristics of gender issues in the economic, social, and demographic aspects, the main OP with specific schemes for financing women entrepreneurship is the European Social Fund (ESF). Under the regulations of ESF (as well as the European Regional Development Fund and the Cohesion Fund) are included gender equity and gender non-discrimination (*Article 16 of Council Regulation (EC) No. 1083/2006*)

Two of the categories of ESF expenditure outlined in Annex IV relates specifically to gender:

- Code 69:

  > Measures to improve access to employment and increase sustainable participation and progress of women in employment to reduce gender-based segregation in the labour market and to reconcile work and private life, such as facilitating access to childcare and care for dependent persons.

- Code 73:

  > Measures to increase participation in education and training throughout the life-cycle, including through action to achieve a reduction in early school leaving, gender-based segregation of subjects and increased access to and quality of initial vocational and tertiary education and training.

According to the Operational Programme Annual Fiche in Bulgaria, there are three measures directly financing women entrepreneurship and/or women entrepreneurship in rural areas:

- Encouraging entrepreneurship in rural areas

Field of Action 2: Establishing a favorable environment for growth and enterprise development; sub-action: better access to finance

European Commission Recommendation to Member States: Make full use of the potential of the ERDF to ensure access to finance for entrepreneurs, especially at an early stage of their activity in the field of agriculture (young farmers) and in rural areas as a whole, including through financial instruments

Name of the measure	Measure 6 "Development of farms and farm holdings," with the following sub-measures: Sub-measure 6.1 "Start-up for Young Farmers"; Sub-measure 6.2 "Start-up aid for non-agricultural activities" Sub-measure 6.4 "Investments in support of non-agricultural activities"
Responsible institution	Ministry of Agriculture and Food
Beneficiaries	Beneficiaries under sub-measure 6.1 are farmers – persons, sole traders, farm holdings, which meet eligibility criteria for the sub-measure. Beneficiaries of sub-measures 6.2 and 6.4 are farmers or micro-enterprises registered as sole traders or legal entities under the Commerce Act, the Cooperatives Act, or the Religious Denominations Act, as well as persons registered under the Crafts Act.
Additional information at:	www.prsr.government.bg www.dfz.bg

- Encouraging women entrepreneurship

Field of Action 3: Imitation examples and reaching specific groups

European Commission Recommendation to Member States: To develop and establish national women entrepreneurship development strategies aimed at increasing the share of women-led businesses.

Name of the measure	Develop a strategy to promote female entrepreneurship
Responsible institution	Ministry of Economics
Beneficiaries	Women who want to develop their own business and women entrepreneurs
Additional information at:	Organizations of women entrepreneurs

- Encouraging women entrepreneurship

Field of Action 3: Imitation examples and reaching specific groups

European Commission Recommendation to Member States: Continue to expand the existing networks of women entrepreneurs and mentors for women entrepreneurs.

Name of the measure	Develop a strategy to promote female entrepreneurship
Responsible institution	Ministry of Economics
Beneficiaries	Women entrepreneurs
Additional information at:	Organizations of women entrepreneurs

Under the implementation the Field Action 3, there are some good examples for projects that encourage women entrepreneurship in rural areas in Bulgaria:

Project title: Women in Europe – new acronym: WE-RUN[1]

OVERALL OBJECTIVE

The project offers new opportunities and innovative instruments to women living in rural areas for improving their qualifications and thus their levels of employability and integration into the labor market mainly through entrepreneurship activities related to the New Yields of Employment (NYE).

SPECIFIC OBJECTIVES

- Identify the existing relations between women from rural areas and the NYE and the emerging sectors in each of the European regions covered by the project. The final goal is recognizing the specific sectors with the greatest potential for being developed by rural women through entrepreneurship activities in each of these regions.
- Detect the best practices in business projects developed by rural women related with NYE and the emerging sectors in each of the European regions covered by the project.
- Improve rural women skills, keeping in mind that this must be a process of empowerment that will allow women to acquire abilities to undertake and create sustainable economic models from their own work, and to take advantage from the ICTs.
- Create a virtual collaborative network of women entrepreneurs from rural areas dealing with NYE and emerging sectors, with the aim of fostering the networking and the exchange of experiences and expertise at European level, not only among new entrepreneurs, but also between them and successful women entrepreneurs already established in the labor market.
- Promote and support the implementation of business projects fostered by rural women who apply business models based on the sustainable management of rural resources related to NYE and emerging sectors.

ACTIVITIES

Activity 1: Diagnosis study on the relation between rural women and NYE and emerging sectors in each of the European regions covered by the project. Main achievements or results are as follows:

- identification of specific sectors with the potential for being developed by rural women through models of self-employment and social economy (third sector),
- identification of best practices already taking place in the regions covered by the project.

Activity 2: Development of educational content and subsequent implementation of a specific training course in entrepreneurship on NYE for rural women, as well as know-how in the use of ITCs. This course (in principle under the formula of presential classes) will include a common part shared by all the regions covered by the project, and a specific part depending on the nature of each of them (nature of the rural women's problems and the sectors considered with the greatest).

Activity 3: Development of a Virtual Community of European rural women and NYE, putting them in contact with each other and with successful entrepreneurs in NYE already established in rural areas, in order to share experiences, knowledge, experiences, and so forth. The educational content developed will be uploaded on the site for greater access, as well as the general information about the project and the rest of the activities implemented in its frame.

Activity 4: Piloting. Each partner, in its own territory, will support and accompany the launch of two business projects promoted by rural women related to NYE and emerging sectors. They will be projects which implement business models based on the sustainable management of rural resources and exploring NYE.

Comparative analysis

A. Problems faced by women entrepreneurs

There are some umpteen problems faced by women at various stages, beginning from their initial commencement of enterprise, to running their enterprise. Their various problems are as follows:

1 Lack of focus on career obligations: Women do not focus on their career obligations in the same manner as they do on their family and personal life, despite having excellent entrepreneurial abilities. Their lack of focus toward their career creates a problem in promoting women entrepreneurship.

2 Economic instability of women: The economic stability of women in most cases is in a very poor state caused by lack of proper education (especially the case of Kosovo) that is crucial for becoming self-dependent. Women in rural areas can't take any entrepreneurial activity. Economic instability is tightly linked to traditional inheritance and ownership rights. Restrictions on ownership over land and other assets for women create instable and unsecure economic basis.
3 Lack of risk-taking ability. The educational system is creating awareness about woman's capacities and their hidden powers to handle economic activities. Most of the women are not performing entrepreneurial activities because they lack proper capacities and risk-taking ability, as they are not taught how to expose and use their abilities.
4 Arrangement of finance and raw material. Arrangement of finance is a major problem that is faced by women entrepreneurs. Their access to external sources of finance is very limited because of their poor economic condition in the society. Therefore, they find it difficult to be an entrepreneur, as they lack the risk-taking ability because of poor financial assistance. Other problems they face are the shortage of raw material and the difficulty in arranging good quality raw material at competitive prices.
5 Cut-throat competition. Women entrepreneurs have to face tough competition not only from the industry but also from their male counterparts. Surviving this cut-throat competition and while producing quality product at competitive price is not an easy task for the women entrepreneurs.
6 Low levels of literacy amongst women. Illiteracy is the root cause of socioeconomic biasness that prevails in the society and that doesn't let women achieve economic independency (this is more relevant for Kosovo). Due to lack of knowledge of latest technology and proper education, it becomes difficult for women to set up their own enterprises.
7 Problems in getting financial assistance by banks and financial institutions. Banks and financial institutions help finance small- and medium-size firm operators to get financial assistance. But these banks and financial institutions don't readily provide credit to women entrepreneurs because they doubt the credit worthiness of women entrepreneurs. The irony is that according to a report by the United Nations Industrial Development Organization (UNIDO), women's loan repayment rates are higher than men's, but still financial institutes doubt their loan repayment abilities.
8 Marketing problems. Women entrepreneurs face problems in marketing of their products as this area is mainly dominated by males and women fail to make a mark in this area. Women entrepreneur also find it difficult to capture the market and make their products popular, and they often take the help of middlemen in marketing their products who often charge high commission from them.

9 Less support toward family. In business, women have to devote long hours, and, as a result, they find it difficult to meet the demands of their family members and society. As such, they become incapable in attending to domestic work and to the needs of their children, which lead to conflict in their personal lives, thus making it more difficult for them to work as a women entrepreneur.

10 High cost of production: High cost of production adversely affects the development of women entrepreneurs. The high cost of factors of production and the raw material makes it difficult for the women entrepreneur to operate in the industry. Government assistance in the form of grant and subsidies enables them, to some extent, to tide over the difficult situations. Other than the high cost of production, women entrepreneurs also face problems of labor, human resources, infrastructure, legal formalities, overload of work, mistrust, and so forth that are associated with every business enterprise.

11 Lack of self-confidence and self-esteem amongst women. A strong mental outlook and an optimistic attitude amongst women are required amongst women to be an entrepreneur. But it has been noticed that women lack these qualities required in setting up their own enterprises. Thus, not having the required confidence that is needed by today's women to move ahead creates resistance in their being a good entrepreneur.

B. Key policy recommendations

- Increase the ability of women to participate in the labor force by ensuring the availability of affordable childcare and equal treatment in the work place. More generally, improving the position of women in society and promoting entrepreneurship will have benefits in terms of women entrepreneurship.
- Increase the visibility of women entrepreneurs. The creation of government offices of women's business ownership is one way to facilitate this. Such offices could have program responsibilities such as providing women's business centers, organizing information seminars and meetings, and/or providing web-based information to those wanting to start and grow a business.
- Incorporate women's entrepreneurial dimension in the formation of all SME-related policies. This can be done by ensuring that the impact on women entrepreneurship is taken into account at the design stage.
- Promote the development of women entrepreneur networks. These are major sources of knowledge about women entrepreneurship and valuable tools for its development and promotion. Cooperation and partnerships between national and international networks can facilitate entrepreneurial endeavors by women in a global economy.
- Periodically evaluate the impact of any SME-related policies on the success of women-owned businesses and the extent to which such

businesses take advantage of them. The objective should be to identify ways to improve the effectiveness of those that should be retained. Good practices that are identified in this way should be disseminated and shared internationally.

- Improve the factual and analytical underpinnings of our understanding of the role of women entrepreneurs in the economy. This requires strengthening the statistical basis for carrying out gender-related cross-country comparative analyses and longitudinal studies of the impact of important developments and policies, especially over time.

Conclusion

Building entrepreneurship is considered an effective tool in combating female unemployment in transition countries. Although the number of women entrepreneurs is growing, research has identified that women entrepreneurs' enterprises are less likely to grow when compared to their male counterparts. Women residing in rural areas are still marginalized and have relatively limited access to information and resources. Overall, poverty is mostly evident among women living in the rural areas. Women entrepreneurs face a wide variety of challenges, both in starting and growing their business ventures. Their special needs and priorities are almost entirely neglected from the macroeconomic development plans of the local governments. Despite the fact that most of them are involved in agricultural activities in their daily life, they lack the know-how and access to markets and also the financial means to invest and develop their farming business. While this fact is recognized by the government, only very limited support targets specifically women both in rural development in general and in agribusiness in particular.

One of the general aims of rural development is to improve the standard of living of the rural population, irrespective of gender or ethnicity. This will be achieved through increased employment opportunities and income of the rural population in farm and non-farm activities, as well as stimulation of entrepreneurship. The sustainable development of rural areas in Kosovo is dependent on the full utilization of its human resource, both women and men. Women present significant part of total population in both countries, as well as of rural population. Based on the latest Labour Force Survey, women in Bulgaria and Kosovo face higher rates of unemployment than men. In addition, only a very small part of working-age women are economically active (i.e. part of the labor force), compared to men. These suggest that despite some progress, gender inequality is still a concern in Bulgaria and Kosovo, given their poor prospects in the domestic labor market. Despite the significant progress in recent years, unemployment remains high, and the level of skills is for the most part low. Many people continue to live at subsistence level. Poverty and migration are particularly prevalent in rural areas and among disadvantaged population groups (including women). Business start-ups are primarily in the service sector, creating little added value. In rural areas, opportunities for business diversification are limited.

The governments of the two countries are developing strategic approaches and planning documents on national level in order to provide the general framework for animation and stimulation of economic initiatives of women in the country. Some of the key objectives of these documents are (i) to increase entrepreneurship among women; (ii) to ensure that public and private partnerships and investments respond to the socioeconomic needs of women; and (iii) to support programs that promote women's access to, control over, and ownership of resources.

Gender equality is a prerequisite for sustainable natural resource management. Women could play very important roles in both rural development and the sustainable development of the countries, in particular the rural women whose economic well-being depends on rural/agriculture resources. Therefore, women make a vital contribution to the improvement of family livelihoods through the utilization of rural resources.

There is little rigorous evidence that either access to finance alone, particularly in small amounts, or business training alone leads to sustained business growth of women's microenterprises. Interventions that combine finance (especially grants) and business training, although more costly, seem to be more effective in supporting women's business start-ups than either finance or business training alone. There is early evidence that business training combined with follow-up technical assistance, and business grants together with business training, albeit more expensive, may be effective in supporting the business growth of existing female entrepreneurs. Overall, there is more rigorous evidence that entrepreneurship programs have been effective in stimulating the creation of women's new microenterprises than in supporting the growth of women's existing businesses, although this is likely due in part to methodological limitations of evaluation designs.

Despite different path of development and existing time lag in ongoing process of implementation of market economy and socioeconomic changes, especially in rural areas – both in Kosovo and Bulgaria – there were evident similar processes. Slowly, gradually, and confidently, women start their own business in rural areas, providing income for the family. They are looking for opportunities to develop their entrepreneurial abilities in both agricultural and non-farm business economic activities, facing the challenges of competing with male entrepreneurs. Women entrepreneurs, while developing their business, contribute to rural development. The specific characteristics that they bring to bear require specific measures and policies to support them.

Note

1 http://naifin.com/org/33/files/site/pdf/brief_presentation-we-run.pdf?1442152143

References

1 Frédéric Delmar and Carin Holmquist, 2004, *Women's Entrepreneurship: Issues and Policies, Center for Entrepreneurship and Business Creation, Stockholm School of Economics*, Stockholm: OECD.
2 Donna J. Kelley, Candida G. Brush, Patricia G. Greene, Yana Litovsky and Global Entrepreneurship Research Association (GERA), 2013, Global Entrepreneurship Monitor 2012 Women's Report.
3 Donna J. Kelley, Candida G. Brush, Patricia G. Greene, Mike Herrington, Abdul Ali and Penny Kew, 2015, Special Report Women's Entrepreneurship.
4 Veneta Andonova and Mira Krasteva, 2016, GEM's Annual Report Women's Entrepreneurship in Bulgaria, Sofia, 2016.
5 European Commission, 2014, Statistical Data on Women Entrepreneurs in Europe: Country Fiche – Bulgaria, Directorate-General for Enterprise and Industry, Directorate D— SMEs and Entrepreneurship, Unit D.1— Entrepreneurship and Social Economy, European Union, 2014.
6 European Commission, 2014, Statistical Data on Women Entrepreneurs in Europe, Directorate-General for Enterprise and Industry, Directorate D— SMEs and Entrepreneurship, Unit D.1— Entrepreneurship and Social Economy, European Union, 2014.
7 EUROSTAT, Labor Force Survey Database. https://ec.europa.eu/eurostat/web/microdata/european-union-labour-force-survey, Accessed on May 18th, 2019
8 KAS, 2007, 2013, *Agricultural Household Survey*, Prishtine: Kosovo Agency of Statistics.
9 Kosovo Statistic Office, 2017. http://ask.rks-gov.net/en/kosovo-agency-of-statistics, Accessed on May 3rd, 2019
10 Bulgarian Entrepreneurial Census, 2005. https://www.gemconsortium.org/economy-profiles/bulgaria, Accessed on May 8th, 2019

7 Female entrepreneurs

An analysis of the entrepreneurial profile of female university students at the Federal University of Alagoas – UFAL

Ibsen Mateus Bittencourt, Jade Demettino, Caio Venâncio de Araújo, Eraldo Souza, and João Batista

Introduction

In the last decades, we were participants to a great number of changes that occurred with indescribable speed and with increasing intensity. We cannot deny that change has always existed in the history of mankind, but that change was without the intensity we are seeing now. Several factors contribute to this, such as economic, legal, political, demographic, environmental, social, cultural, and technological, that act in a combined and systemic way in a dynamic field of forces that produces unimaginable results and generates unpredictability and uncertainty for society.

Uncertainties bring insecurity, and they act as barriers for many people; in times of crisis, the only plausible way out of this scenario is to be entrepreneurs. Faced with this situation, many women have been undertaking the course in the State of Alagoas. However, it is necessary to understand this phenomenon.

The study of entrepreneurship has grown significantly lately due to the importance of the theme in the academic, economic, and social environments. Therefore, entrepreneurship has become, according to Cerizza and Vilpoux (2006), an icon capable of promoting viable alternatives to behavioral changes, forming a differentiated class with a systemic view of economic, environmental, and social situations.

Despite the exponential growth of the study of entrepreneurship, there is still a great deal of divergence regarding the characteristics of an entrepreneurial person. Several studies have already been carried out with the objective of identifying them, but there is still controversy considering whether they, in fact, exist and are correct. However, what should be noted is that many researches point to characteristics, competencies, abilities, attitudes, deliveries, postures, and so forth, but often in a positivist and very pragmatic perspective, and it is necessary to look deeper, with a more interpretative view, on the study of entrepreneur skills.

This study presents some considerations on a first look about the potential of female university students, but it is not yet a conclusive research and is still in its initial phases. The next steps will consist of a fully qualitative research, including the identification of some female university students with entrepreneurial potential to be part of the study using narrative research with an interpretative view of Sandberg.

Entrepreneurship and female entrepreneurship

It may be noted that in recent years, the entrepreneurship has grown considerably, not only in Brazil, but also worldwide, and there is an increase in the number of women involved in entrepreneurial activities.

Women usually undertake motivation for opportunities or primarily for personal needs. According to data from GEM (2007), 42% of 14 million Brazilian entrepreneurs are women, and that places Brazil in the thirteenth place when it comes to female entrepreneurship in the world. These numbers can be large or small, and may vary depending on the country. For Brazil, which has 51% of its population composed of women, according to the latest data from the 2010 census, the numbers show the strength that women have had in recent years when it comes to entrepreneurship. We can list the desire for achievement and independence, perception of market opportunities, difficulties in career advancement, among others, as motivational aspects for these women to become entrepreneurs. Other researches also showed that countries with a growth in female entrepreneurship are poor or developing countries. According to the GEM (2007), some countries rank among the highest female participation in the entrepreneurship rate as Peru (26%), Thailand (26%), Colombia (19%), Venezuela, Dominican Republic (14.5%), China (13.4%), and Brazil (12.7%).

What was previously a concern and a reason for great discussions in the labor market is today one of the main motivational agents for women to become entrepreneurs, such as the difficulty of advancing in their professional careers in the companies where they work. It was soon noticed that these women find in this challenge an opportunity to grow in other ways, which means they do not put themselves in a box and wait for things to happen; on the contrary, they recognize that there is still a prejudice in some areas and functions, and through that they return in the current scenario of capitalism with a large and important function, which is to become entrepreneurs. Another fact is that women seek their financial, social, and personal independence, and, in entrepreneurship, find this opportunity.

In a perspective focused on the State of Alagoas, it is important for Alagoas women to undertake participate in entrepreneurial activities for the generation of employment, income, and development of the State, because, nowadays, reality of social needs are present, where the government cannot meet all of the needs, whether due to incapacity or lack of will; no matter the reason, these needs exist, and thus there is a need to have new entrepreneurs with a comprehensive vision for social, political, and economic issues. The women need to have a great participation in this, but they live in a state where a great part of its population is functional illiterate and that does not have access to a good education; therefore, not only the need to improve this reality grows, but also the ability of entrepreneurs to emerge to lessen these problems; we have no place to empower these people, nor do we have the structure to carry it out. That is why the great majority of ventures that can move forward do so because their entrepreneurs do not give up for whatever reason and usually have the will to do something different for society. However, often these entrepreneurs are still people who come from families that have good financial conditions, but we must now have great entrepreneurs out of the masses as well, and women play a fundamental role in this process, since it is they who will be able to take this entrepreneurial need to this great mass – that is, more the women entrepreneurs, more would be the existence of social entrepreneurs.

Development of entrepreneurial competences

The concept of competences has been discussed for many years. According to Brandão and Guimarães (2001), by the end of the Middle Ages, the term was associated specially with the judicial language. It was related to the capacity, given to somebody or some institution, to evaluate and judge certain questions. At that time, the concept incorporated the social acknowledgment regarding someone's capacity to speak about a given subject, and since then it has become, in a more generic way, a reference for the process of qualifying the individuals capable of performing a given work or activity.

The term competences gained prominence in the field of organizational studies with McClelland's work in the 1970s and Boyatzis' in the 1980s, exploring the concept in the managerial context (Bittencourt, 2005; Zampier, 2010). After these two authors, the term continued to be explored, and began to develop very quickly with the development of new theoretical approaches. Dutra et al (2006) in their studies presented two main approaches: (i) the North-American one, which has as exponents McClelland (1972 and 1973) and Boyatzis (1982), and later Spencer and Spencer (1993), and (ii) the European approach, which has as exponents Sandberg (1991), Zarifian (2001), and Le Boterf (2003).

With the development of skills, entrepreneurs can create new business opportunities capable of generating a huge impact, so it is important to be prepared to deal with adverse market situations and the many issues which come with it. Faced with this scenario, it is crucial to be prepared to deal with certain setbacks. According to Bittencourt et al. (2015 and 2016), entrepreneurs need to have certain competences, skills, knowledge, and attitudes.

Regarding competence, it is the capacity to be visionary, with a sense of responsibility and solidarity, and knowing how to interact with different segments and interests in all sectors of society. With the concept of skills, it is understood that a clear vision is necessary, and to also have initiative, balance, being participative, and know-how to work as a team. As for knowledge, it emphasizes that it is necessary to know how to seize opportunities, have managerial competence, be pragmatically responsible, and know how to work in a business way to solve problems. Finally, regarding attitude, it affirms the importance of being dissatisfied and indignant with injustice and social inequality, which means that entrepreneur women have the same characteristics as their men counterparts.

Entrepreneur women use all the knowledge, motivations, attitudes, visions, and directions to generate impact, and this is related to the life plan, values, and personal characteristics of each one. This positioning is a part of each person's different personality traits, skills, and knowledge that reflect in the attitudes that generate impact. According to Le Boterf (2003), the traits are influenced by the life experience and perception of each one, and by their traditional and familiar education. For Antonello (2005), entrepreneurial competence is a set of knowledge, skills, and attitudes that enable an individual to print their vision, strategies, and actions in the creation of value (tangible or intangible) for society.

According to Zampier et al. (2012), the competencies necessary for the full performance of the entrepreneurial role change with the specific context of each business, so the entrepreneurs must develop another competence called contextual reading capacity. With the development of this competency, the entrepreneur begins to critically analyze several situations, adapting to different realities, acting with parsimony, and thinking about the business in a strategic way to generate the greatest possible impact.

Methodological procedures

It is a research, with a qualitative approach, of descriptive nature and temporal perspective of transversal cut with longitudinal approximation in which the data were collected in November 2013, through a documentary research and questionnaire. Fifty questionnaires were validated from university students who participated in the entrepreneurship actions and programs of the Federal University of Alagoas (UFAL) in partnership with Endeavor, SEBRAE, and Aliança Empreendedora, in addition to the Pontapé Entrepreneurship program.

Analysis and data discussion

This section is divided in three parts, the first and second presenting the Pontapé program and the Bota pra Fazer Endeavor course, respectively, and the third part identified the entrepreneurial profile of the female university students and their need to be entrepreneurs.

Pontapé

The seminar 'Pontapé – Every great idea needs one' comes with the proposal to stimulate in the university students the will to be entrepreneurs. Thus, the initial seminar had the following questions. Have you ever had a great idea? How about taking this idea off the paper? With such questions, the event uses a panel of speakers, with usually 02 (two) being local entrepreneurs and 01 (one) a consultant who deals with market trends and who can present solutions to the students' great concerns.

Thus, the seminar becomes an instrument to induce the entrepreneurial spirit in the young students who participate in the Pontapé program. The seminar began in September 2013, with its first edition being held at the UFAL. Till date, further 25 editions were held, involving a total audience of approximately 4,300 students. Pontapé then becomes the largest seminary of decentralized entrepreneurship in the state of Alagoas, held in the IESs of the capital and interior, in the main regions of the state, such as the coast, wilderness, and hinterland.

The event has a shared management between the State Secretariat for Economic Development and Tourism (SEDETUR), the UFAL, and the Brazilian Support Service to Micro and Small Enterprises (SEBRAE/AL). Because of this initiative, the public's interest in the creation of new businesses and the actual effectiveness of some ventures are being already observed. Some of these initiatives are already in the process of being incubated at universities.

Characterization of the Bota pra Fazer sample

One of the programs for teaching entrepreneurship in the country, named 'Bota pra Fazer,' enables educational institutions to broaden their entrepreneurial education offer, offering more qualified content, connected with the reality of entrepreneurship in the country and in the world. This program was implemented in Alagoas, through its Federal University, in September 2013, with the objective of training 2,400 students in one year. To support this program, 20 teachers were trained as facilitators and followed classes of approximately 30 students.

The first groups of the Bota pra Fazer program had 700 students enrolled in five cities of Alagoas (Maceió, Arapiraca, Delmiro Gouveia, Santana do Ipanema, and Palmeira dos Índios) simultaneously. The program was concluded in September 2014, with more than 1,900 students trained, and the general satisfaction of the students measured 8.7 (in a scale of 1 to 10), according to a research conducted by Endeavor, in partnership with the UFAL. The Bota pra Fazer methodology differs from traditional higher education entrepreneurship, with the objective of enabling the students to acknowledge and develop their entrepreneurial capacity, learn to identify opportunities, and create new business (ENDEAVOR, 2014), thus offering a more practical knowledge and stimulating the creation of new initiatives in the participants.

The entrepreneurial profile of the female university students

To identify and analyze the entrepreneurial profile of the female university students, a secondary research was not used. Initially, some offers were made of the Endeavor Bota pra Fazer course and some editions of the Pontapé – Every idea needs one course. Some questions were asked to verify the entrepreneurship intentions of the female university students in order to know what influenced them the most in the decision of becoming entrepreneurs and what led them to such direction while they are still university students of the UFAL.

Regarding the socioeconomic profile, it was identified that 46% of the female students were between 21 and 25 years, 21% were less than 20 years, and 16% were between 26 and 30 years. This means that 83% of the female students who wanted to be entrepreneurs were less than 30 years old, a data that is surprising considering the specificity of the State of Alagoas, which is a place without many options for employment and career advancement.

It is interesting to compare the low age of the female students with their family income: more than 60% of the students have a family income lower than three minimum wages, which is considered a relatively low income, because the family income is obtained by the sum of the persons living under the same roof by definition, the spouse, the female companion, the male companion, the non-emancipated child, of any condition, under the age of 21 or invalid.

In Figure 7.1, it can be verified the questioning that was made to the female students, the question being if they had a business that was in operation; it was found that 67% of the students never had a business, followed by 15% of entrepreneurs who had some business that was in operation. These data show that women think of being entrepreneurs to be able to impact the economy of the State of Alagoas in some way.

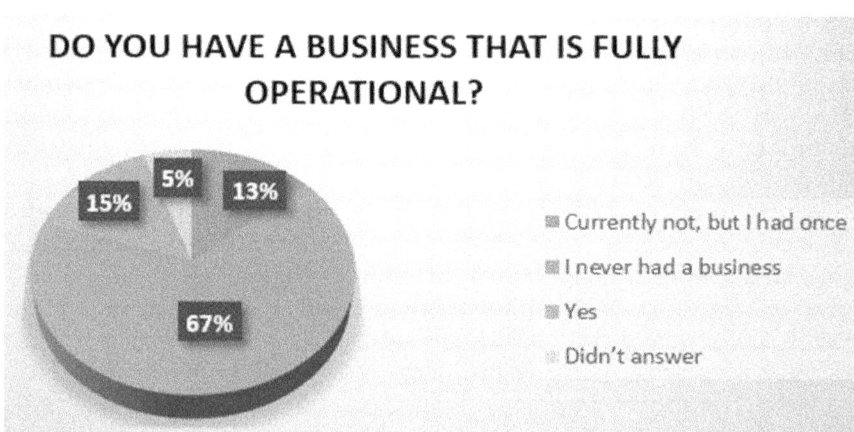

Figure 7.1 Do you have a business that is fully operational?
Source: Primary data.

When we questioned which course each student was taking, the interest was to find out from among the group of women surveyed, which course had the largest participation of women who wanted to be entrepreneurs. In Figure 7.1, it can be verified that the course that more women took the business course with intention to be entrepreneurs, which was already expected due to the specificity of the course and the area (Figure 7.2).

To identify the potential and the willingness of the female university students to be entrepreneurs, the following questions were asked during the survey to enable them to question themselves and then answer: (i) I'm researching opportunities to start a business; (ii) I am saving money to start a new business; (iii) I'm reading books about opening a business; (iv) I am planning to open my own company; and (v) I'm spending time learning how to start a new business. To answer these questions, the female students had to put the following on a scale: false; more false than true; neither true nor false; truer than false; true.

In Figure 7.3, you can see the evolution of the female students' entrepreneurial thinking. On analysis of the set of columns in the graph, it is

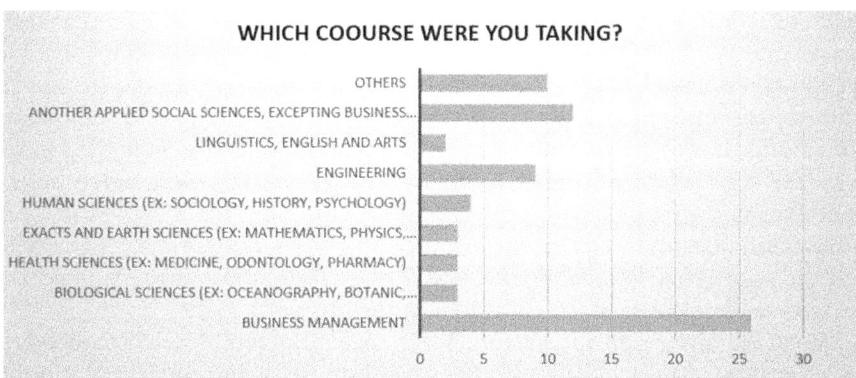

Figure 7.2 Which course were you taking?
Source: Primary data.

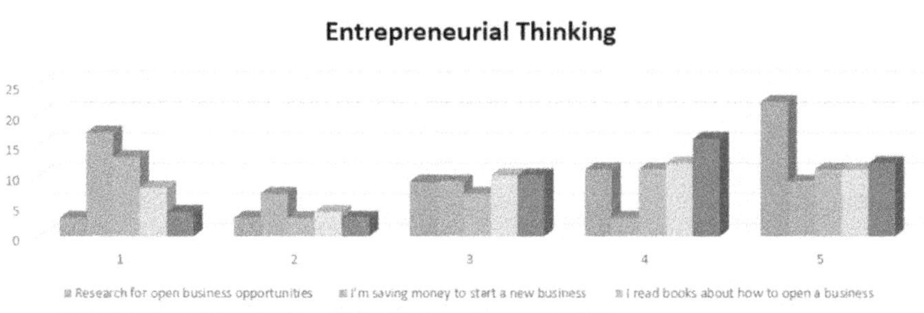

Figure 7.3 Entrepreneurial thinking.
Source: Primary data.

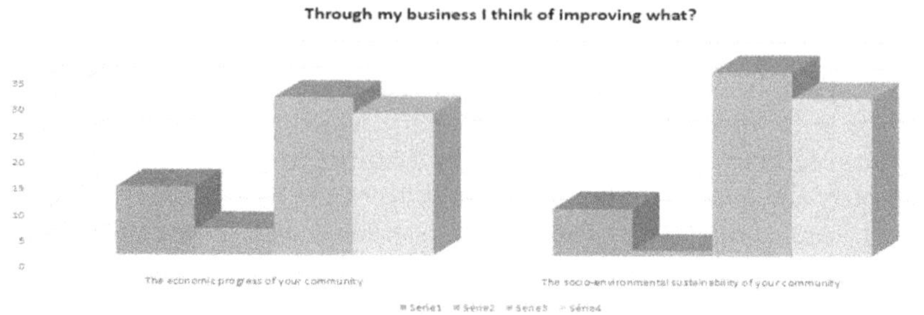

Figure 7.4 Through my business I think of improving what?
Source: Primary data.

noticed that the set of columns of groups 1 and 2 refer to the answers considered as false and more false than true, respectively, group 3 corresponds to the column of the medium that was neither true nor false, and groups 4 and 5 was truer than false and true, respectively.

There is a definite interest in entrepreneurship among the female students surveyed, and there is a growing curve to all the questions asked, except when asked if they were saving money to start a new business. This question posed as a point off the curve because many said they were not saving money to be able to open a business, and this fact may have occurred due to the profile of students living with less than three minimum wages.

Based on questions – the economic progress of your community or region and the socio-environmental sustainability of your community or region – many considerations can be drawn from the answers.

Figure 7.4 shows an increase in the female students' level of collective consciousness. Many young people are willing to be entrepreneurs and do good, which means that they want to be entrepreneurs to earn money, but also to generate a social impact.

Final considerations

With the collected data, the objectives established for this work were achieved, which were to identify and analyze the entrepreneurial profile of students at the UFAL, to verify their potential to identify business opportunities, and their impact on society with their work and entrepreneurial potential.

Through the research it was possible to observe that the female students who wanted to be entrepreneurs are young, in the range of 21–25 years of age, which comprises a total of 46%; however, this percentage increases even more if we take as basis the students up to 30 years of age; with this angle, the range would comprise a percentage of 83% female students with entrepreneurial potential. This fact is justified by the students themselves wanting to be entrepreneurs to be able to change their condition of life and their family. The data indicate that 67% of the students interviewed never had their own business and that this wish to be entrepreneurs also arises with college education, with the study highlighting that most of the students want to undertake baccalaureate courses in business management.

Although some female students have verbally reported to the current researchers their planning difficulty, being able to raise capital to open a business, and clearly define their goals and control their activities, most pointed out that they are seeking new opportunities to open a business; they are reading books, news, and newspapers on how and why to open a new business; they use the time they have available to learn more through courses, trainings, and classes, learning how to open a business in the best possible way.

What draws attention is the fact that the female college students don't want only to be entrepreneurs: they want to be entrepreneurs to earn money and generate high impact in the society. The question then is as follows. Why don't make money and generate social impact? This can be verified because most of the students were concerned not only to open their own business, but also wanted to generate economic progress in their community or region, taking into account the socio-environmental sustainability aligned with the economic and financial sustainability of the business, which means, it is only possible to generate the expected impact for society if the business has a profit.

It should be emphasized that further research is needed to increase the knowledge about the entrepreneurship of female university students and their entrepreneurial potential to generate high-impact business for society.

References

Antonello, Claudia Simone. A Metamorfose Da Aprendizagem Organizacional: Uma Revisão Crítica. In: Ruas, R. L.; Antonello, C. S.; Boff, L. H. (Org.). *Os Novos Horizontes Da Gestão: Aprendizagem Organizacional E Competências.* Porto Alegre: Bookman, 2005, pp. 12–33.

Bittencourt, Claudia. *Gestão De Competências E Aprendizagem Nas Organizações.* São Leopoldo/Rs: Unisinos, 2005.

Bittencourt, Ibsen; Janette Brunstein; Angelo Antônio Cavalcante Martins; Paulo Henrique Desidério and Carlos Antônio Cardoso Sobrinho. Systematic Review of the Literature Social Entrepreneurship and Skills Development: An Analysis of Past 10 Years. *International Journal of Innovation*, V. 4, N. 1, pp. 33–45, 2016.

Bittencourt, Ibsen Mateus; Angelo Antonio Martins; Carlos Cardoso; Paulo Desidério; Renato Neder and José Carlos Marques. Empreendedorismo Social, Seus Pressupostos E Sua Aplicação No Desenvolvimento De Competências. *Ciaiq2015*, V. 3, p. 35, 2015.

Boyatzis, Richard. *The Competent Manager*. New York: John Wiley & Sons, 1982.

Brandao, Hugo Pena; Tomás De Aquino Guimaraes. Gestão De Competências E Gestão De Desempenho: Tecnologias Distintas Ou Instrumentos De Um Mesmo Construto? *Revista de Administração de empresas*, São Paulo, V. 41, N. 1, Mar. 2001. Disponível Em Www.Scielo.Br/Scielo.Php?Script=Sci_Arttext&Pid=S0034-75902001000100002&Lng=Pt&Nrm=Iso. Acesso Em 28 Jul. 2014. Doi10.1590/S0034-75902001000100002

Cerizza, A.; O. Vilpoux. Empreendedorismo E Empreendedores: Uma Revisão Bibliográfica. In: Simpósio De Engenharia De Produção, 13, 2006, Bauru. Anais... Bauru: Unesp, 2006. 1 Cd-Rom.

Dutra, Joel Souza;_André Luiz Fischer; Roberto de Lima Ruas and Lina Eiko Nakata. Absorção Do Conceito De Competência Em Gestão De Pessoas: A Percepção Dos Profissionais E As Orientações Adotadas Pelas Empresas. Anais Do Xxx Enanpad-Encontro Da Associação Nacional Dos Programas De Pós-Graduação Em Administração, Salvador, Ba, Brasil, pp. 23–27, 2006. Disponível Em: Www.Anpad.Org.Br/Enanpad/2006/Dwn/Enanpad2006-Gpra-2578.Pdf Acesso Em 10 Jan. 2014.

Endeavor. Entreprenual City Index, 2014. http://endeavor.uberflip.com/i/528453-2014-endeavor-brazil-entrepreneurial-city-index/0? Accessed on June 14th, 2019.

Gem – *Global Entrepreneurship Monitor. Empreendedorismo No Brasil*. 2007. Disponível Em: Www.Sebrae.Com.Br/Sebrae/Portal%20sebrae/Anexos/Gem-Brasil-2007.Pdf Acesso Em 10 Ago. 2015.

Le Boterf, Guy. *Desenvolvendo A Competência Dos Profissionais*. Porto Alegre: Artmed, 2003.

Mcclelland, David. *A Sociedade Competitiva: Realização E Progresso Social*. Rio De Janeiro: Expressão E Cultura, 1972.

———. Testing for Competence Rather than Intelligence. *American Psychologist*, Washington, V. 28, N. 1, Jan. 1973. Disponível Em: < Http://Psycnet.Apa.Org/Journals/Amp/28/1/>. Acesso Em: 10 Abr. 2013. doi:10.1037/H0034092

Sandberg, Jörgen. *Competence as International Achievement: A Phenomenographic Study*. Occasional Paper 91.4. Melbourne: Eradu, 1991.

Spencer, Lyle; Signe Spencer. *Competence at Work: Models for Superior Performance*. New York: John Wiley & Sons, 1993.

Zampier, Marcia. Desenvolvimento De Competências Empreendedoras E Processos De Aprendizagem Empreendedora: Estudo De Casos De Mpe´S Do Setor Educacional. (2010). Dissertação Da Universidade Federal Do Paraná Do Programa De Pós-Graduação Em Administração. Disponível Em: Http://Dspace.C3sl.Ufpr.Br/Dspace/Bitstream/Handle/1884/23979/Dissertacao%20final%20050510.Pdf?Sequence=1 Acesso Em 01 Jul 2014.

Zampier, Marcia, Adriana Roseli Wunsch Takahashi; Bruno Henrique Fernandes. Sedimentando As Bases De Um Conceito: As Competências Empreendedoras. *Regepe-Revista De Empreendedorismo E Gestão De Pequenas Empresas-Issn 2316-2058*, V. 1, N. 1, 2012. Disponível Em: Www.Regepe.Org.Br/Index.Php/Regepe/Article/View/16/14. Acesso Em 10 Dez. 2014.

Zarifian, Philippe. *Objetivo Competência: Por Uma Nova Lógica*. São Paulo: Atlas, 2001.

Part III

Learning and choosing type of entrepreneurship

8 Female entrepreneurs in the generation of high-impact business in the State of Alagoas

Ibsen Mateus Bittencourt, Angelo Antônio Martins, Nilson Leão, Jade Demettino, and Caio Venâncio de Araújo

Introduction

High-impact entrepreneurship is still little explored in Brazil, both in academic environment and in terms of public policies, and its concept generally leaves room for doubt. That is why public policies aimed at leveraging this type of entrepreneurship have been gaining space within the political agenda at state and federal levels (Bittencourt et al., 2015 and 2016). The Startup Brazil Program is an example of these initiatives, created by the federal government to support and leverage high-impact business.

The term high impact has been fostered by Endeavor, a non-governmental institution of American origin that has been in Brazil since 2000. The institution conceptualizes this term as follows. Being a high-impact entrepreneur means revolutionizing industries and the environment in which it operates, generating income and job opportunities, providing social mobility, and inspiring future generations of entrepreneurs (Endeavor, 2015).

For this kind of entrepreneurship to be fostered, especially among university students, it is necessary for higher education institutions to realize that entrepreneurial education is the most appropriate way to transform ideas into high-impact business. According to Lopes and Teixeira (2010), entrepreneurship education enables the individual to be able to recognize opportunities not detected by others, to gather and manage resources, and to be able to act in situations involving risk, while others would hesitate.

Entrepreneurial education and high-impact business

High-impact entrepreneurs have characteristics that set them apart from conventional entrepreneurs, among them are the following: (i) they dream big; they have ambition and ability to see things in the long term; (ii) they have a spark in their eyes; they have a passion for what they do, and therefore, they always do more and better; (iii) they innovate; they know that to differentiate themselves it does not help to make things in the same way as their competitors; (iv) they make things happen; they have the capacity to execute with excellence; and (v) they are ethical; they do things with transparency, management, and professionalism.

Entrepreneurial education has been the target of teaching institutions throughout the world, each one focused on its regional contexts. In regions with no entrepreneurial tradition, schools and universities face the challenge of initiating this process, finding experienced educators and gathering the necessary resources. In other regions, entrepreneurship education is seen as a tool to stimulate economic development. There are also regions where entrepreneurial education is recent and in the process of experimentation, while at the same time, there is already a global network of entrepreneurship educators that allows sharing of the best practices in this regard.

Huber, Sloof, and Praag (2012) conducted an analysis of the effectiveness of entrepreneurship education programs at elementary schools in the Netherlands and were positively surprised to find that the programs have a strong and positive effect on the development of non-cognitive business skills. Rocha and Freitas (2014) affirm that entrepreneurial education has presented a range of different approaches in its pedagogical process. Faced with the challenge of training entrepreneurs, the expected behavior of the student is in line with the knowledge, skills, and attitudes that make up the entrepreneurial subject. The authors propose that, in order for the entrepreneurial formation to be able to involve a series of learning contents, it is necessary to organize several methodologies according to the pedagogical applications.

The new challenge of educational institutions is to include the teaching of entrepreneurship as part of all the offered higher courses, independently of the knowledge area, focusing on the development of the students' entrepreneurial capacity, and as a tool to support the development of new and innovative activities, seeking to generate new sources of employment and income and the consequent local and regional development, since this is one of the fundamental themes of entrepreneurship.

According to Dolabela (1999), there is still no scientific answer as to whether it is possible to teach someone to be an entrepreneur, but it is known that it is possible to learn how to be an entrepreneur, and for this reason, it is fundamental to create a proper learning environment. For Dornelas (2008), the entrepreneurial process can be taught and understood by anyone. Kuratko and Hodgetts (2004) affirm that an entrepreneurial perspective can be developed in individuals. In this sense, Henrique and Cunha (2006) highlight that IESs have added the teaching of entrepreneurship to their school program, contributing to the training of professionals capable of starting a business, seeking innovations within the organizations, and acting as entrepreneurs, thereby contributing to the continuous insertion and survival of organizations within ever more complex environments. For Desidério, Bittencourt, and Sobrinho (2016), the stimulus for the development of internal entrepreneurial actions in companies can boost innovation and guarantee its permanence through challenges presented in a competitive scenario

Challenges and entrepreneurship opportunities in the State of Alagoas

The strategic actions developed provide the state with a favorable environment for the development of entrepreneurship. In 2013, it was announced that the General Law would be included in all the municipalities of Alagoas. The Law was created with the objective of enhancing the development and competitiveness of micro and small enterprises in Brazil. It provides benefits in many aspects, such as simplification and debureaucratization, facilitation of market, credit and justice access, encouragement of innovation and export. After their total implantation in the municipalities, 93% of the local companies already are framed within the legislation. With the implementation of the National Network for Simplification of Registration and Legalization of Companies and Businesses (REDESIM), the process of businesses opening was debureaucratized, bringing comfort and ease to micro entrepreneurs. In December 2013, Alagoas became the first state in Brazil to have total system coverage. Another initiative that contributed to strengthen small businesses in the state was the increase in the ICMS tax to the sub-ceiling of MSEs to R$ 1.8 million. The micro and small companies included in the Simples Nacional program that earned below this revenue were exempt from the collection of ICMS and ISS taxes. It is worth highlighting the significant investment made by the state in partnership with the Federal Government in 2014, which amounted to the sum of R$8,000,000.00 (eight million reais) invested in innovative MPEs, and the resource is used to purchase machinery and consulting, among others. Another significant advance was the launch of the government purchases program – Compra Alagoas – which regulates the acquisition of public purchases from the state benefiting the MPE, in accordance with the General Law and the legal instruments published in the state.

These initiatives should be potentialized mainly due to the implementation of the Technology Park in the Jaraguá neighborhood of Maceió/Al, which has already announced an auction notice for the completed work, and is expected in the coming years. Between 2007 and 2013, the gross domestic product (GDP) of Alagoas increased by 38%. The increase still reached the Human Development Index (HDI), which rose 19% between 2000 and 2010. These results reflect the gains that have been generated by the current initiatives that promote entrepreneurship in the region as a source of development. However, many of the actions currently being developed will only have their results visualized in the long run.

Brazil is considered, based on the world ranking of entrepreneurship, one of the most entrepreneurial countries in the world. According to Bernardo et al. (2013), there are innumerable factors that lead people to entrepreneurship, such as an alternative to unemployment or to utilize the idle time they have after they retire. There are also those who see in entrepreneurship an opportunity to trace their own paths without having to be answerable to any boss or manager, among others. Entrepreneurship can be a way of improving the quality of life of the population through the generation of jobs and income. In Alagoas, despite the unfavorable picture of socioeconomic indicators, the growing stimulus to local entrepreneurship has already been reflected in some substantial changes in some indicators, such as the HDI. However, current actions should be observed more effectively in the future, mainly the activities linked to the stimulus of the young entrepreneurs, as they can verify new business opportunities when observing the favorable scenario.

Another alternative to boost local entrepreneurship is related with the need to create an effective project for start-ups (companies in an initial stage of technological base) that makes it possible to provide entrepreneurs with effective and financial support, as is already the case in other states. It is hoped that with these initiatives, the state can improve its economy by opening new businesses and consequently offering more job opportunities, and generating income for the population and thereby enabling economic growth and development.

Methodological procedures

The research methodology was quantitative-qualitative (Creswell, 2012). A structured questionnaire was applied with female university students from several areas of knowledge, with a return of 75 answered and validated ones according to the inclusion criteria of the research. The theoretical contribution was oriented toward the universe of entrepreneurship and high-impact business.

Sample characterization of the Bota pra Fazer program

One of the programs for teaching entrepreneurship in the country, 'Bota pra Fazer,' "empowers educational institutions to expand their offer of entrepreneurial education, offering more qualified content, connected with the reality of entrepreneurship in Brazil and in the world" (Endeavor, 2014). This program was implemented in Alagoas, through the UFAL in September 2013, with the objective of training 2,400 students in one year. To support this program, 20 teachers were trained as facilitators and followed classes of approximately 30 students.

The first groups of the Bota pra Fazer program had 700 students enrolled in five cities of Alagoas (Maceió, Arapiraca, Delmiro Gouveia, Santana do Ipanema, and Palmeira dos Índios) simultaneously. The program was concluded in September 2014, with more than 1,900 students trained, and the general satisfaction of the students reached 8.7 (in a scale of 1 to 10), according to a research conducted by Endeavor, in partnership with the

UFAL. The Bota pra Fazer methodology differs from traditional higher education entrepreneurship, the objective of this program being to enable students to acknowledge and develop their entrepreneurial capacity, learn to identify opportunities, and create new business (Endeavor, 2014), thus offering more practical knowledge and stimulating the creation of new initiatives for the participants.

Socioeconomic profile

For the analysis of the profile of the female students researched, it was not used any type of primary data. All the questionnaires received were used and, for them to be interviewed, the inclusion criteria was participation in the Endeavor Bota pra Fazer course.

The students were asked some questions to verify their socioeconomic profile, which was very important to identify if the gender, level of family income, age group, and marital status would influence in any way the intention to be entrepreneurs.

Figure 8.1 shows the age range of the researched students; it was important to know at what age there was the greatest desire to be entrepreneurs – 46% of the students are aged between 21 and 25, and 21% are under the age of 20. According to the data of the NTI / UFAL (2015), these two groups comprise the largest number of UFAL students.

Regarding the income, 26% of the students have a family income between 1 and 2 minimum wages, while 19% have between 3 and 5 minimum wages (Figure 8.2). When analyzing the data in Figure 8.3 and crossing between the family income, it is surprising that 31% of the students do not work, only studying and thinking about being entrepreneurs.

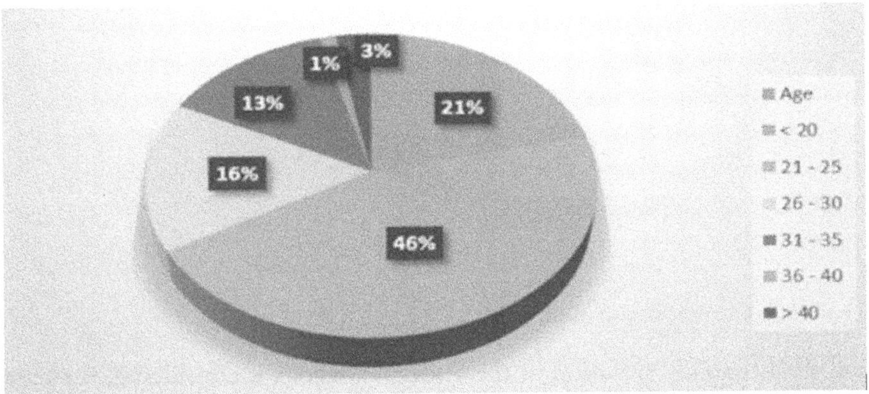

Figure 8.1 Age group.
Source: Primary data.

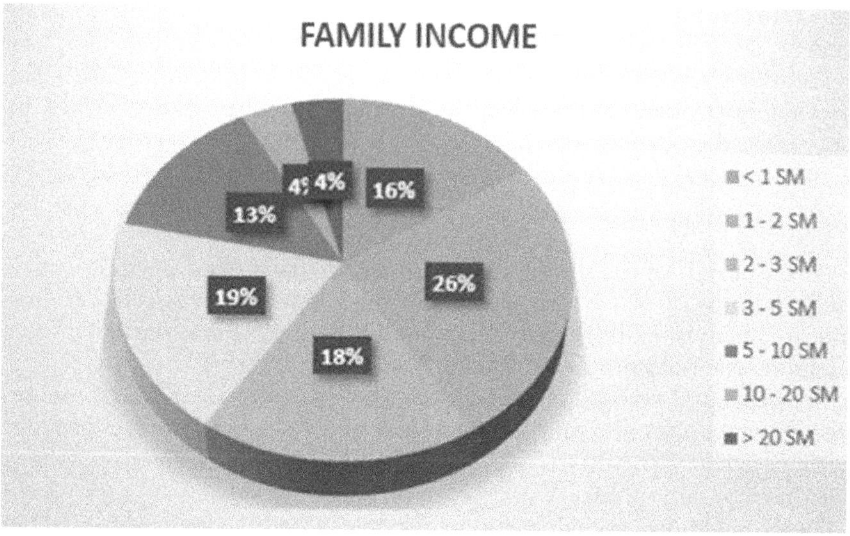

Figure 8.2 Family income.
Source: Primary data.

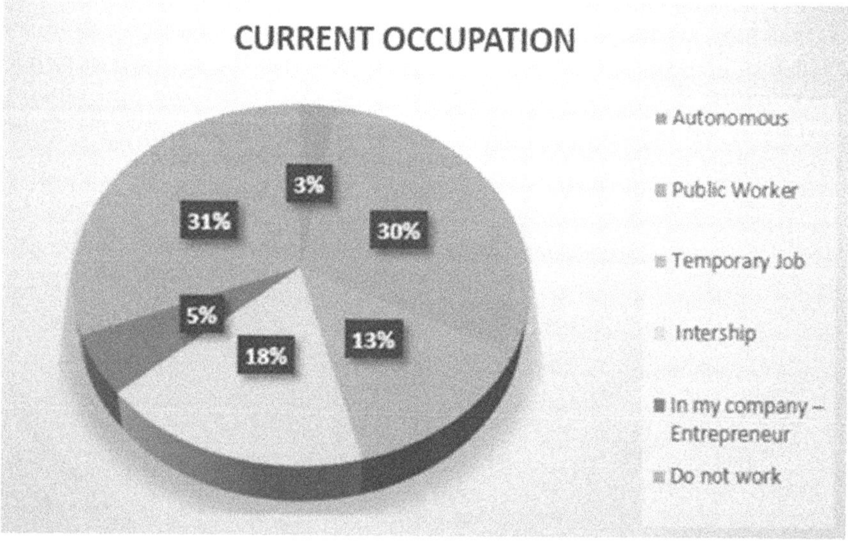

Figure 8.3 Current occupation.

If the economic situation of the State of Alagoas is considered, the data are not surprising, as many female students reported experiencing financial difficulties which made them think of being entrepreneurs in order to change their living conditions. According to the Decree 6214/2007, the family income is obtained by the sum of the people living under the same roof, as intended, the complaining party, the partner, the spouse, the husband, the non-emancipated son, under any condition, under 21 years or disabled, the parents, the non-emancipated son, under any condition, under 21 years of disabled.

Academic training versus intention to be an entrepreneur

The information was related to the teaching of the female student: identifying which institution she studied; whether it was public or private; whether she was an undergraduate or graduate student; if she had already studied some subjects related to entrepreneurship and what discipline was this; whether she was thinking of starting a business or if she had one already; and finally if the student felt prepared to be entrepreneur before the course or if they felt better prepared after the course.

From this analysis, it was concluded that female students came from several educational institutions; 74.66% of the students studied at UFAL, of which 83.33% were undergraduates and only 14.66 % were postgraduates. It was also identified that 50.66% of the students had not attended any discipline related to entrepreneurship, while 49.33% had attended. Of the students who had answered that they had studied courses, introduction to entrepreneurship was the course that was considered with high regard, as can be verified in Figure 8.4:

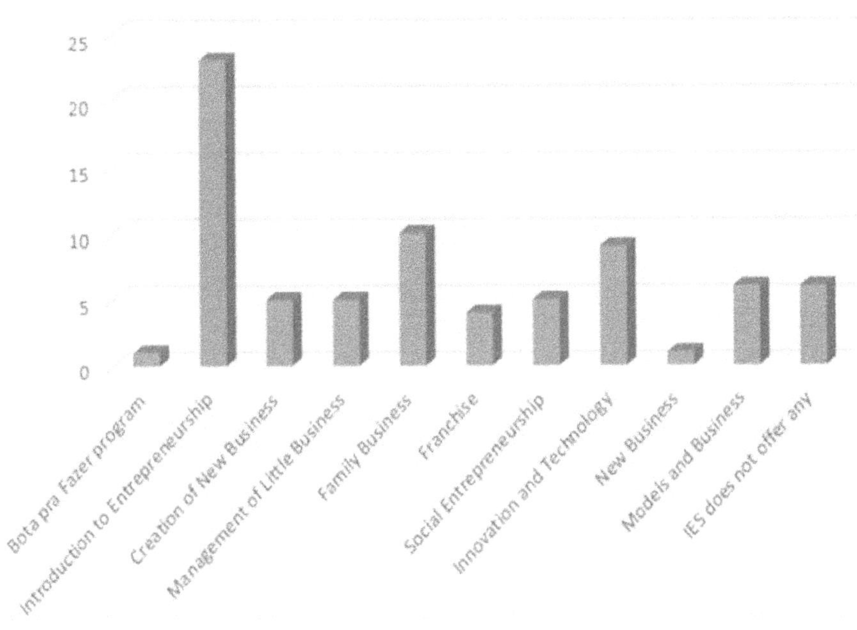

Figure 8.4 Entrepreneurship courses.
Source: Primary data.

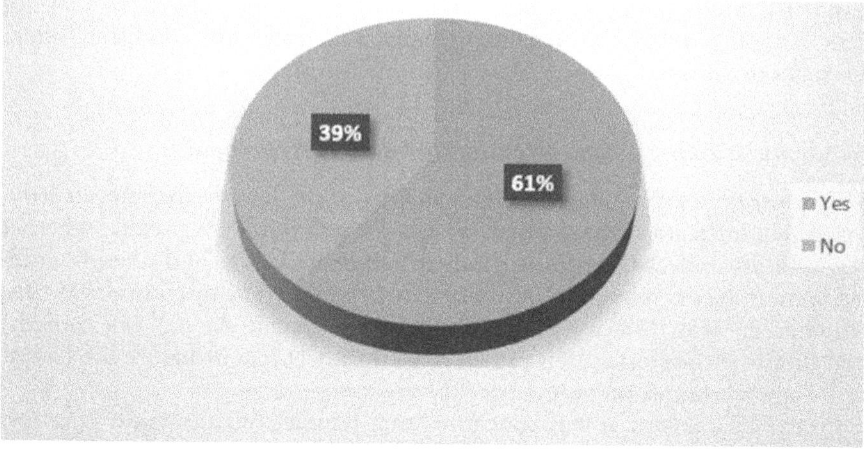

Figure 8.5 Intention to open a business.
Source: Primary data.

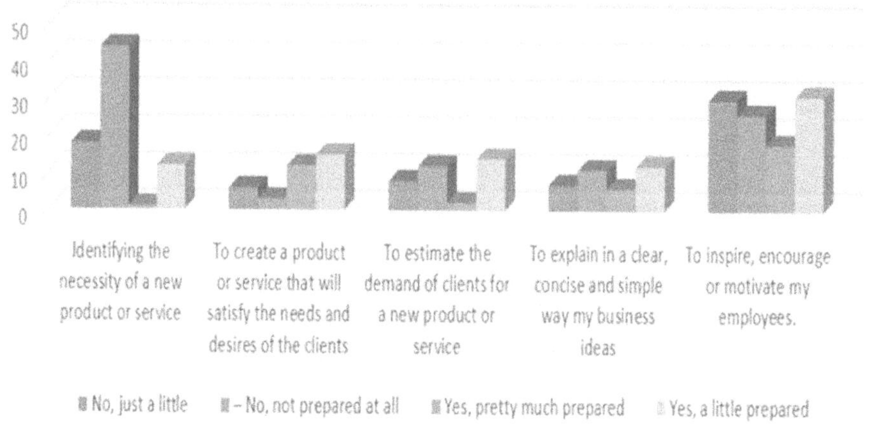

Figure 8.6 Did you feel prepared to.
Source: Primary data.

According to the research data presented in Figure 8.5, 61% of students think about starting a business, while 39% do not know or are still in doubt.

In Figures 8.6 and 8.7, it is possible to verify the evolution of the thought process and the attitude of the students in relation to the condition of knowing if they could or should be entrepreneurs. It is noticed that the students feel better prepared after having contact with some disciplines and with courses aimed at entrepreneurship.

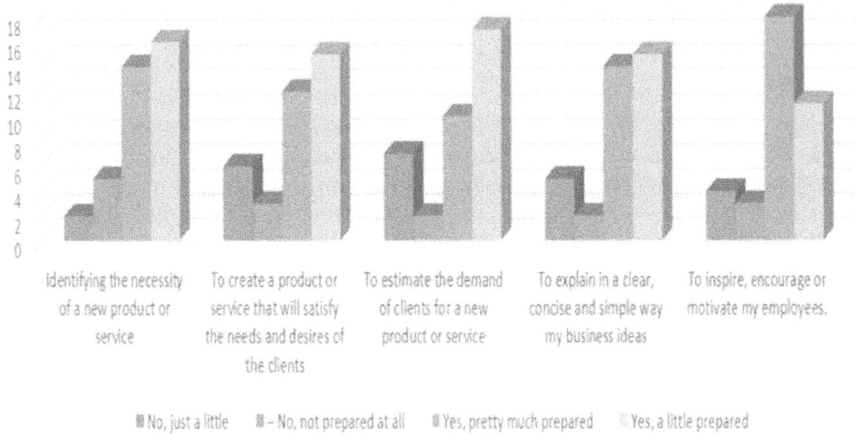

Figure 8.7 Do you feel prepared to.
Source: Primary data.

Final considerations

The results show that 61% of the students think about starting a business; however, the majority never studied or had contact with disciplines directly related to entrepreneurship. Two categories and five subcategories were analyzed. Students were asked if they felt prepared before or after the Bota pra Fazer entrepreneurship course? The subcategories were as follows:

i identifying the need for a new product or service;
ii creating a product or service that will meet the needs and desires of customers;
iii estimating customer demand for a new product or service;
iv Explaining in a clear, concise, and simple way the business ideas; and
v inspiring, encouraging, and motivating the employees. It was found that students felt unprepared to start a business before the course, but the effects of the training are felt in the post-course analysis, where the indices of those who felt much better prepared increased considerably.

Currently, more than 1,900 students have already participated in the program in five cities in the State of Alagoas (Maceió, Arapiraca, Delmiro Gouveia, Santana do Ipanema, and Palmeira dos Índios), and the overall satisfaction reached an 8.7 level (in a scale of 1 to 10). However, many other actions are planned to broaden the reach and spread entrepreneurship in all regions. It is hoped that with these initiatives, the State may have more entrepreneurs sensitized to act, improving the economy through the creation of new businesses of high impact, besides offering more opportunities of employment, generating income for the population, and allowing the growth and social and economic development.

References

Bernardo, N., Vieire, E. T., & De Araujo, E. A. S. (2013). A Relevância Da Atividade Empreendedora Para O Desenvolvimento Econômico De Um País. *Revista Científica On-Line-Tecnologia, Gestão E Humanismo*, V. 2, N. 1, pp. 1–11.

Bittencourt, I., Brunstein, J., Martins, A. A. C., Desidério, P. H., & Sobrinho, C. A. C. (2016). Systematic Review of the Literature Social Entrepreneurship and Skills Development: An Analysis of Past 10 Years. *International Journal of Innovation*, V. 4, N. 1, pp. 33–45.

Bittencourt, I. M., Martins, A. A., Cardoso, C., Desidério, P., Neder, R., & Marques, J. C. (2015). Empreendedorismo Social, Seus Pressupostos E Sua Aplicação No Desenvolvimento De Competências. Atas: Investigação Qualitativa Nas Ciências Sociais. *Ciaiq2015*, V. 3, pp. 102–107.

Creswell, J. W. (2012). *Projeto De Pesquisa: Métodos Qualitativo, Quantitativo E Misto*. 3. Ed. Porto Alegre: Artmed.

Desiderio, P. H. M., Bittencourt, I. M., & Sobrinho, C. A. C. (2016). Aprendizagem Organizacional E Intraempreendedorismo: Aproximações Com Olhar No Projeto Mostra Algar Inovação. *Revista Capital Científico-Eletrônica (Rcc•e)-ISSN 2177–4153*, V. 13, N. 4, pp. 10–26.

Dolabela, F. (1999). *Oficina Do Empreendedor*. 6. Ed. São Paulo: Editora De Cultura.

Dornelas, J. C. A. (2008). *Empreendedorismo: Transformando Ideias Em Negócios*. 3 Ed. Rio De Janeiro: Elsevier.

Endeavor. (2014). 5 Conselhos Valiosos Para Se Ornar Um Empreendedor De Alto Impacto: Os Aprendizados De Empreendedores Endeavor Ao Redor Do Mundo. Ebook, Endeavor Brasil, 2015. Disponível Em: Https://Endeavor.Org.Br. Acesso Em: 23 Mar. 2015.

Endeavor. (2015). Programa Bota Pra Fazer. Disponível Em: Www.Endeavor.Org.Br/Institucional/Programas/Educacao. Acesso Em 29 Maio 2014.

Henrique, D. C., & Cunha, S. K. (2006). Metodologias, Recursos E Práticas Didático- Pedagógicas No Ensino De Empreendedorismo Em Cursos De Graduação E Pós-Graduação Nacionais E Internacionais. In: Encontro Nacional De Programas De Pós-Graduação Em Administração, 30, Salvador.

Huber, L. R., Sloof, R., & Praag, M. V. (2012). *The Effect of Early Entrepreneurship Education: Evidence from a Randomized Field Experiment*. Tinbergen Institute Discussion Paper.

Kuratko, D.F., & Hodgetts, R. M. (2004). *Entrepreneurship: Theory, Process and Practice*. 6 Ed. Mason: Thomson. (The Entrepreneurship Series).

Lopes, R. M. A., & Teixeira, M. A. A. (2010). Educação Empreendedora No Ensino Fundamental: O Caso Da Educação Municipal De São José Dos Campos. In. Lopes, R. M. A. (ORG.). *Educação Empreendedora: Conceitos, Modelos E Práticas*. Rio De Janeiro: Elsevier, p. 35.

Rocha, E. L. C., & Freitas, A. A. F. (2014). Avaliação Do Ensino De Empreendedorismo Entre Estudantes Universitários Por Meio Do Perfil Empreendedor. *Revista De Administração Contemporânea*, V. 18, N. 4, Art. 5, pp. 465–486, Jul. /Ago, Rio De Janeiro.

9 Some thoughts on leadership and entrepreneurial education of Brazilian women

Mary Rosane Ceroni, Berenice Carpigiani, Maria Elisa Pereira Lopes, and Ana Maria Porto Castanheira

Introduction

Nowadays, the concept of entrepreneurship takes on several outlines, deployments, and impacts, mainly for the modalities and strategies concerning innovative socio-educational and corporate projects. Among those deployments, the paradigm of entrepreneurial education emerges as a differentiating factor for sustainable human development, pointing out entrepreneurship as a facilitator of social and corporate innovation, involving the participants in the development of management processes concerning integration, sustainability, and solidarity, adding value and differentiation by using projects outcomes and entrepreneurial education dynamics/optimization.

It is possible to notice that since the end of the 20th century, the theme entrepreneurship has been the object of more attention from governments, entrepreneurs, workers, and society in general. In that context, a quest has been made to broaden the entrepreneurial ability, which, until recently, was strictly associated with people's formal qualification (human capital) in organizations. When seeking to understand the adult female universe, it is necessary to rethink variables such as labor, intellect, and professional status (visible aspects).

Entrepreneurial education is vital for the development of organizations and countries. Brazilian higher education is experiencing urgent didactic and pedagogical processes for relevant proposals concerning the effective implementation of academic measures that are prophylactic and efficient with regards to the world of labor. Thus, it presents as an evident fact, entrepreneurship, lived in the different sectors of human activity, as an unfinished product of a brief historical evolution, whose synthesis the present study is also responsible for registering. "[...] Higher education is expected to produce graduates who are not only individuals looking for work, but also ***entrepreneurs*** and successful job creators." (UNESCO,1995, p.187)

The principle of a dominant organization is aimed at developing leadership, with the purpose of offering opportunities of bringing out the best in people and responding quickly to changes. Hence, according to Motta (1998), leadership has been defined as "the process in which an individual influence other to commit to the search of shared objectives" (p. 210). According to Tenório's perception (1998), leadership is a "[...] set of abilities and knowledge that need to be learned, developed, and perfected" (p. 85).

Thus, it is possible to understand that the purpose of leaders in an organization must be to improve the performance of the people involved in an organization and the material resources. They have to improve the quality of services, give people pride in the work they do – presenting in their actions voluntary work maintained competently, in order to maximize effectiveness in the proposed objectives and ensure the continuity of public support and ethically constituted actions.

The concern with the female identity construction in different areas, including the universe of work, has generated rather unclear investigations. Different family formats, unrestricted access to information and technology, fierce media exposure, among other present phenomena, need to be carefully incorporated into the reading of how the female human mind develops today.

From this perspective, the Brazilian female leadership, by the means of entrepreneurial education, reveals the ability to act as a change agent, with cooperative attitude, sociability, high persuasion power and group influence, and the ability to evaluate, synthesize, and organize knowledge by creating by her own example an environment of enthusiasm. By maximizing the opportunity of co-responsible action of people (those who actually make the commitment to an organization), – in which the organization and people are authentic and fair; it is important that you perceive the parties and the whole and understand their relationships – a holistic view of leadership. It is significant in a process of change, adapting the individual to the transformations present, in a society that restructures and recomposes at every moment.

Methodology

In order to study human development, especially women's development, it is necessary to be committed to curiosity about the mechanisms governing the mental world, being sure it will not finish, for the good reason that human psychological possibilities are endless. But it is also committed to understanding the "things of culture" – of ever-growing technologies, question-raising ethics, policies and economies on the go. Simple rhymes for such complex issues (Carpigiani, 2012). A perspective and possibility of acting of the enterprising woman today is related to impasses and possibilities in human relationships that challenge creativity, innovation in search of rediscovering, and revaluing life, relationships interpersonal personnel, institutions. This puts organizations in the face of situations that drive to discover the new in relations between employees and leaders. What brings other challenges to the authors of this study: to discuss "what", and "how" the entrepreneurial leader needs to learn; the analysis of the education of brazilian women and her leadership for entrepreneurship in working relationships, related more to nonlinear issues than linear issues, such as: having personal capacity to agglutinate and influence people to carry out objectives; effects or results in the field of human relations.

Discussion

The notion of entrepreneurship emerged as an art of creativity, negotiating ability and conditions to solve the problems affecting a person and her community, whether in a marketing competition, in a social issue, or in something related to the public good, according to Souza Neto and Ceroni (2015). The same authors (Souza Neto and Ceroni, 2015) signal that we could characterize the entrepreneur as someone "who generates positive value for collectivity", when referring to Dolabela (2006, p. 206 apud Souza Neto and Ceroni, 2015, p. 365).

Schwenkow and Ceroni (2015, p. 707) highlight the considerations made by Dornelas (2014, p. 9): "In Brazil, being successful as an entrepreneur is not an easy task, but those who succeeded become a reference because of the boldness, creativity, innovation, and persistence that are usually associated with these differentiated individuals". Schwenkow and Ceroni (2015, p. 707) noticed that "[...] entrepreneurship has been a primary debatable theme in the several public and private instances. The country has finally given the due importance to entrepreneurship". One can learn from those examples and use this learning to improve their chances of success.

The roles of the organization leaders identified by Nanus and Dobbs (1999 apud Prado; Souza Neto; Ceroni, 2007) and the features found by Kouzes and Posner (1993 apud Prado; Souza Neto; Ceroni, 2007) and defended by them suggest a relationship matrix between both aspects that may be used as a way of analyzing the leader's way of working in organizations, where in the vertical axis it is possible to situate the characteristics – honesty, concern for the future, motivation, and competence in the other roles played: visionary and strategist, specialized politician, trainer, and change agent (Prado; Souza Neto; Ceroni, 2007).

It is noticed, then, that honesty and other characteristics intersperse in all the roles, acquiring in each one its own specificities. The role of female leadership in organizations starts to be, thus, the one of motivating people to take on an active role; this means making a sincere effort to understand the needs, aspirations, and feelings of all people involved and committed to it and to the organization. This communication action demands constant evaluation that contributes to reestablish more reciprocity between the parts.

In this context, it is possible to understand the path to adequate exercise of Brazilian women – efficient, efficacious, and effective leadership contemporarily is to be able to make people want to contribute and feel fulfilled as human beings; to appreciate challenges; to use her power and persuasion with assertiveness; have the ability to unlearn and learn again; stimulate everyone's self-assessment as a personal and professional process; valuing innovative creativity, invigorate individual and/or group fulfillment; implement autonomy; foster interpersonal relationships; raise awareness by example and not by discourse; maximize satisfaction and people's performance.

It is considered that regarding leadership at work in contemporaneity, the entrepreneur Brazilian woman, in the unequivocal duty of seeking self-development, has a wise and serene attitude concerning the anxious moments which occasionally arise, controlling her impulses, getting motivated even facing adversity, being persistent in her objectives, being sensible to realize what other people are feeling, being aware of her own feelings, and, finally, having altruistic perception of her own feelings and of others' to manage conflict, negotiate, and undertake, especially focusing and managing *with* people and not managing people.

Ceroni (2010) presented the study made by Aburdene and Naisbitt (1993 apud Ceroni, 2010, p. 220–221) based on a research of more than 30 years about traditional leadership and "new" leadership, further recognized as female leadership, and groups the behaviors with the purpose of showing the features of that leadership (Table 9.1).

From the analysis of those features, it is possible to think about commitment and action, with their limits and possibilities. The contemporary female leadership is challenged to seek learning and develop new abilities; to be willing

Table 9.1 Features of traditional and contemporary leadership (Aburdene & Naisbitt, 1993, 119–120)

Traditional Management	*Leadership / Female Leadership*
Restructuring	
Objective: control	Objective: change
Hierarchy	Network
Levels	Connections
Strict	Flexible
Imposes discipline	Values criticality
Mechanical	Holistic
Impersonal/objective	Personal
Criticism of the action	Mutual agreement aiming results
Compartmental	Systemic
Training	
Demands respect	Invites to speak up
Command and control	Change
Punishment	Reward
Here is what we are going to do	How can I help you
Basic line	Vision
Imposes discipline	Values creativity
Gives orders	Acts as example
Teaching	
Transmission of orders	Facilitating/mediating
Military archetype	Educator archetype
Opening	
Information control	Information availability
Maximum/minimum threshold	Scope of action
Knows all the answers	Formulates the right questions
Keeps people "walking on thin ice"	Stimulating environment for growth

to be proud of her ability to absorb the new; and to make hope her certainty, understanding her personal fulfillment is linked to her emotions – where you can find a reason to live, to live together with others (Ceroni, 2010).

This refers to the contemporary Brazilian woman to make a difference in human relations (reflecting her vision and joint actions), in the group she leads, that is, her role is to collaborate with the transformation of the reality experienced: perfecting the educational process; providing a deeper meaning to life and work.

In theory, this means: the search for the formation of the human person in completeness. In practice: the search for an increasingly efficient, effective and, consequently, effective work – encouraging healthy interaction in the institution to which it is linked; creating spaces where an increasing number of facilitators/multipliers are eered in the process, in the mutual effort to produce and propagate new ideas and actions among the qualities it must present in a democratic society (Ceroni, 2010, p. 221).

It is hoped that the entrepreneurial leader in contemporary times may face a favorable environment in which people make themselves available and can develop ever renewed constructive skills and criticism.

To the one who studies human development, who stops and tries to understand the adult female universe, is given the task of rethinking variables such as work, religions, intellect, finance, body aesthetics, beauty, sensuality, professional status, sexual freedom, and space for decisions in the harsh financial area. These are all visible ingredients. What other ingredients will this researcher find, when he dares to cross the visible and look at another plan, maybe not so visible, of the woman development? He may find, for example, a new way of building and expressing competitive components, or a new shape for expressing affection, with a new perception concerning relationship possibilities with other women or men. He may find a new perception regarding the concept of motherhood. To all these variables it is necessary to add the equally expected role of the entrepreneurial woman, which leads us to seek to understand at what time entrepreneurial education is currently located and its repercussion on the actions of women entrepreneurial leaders.

Lopes (2010) comments that the teaching of entrepreneurship was born in the United States and has spread across several countries and has its origins in '[...] Business Management courses, almost as a practical need' (p. 6). However, today the focus is not only in small companies' management: there are several methodologies, proposals, and environments on which the teaching of entrepreneurship is being developed.

Lopes (2010) also points out that '[...] aware of the existence of education for the training of entrepreneurs [...]' (p. 12), it is necessary to seek answers for three questions, which are as follows:

Is it possible to educate an entrepreneur? What can be taught to this future entrepreneur? If the entrepreneurs already exist in society, why lose time discussing education for entrepreneurs, without even knowing if there is any advantage in offering education to future entrepreneurs?

When seeking answers to these questions, also based on studies performed by other authors (Kim; Aldrich; Keister, 2003; Sexton; Bowman, 1984), Lopes (2010) states: '[...] education can, for sure, help the rising entrepreneur and, thus, it is important to discuss "what", and "how" the future entrepreneurs needs to learn' (p. 13). In that context, Dolabella (1999) proposes a methodology that stimulates learning by the means of discovery processes, without right answers, involving the leaner in an entrepreneurial culture.

An important agreement point with Lopes (2010) and that cannot be left out of the entrepreneurial education programs is related to the ethical and moral standards.

One of the factors for success in entrepreneurship is the understanding of the sex issue, the understanding that women, in general, develop a singular style when they manage, considering that this approach of leadership is the result of learning since childhood, learning about values, behaviors, and interests more directed at cooperation and relationship. Despite the fact this style is present among women, one cannot radicalize it as being exclusive of women.

Loden (1988) notes that the qualities which define female leadership are not characteristics limited exclusively to women. Those features certainly are also found among men. There are some women who feel at ease displaying a predominantly masculine leadership style, as there are men who believe the female approach is more natural. But the key difference is that women, as a class, display those particular leadership characteristics more noticeably than men. The fact the female leadership is a generalization, and may not be applicable to all individuals, does not make it less valid, relevant, or meaningful (Loden, 1988).

Loden (1988) states that female leaders, when working in teams or managing a team task, place cooperation over competition, encouraging open communication and requiring the employee's contribution to establish goals everyone agree with; encourage creativity and increasing autonomy among the team members; as well as manage the relationships and their own feelings.

In this sense, personal competence is favored, on which certain abilities are more remarkable: **1- ability to perceive:** ability of understanding non-verbal clues; put yourself in the other person's shoes, both literally and figuratively, and understand their feeling or reactions; **2- ability to listen:** paying a lot of attention to what is being said by others and how it is being said; use non-verbal clues to boost open discussions; allowing people to complete their lines of thoughts without interrupting them; **3- managing feelings:** being in tune with other people's feelings and the environmental conditions that unleash several feelings; using their reactions to those feelings as an emotional gauge within the group; expressing feelings as a method to increase communication and asking other people's feelings statements; spontaneously reacting to situations; taking the feelings into consideration when making decisions; **4- intimacy/authenticity:** developing personal harmony with others; sharing personal data and encouraging others to do the same; concentrating on the individual as a whole, and not only as an employee; 5- **use of her position:** positioning others clearly and directly about their performance, focusing on the actions; requiring positioning from the coworkers and employees; using the positioning to modify coworkers and employees; using the positioning to modify her behavior; 6- **calculating the personal impact** (Loden, 1988, p.120): understanding the impact of her behavior over others; recognizing how she is being perceived as a result of the consequences of her actions while building relationships.

The social practice of each leader takes on its own characteristics in the organization in which it operates. Specialists insist regarding indispensable attitudes, values, and qualities of those who are at society disposal (Prado; Souza Neto; Ceroni, 2007). Under that perspective, the contemporary Brazilian woman, in the exercise of her leadership, must be aware of the intentionality of her role and her actions – reflection of her ideology. Her performance in an increasingly complex environment requires the use of all her resources, energy, and talents. Because she is aware of her role in society, the woman becomes able to observe and become sensitive to the values that compose the reality complex in its multiple aspects. Personality, coherence, and moral integrity are indispensable qualities educator entrepreneur leader must have, a leader who proposed to participate and collaborate to society, who seeks everyone's well-being. Also, the knowledge and acceptance of her own worldview are essential, so she can give sense to the educational entrepreneurial action she is dedicated to. It is evident the contemporary woman needs to present peculiarities to the role she performs, regardless of the type of organization in which she performs.

Prado, Souza Neto, and Ceroni (2007) presented the study of Kouzes and Posner (2007) that pointed out four fundamental features to the making of the leadership, presented as follows: *honesty* refers to deserving trust, and this characteristic is basic for leadership, because the donations offered by sponsors and the image in society depend on it; *concern for the future,* because people who work in the third sector hope they can contribute to society and improve themselves – they are idealist and dream about a better future; *motivation,* because people appreciate a leader who encourages them to offer their best, and the third sector organizations are a conducive environment to reach that personal goal; *competence,* because the ones who are led will feel motivated by leaders who can help them become more efficient and hope those leaders are competent to guide them toward meeting the organization goals.

Conclusion

By observing the personal and socially imposed challenges imposed on the Brazilian woman, and the new routes that she has been taking on before the social-political-ethical-educational phenomena, it appears the emergent purpose of the present research is to (re)think the role of the Brazilian women in contemporaneity, her leadership, and her education, establishing relevant interactivity and dynamic connection to make a prospective and proficient action in the world of work safely viable.

By entrepreneurial education, the educational actions of the female leadership point to collective decision and construction, offering opportunities of experiencing local and global realities at the same time, introduced in the everyday experiences of people, contributing to the training of the entrepreneur Brazilian woman leader.

The professional applicability of entrepreneurship presents its relevance by proposing to the Brazilian woman, the eternal learner, the importance of situating herself in today's world, criticizing and understanding the numerous pieces of information that harm her on a daily basis; there is the need of a multivalence in her own development related to the changes in professional activities and personal situations, many times during life (Ceroni, 2010). Thus, for elaborating life projects, dialogues, interrelations, and integration are necessary. In the essential sense of creating a favorable environment which consolidates the historical-critical subject situation, as the etymology of the world criticism teaches (criticism understood as *act of judging*), and creative subject, this entrepreneur leader [...] can make the difference in the contemporary society, where she lives and coexists, where her feeling of belonging and her resilient attitude manifest themselves by the means of completeness, oneness of her actions in the world of work, as Ceroni states (2010).

For the development and ongoing education of the Brazilian woman leader entrepreneur contemporarily, especially so it is indeed achieved, a process of conceptual clarification is necessary, which presupposes a certain degree of intellectual and practical leadership maturity – an acquisition in the reflective and experiential process. Thus, entrepreneurial education contributes significantly. Besides the development of new knowledge, entrepreneurship in education favors new ways of approaching reality in work and life, in society environments, and in new readings of the social-economical-cultural dimensions of human communities.

It is possible to conclude that, in Brazil, entrepreneurial female leadership in contemporaneity needs self-knowledge, self-assessment, and self-development; needs to have an understanding of the consequences of her own actions and of the actions of each person involved and committed, in favor of general global efficacy; needs to be focused in the search for self-improvement and self-education, continuously. And it is her example, mainly with her ethical behavior and her competencies, that makes people follow her, with the aim of creating appropriate environments on which people's potentials may arise (Ceroni, 2010). The accomplishment of that posture brings as a result the appreciation for the human being, for the woman herself in contemporaneity, feeling more and more involved and committed; finding a proper place to live and work with dignity, today and tomorrow.

Recommendation

It is possible to notice that the properties of agents and organizations have been changing significantly, making it difficult to predict future paths. The problems that arise naturally must be presented to that agent, as a safe means of development, in relevant stimuli and special motivation for the everyday struggles. Overcoming challenges is an effort which results from persistence, that is, from the excellent opportunity of revealing oneself, managing values of any nature for the benefit of life and collectivity – developing the dormant abilities that may, significantly, contribute to a person's emotional balance, and to take on one's humanity, and, consequently, to fulfill oneself and meet the real needs of the collective.

What is required from the leadership is that people who are responsible for the work teams, is competence – allying the ethical-political perspective to the technical dimension, as well as the quality in relations, the critical awareness and the firm purpose of meeting their society and the historical moment of real needs.It is possible to notice the contemporary woman needs to retain in her power, with perceptible excellence, interpersonal competence – expression of how and what to do with the educational purposes and the social quality (Prado; Souza Neto; Ceroni, 2007).

In that context, new ways of performance are demanded in terms of planning and management. Educational leadership needs to broaden the vision of female leadership under the perspective of integrated action and ethical behavior; it must contribute to settle and strengthen the proposals of different groups which make up the work group, as well as motivate people to take on responsibly the society destinations – not allowed to be negligent concerning experience, motivation, collaboration techniques, providing conditions so people engage and become co-responsible in the work environment, according to studies developed by Ceroni (2007).

The objective of those considerations is providing the female leadership at work a significant and relevant working style according to her own experience. Learning is centered in specific behavior qualities that happen in the interpersonal relationships, compliant with the changes that have been happening in the society that have demanded an entrepreneurial education.

The leaders in the organizations must apply their competences according to the role they perform in the organization. According to Nanus and Dobbs (1999), those leaders' roles may be classified into two axes. One axis refers to the organization's orientation to time and varies from being concerned with present operations to the future possibilities. The other axis refers to the organization's orientation concerning internal or external focus and varies from 'outside' to 'inside.' Women's performance in the work environment under those axes biases results in four sets of performed roles: *strategist visionary leader:* concerned about the future of the organization, builds a guiding vision, and helps design strategies to achieve it.

She gets involved in the big issues of the organization that influence her future; *leader as politician and specialist:* action characterized by the defense of the public served by the organization and who are specialists in building relationship networks; *leader enabler:* this role concerns building and developing work teams, generating hope and safety; *leader as a change agent:* refers to the leaders' roles in preparing the organization for the future, making decisive choices and influencing decisions, and establishing alliances with several partners.

Based on the considerations examined herein, it is possible to deduce that the coherence between personality and the authentic behavioral expression of the female leadership in the work environment is what matters. It is necessary, consequently, to remember all the time that the social-political context on which the organization acts is a part of the scenario, as well as the personal, professional, and organizational harmony preservation.

References

Aburdene, Patrícia; Naisbitt, John. (1993). *Megatendências Para As Mulheres. Tradução De Magda Loes.* Rio De Janeiro: Rosa Dos Tempos.

Carpigiani, Berenice. (2012). Desenvolvimento Humano: Entre O Natural E A Cultura. In: Lima e Dias, Marian Avila; Fukumitsu, Karina Okajima; Melo. Aurélio Fabricío Torres de. *Temas Contemporâneos Em Psicologia Do Desenvolvimento.* São Paulo: Vetor, pp. 161–196.

Ceroni, Mary Rosane. (2007). Desafios Para A Gestão Escolar Na Contemporaneidade. In: *Congresso Municipal de Educação de São Paulo.* O Ensino Municipal De Educação, 09 E 10 / Novembro/ 2006. Secretaria Municipal De Educação. São Paulo: SME, pp. 95–99.

———. (2010). A Mulher Brasileira Na Contemporaneidade: Liderança, Educação E Interdisciplinaridade. In: Bertolin, Patrícia Tuma Martins; Andreucci, Ana Claudia Pompeu Torezan (Orgs.). *Mulher, Sociedade E Direitos Humanos.* São Paulo: Rideel, pp. 211–232.

Kouzes, James M.; Posner, Barry Z. (2007). The Leadership Challenge. Philip Emery, U.K. In: Prado, Carlos Roberto; Souza Neto, João Clemente; Ceroni, Mary Rosane. *Filantropia, Ética E Gestão Nas Ongs.* São Paulo: Expressão E Arte Editora, pp. 62–63.

Loden, Marilyn. (1988). *Liderança Feminina: Como Ter Sucesso Nos Negócios Sendo Você Mesma.* São Bernardo Do Campo: Bandeirante.

Lopes, Rose Mary A. (Org.). (2010). *Educação Empreendedora: Conceitos, Modelos E Práticas.* Rio De Janeiro and São Paulo: Elsevier and SEBRAE/SP.

Motta, Paulo Roberto. (1998). *Gestão Contemporânea: A Ciência E A Arte De Ser Dirigente.* Rio De Janeiro: Record.

Nanus, Burton; Dobbs, Stephen M. (1999). *Leaders Who Make A Difference: Essential Strategies for Meeting the Nonprofit Challenge.* San Francisco, CA: Jossey-Bass.

Prado, Carlos Roberto; Souza Neto, João Clemente; Ceroni, Mary Rosane. (2007). *Filantropia, Ética E Gestão Nas Ongs.* São Paulo: Expressão E Arte Editora, pp. 63–64.

Schwenkow, Dirk Thomaz; Ceroni, Mary Rosane. (2015). Acompanhamento De Um Grupo De Três (3) Jovens Empreendedores Por Um Business Angel. In: Ghobril, Alexandre Nabil; Perez, Gilberto; Castilho, Pedro Vera [Org.]. *Modelo Da Tripla Hélice: Temos De Fato Ecossistemas Empreendedores?* Anais Do VIII Workshop Empreendersur. São Paulo: Universidade Presbiteriana Mackenzie, pp. 706–718. E-Book: ISBN: 978-958-58070-4-4. Disponível Em: Http://Emprendesur.Net/?Page_Id=317&Lang=Pt

Souza Neto, João Clemente; Ceroni, Mary Rosane. (2015). Formação Do Professor E Do Educador Social Para O Empreendedorismo. In: Ghobril, Alexandre Nabil; Perez, Gilberto; Castillo, Pedro Vera [Org.]. *Modelo Da Tripla Hélice: Temos De Fato Ecossistemas Empreendedores?* Anais Do VIII Workshop Empreendersur. São Paulo: Universidade Presbiteriana Mackenzie, pp. 364–375. E-Book: ISBN: 978-958-58070-4-4. Disponível Em: Http://Emprendesur.Net/?Page_Id=317&Lang=Pt

Tenório, Fernando Guilherme (Coord.). (1998). *Gestão Social: Metodologia E Casos.* Rio De Janeiro: Fundação Carlos Vargas.

UNESCO – Documento Para (1995). Política De Mudança E Desenvolvimento No Ensino Superior. In: *Educação Brasileira.* Gabinete Do Reitor: Universidade De São Paulo –1995; Tradução De: Laura A. Ferratini Fusaro. Brasília: CRUB, Vol. 17, No. 34, pp. 153–221.

10 Kosovo women's role in the development of local business

Hamdi Shaban Hoti and Bekim Berisha

Introduction

The role and importance of Kosovo women in developing general business and societies should be one of the main priority of Kosovo society, where gender equality is an immediate necessity today. Therefore, equality between genders should be part of every strategy to make business and society sustainable in the economic aspect of the future. The education of women in the past constituted about half of economic growth in OECD state in last 50 years, and this obligates more commitment to help women to achieve higher levels of education and to practice gender equality in education. It's evident that in states where gender equality is at lower level, economic development is slow, and it faces mores obstacles in poverty alleviation than the state where gender equality is at a better level. In registration agency business (MTI), 2014 9121 businesses were registered, of which 7383 owners were male, 1471 owners were female, and 267 were not registered in the base of gender. On the basis of these data, women appear not to be doing well in terms of the employment rate in Kosovo. The overall rate of unemployment is 30.9%. From this cipher, it results that 40% of unemployed are women, 28.1% are male, while the unemployment rate among young people aged 15–24 years is 55.3%. Report of 2013 shows that 21.1% women in Kosovo are part of the labor market, while just 13% of them are owners of SMEs. This is among the lowest rates of unemployment in the region. Cooperation for advancing it will open new opportunities for women and contribute to them working in the business sector. Gender equality is the cornerstone in the process of democratic development of a nation. Therefore, it is necessary to take into account all the gender inequalities that characterize the family, the community, the labor market, and the society in general.[1]

The role and importance of women in development of business

Women, today, consider that they are as powerful as male in business direction and they know that they are authoritative, but also know how to be friendly. Women who are in leadership of private business or essential public institution in Kosovo have created a new culture of management and leadership because they are innovative, more active, and have inherited the traditional experience in different jobs; they know to take responsibility and decision at the right time. Kosovo women are considered to have an excellent talent for the development of business from a considerable number of local and international enterprises. Moreover, commitment of women in Kosovo business life is too far of expected level even they still play an essential role in the development of business wherein this role, they have a direct impact in growing of general economy of the state. Women are powerful when they are take up a job with proper payment, or when they are leading their business. The entry of women in the formal economy as an employer or a businesswoman allows them to ensure welfare for themselves and their family, their role in the development of economy, and their role in creating new job positions. The empowering of women in the private sector is good for advancing and developing the Kosovo society. This includes some of the chance for developing business in the private sector, with higher productively and stronger flexibility, as well as market segmentation for a new product that can grow in the future; private sector always presents significant opportunities and is uncontested in the creation of new opportunities for employment of women.[2]

Women in leadership position

Representation of women in leadership position and in decision-making role continues to be a challenge worldwide. This problem is not limited only to developing countries, but it is widespread international phenomenon nowadays. Women take only 18% of the parliamentary seats and only 16% of the world's ministerial positions. Percentage of women operating as leader of states and as government officials is deficient – only 5% in 2011.

Therefore, women are inadequately represented in decision-making position and other positions of the government, responsibility, and leadership, despite the level of formal employment of women in the last decade. As regards their participation in the labor market, schooling, and diplomas obtained, women are behind men. What is the reason for the underrepresentation of women in leadership positions and what stops them from achieving leadership positions? As it is stated in many studies, women do not have any difference biologically in performance and personality traits. Women need two aspects to represent and to take a position in the society: financial and emotional independence. Except this, Eagly and friends stated that (2003) it does not have significant differences between the way they lead for women and men.

On the other side, they found more similarities than differences in leadership of women and men, and the style of leading of some women can be more effective than men. So, underrepresentation of women in leading roles and in decision-making positions is not attributed to difference in 'nature' and 'biological' between the gender. *The New York Times* is covering the events for women in the business report, stating that war of equality for women is far from over. Moreover, 'the situation for women in the world it is not what is supposed to be. We are making back steps,' citing violence against women and human trafficking as urgent concerns. 'Lets we remind, if someone who speak so its our obligation and privilege to use that voice for them who can't speak and say what they want.' US President Barack Obama, regarding the role of women, states as follows: The world in the 21st century is the diversity world, where men and women divide together responsibility as the office and in family life. Diversity makes ok not only companies, but it provides and useful things for society and the economy as a whole. 'The rise of women means the growth of our economy and the growth of our state… We must ensure that someone in on their arms.'[3]

Leader women with world size

In past years, especially in 2016, there have been significant changes in different places of the world regarding leadership from women, even in politics, which is changing in favor of women; new development shows that they do not need to fight for high representation in politics of different states. The strong points in favor of women generally are seriousness at work, great responsibility, and high integrity. It is now ten years since 'iron lady' Merkel led Germany, and now two 'other iron lady' seem to be on the right path to take over two of the dominant states in the world. In one of them, we have German Chancellor Angela Merkel. For ten years she served as chancellor in one of the dominant states in the world, and she is a politician as well as one of the most eminent scientists. She studies in physics, but engaged in politics after the fall of the Berlin wall in 1989. From 2000 onward, she led the Christian Democratic Union Party in Germany. Mrs. Merkel holds the title of the first woman in the history of the German state that led Germany as a chancellor. Meanwhile, from July, Theresa May started officially to work as a prime minister and new leader of Conservative in Great Britain. May was one of the ministers with more experience in the cabinet of Prime Minister Cameron, where she served one of the most difficult roles, and she has received support for her new position. She was home secretary for six years.

Theresa is the second woman in the history of United Kingdom to hold the prime minister post. May is famous not only for her political ambitions but for the fact that she is as fierce as Margaret Thatcher.

Hillary Clinton qualifies as a potential winner of the presidential election against businessman Donald Trump. Fifteen years ago, she was known as former President Bill Clinton's wife, but now she is known as a leader in America. Hillary Clinton has always focused on equality of gender, racism in the USA, increase in minimal monthly salary limit, and improvement of health system generally.

Employment in Kosovo according to gender

From all of the population in working-age group, 25.2% were employed. The scale of employment was higher for men than for women: 38.7% of men in working age were employed compared with 11.3% of women in working age. In four years (2012 to 2015), the scale of employment has undergone few changes, increasing about 3% from 2012 to 2013, a decrease of about 1.5% from 2013 to 2014, and again a decrease of 1.7% from years 2014 to 2015 (Figure 10.1).

Employment according to age group and education level in Kosovo

The scale of employment in the age group was higher among the persons aged between 45 and 54 years. Only 3.7% of new women and 9.5% of women between 55 and 64 years old were employed. For men, the scale of employment was higher for age group 35 to 54 years (about 60%), and lower for youth (12.9%). During the analysis of higher level education we can see more than 60% have graduated from professional secondary school, and over one-fourth (27.5%) have graduated from tertiary education. Table 10.1 illustrates that requirements for jobs are high in a government position, where half of those employed (58.4%) have finished higher education.

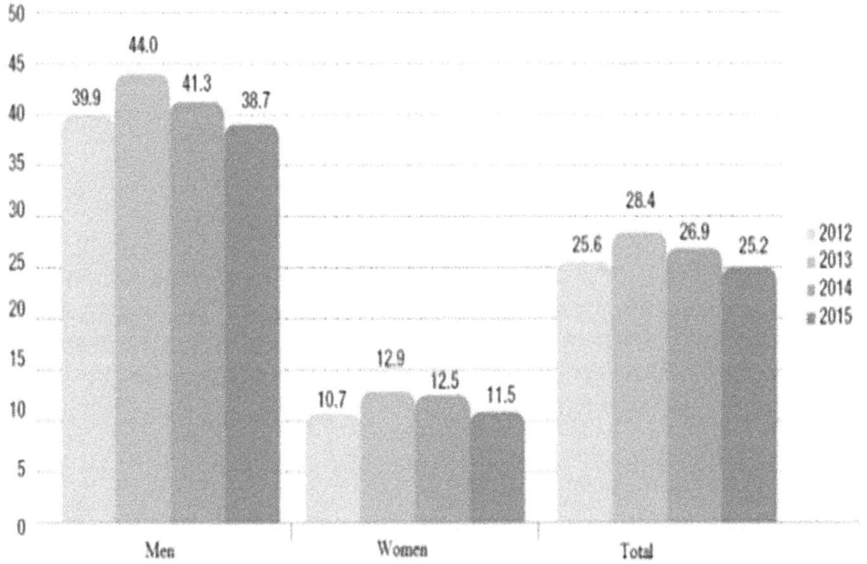

Figure 10.1 The scale of employment according to gender and years in %.
Source: Labour Force Survey, 2012–2015, Kosovo Statistics Agency, 2016.

Table 10.1 Number and scale of employment according to gender and age group

Kosovo 2015	*Men*	*Women*	*Total*
Employment (in thousands)			
15–24	23.2	6.1	29.3
25–34	58.8	17.7	76.5
35–44	60.3	17.6	77.9
45–54	54.8	18.5	73.3
55–64	32.9	7.1	40.0
Total: 15–64	230.0	67.0	296.9
Employment (%)			
14–24	12.9	3.7	8.5
25–34	42.6	14.4	29.3
35–44	56.6	15.1	34.9
45–54	56.8	17.5	36.2
55–64	45.2	9.6	27.2
Total: 15–64	38.7	11.5	25.2

Source: Labour Force Survey, 2012–2015, Kosovo Statistics Agency, 2016.

Table 10.2 Employed status according to gender in %

Kosovo 2015	*Men*	*Women*	*Total*
Employment status (%)			
Employee	68.6	79.4	71.1
Self-employee with employees	7.5	1.9	6.2
Self-employee without employees	15.7	11.9	14.8
Family employee unpaid	8.2	6.8	7.9
Total	100	100	100

Source: Labour Force Survey, 2012–2015, Kosovo Statistics Agency, 2016.

Employment status according to gender in Kosovo

In 2015, a total of 71.1% were employed, 6.2% was self-employed and had other employees, 14.8% were self-employed without another employee, and 7.9% were family workers (Table 10.2). Most of the employed women had employee status, 79.4% compared with 68.6% of male. One-fourth of men were self-employed compared with 13.8% of women.

Employment professions in Kosovo

In 2015, most of the employees had a working position in service and sale sector, in elementary professions, as professional and handicraft workers, and in trade. Half of the employed women were professional, technical and

Table 10.3 Employment professions according to gender in Kosovo

Kosovo 2015	*Men*	*Women*	*Total*
Employment according professions (in thousands)			
Lawmaking, official, high manager	22.4	3.2	25.6
Professionals	28.4	22.4	50.8
Technical and related professions	13.3	7.3	20.6
Employee	9.0	6.4	15.4
Service employee and salary employee in shops and market	40.9	11.2	52.1
Qualified employee in agriculture and fisherman	2.6	0.1	2.7
Handicraft workers and trade	35.7	6.7	42.4
Factory operators and machinery and fitter	19.6	0.5	20.8
Elementary professions	59.6	9.5	69.1
Total	231.5	67.3	298.8
Percentage of employment according to professions (%)			
Lawmaking, official, high manager	9.7	4.8	8.6
Professionals	12.3	33.4	17.0
Technical and related professions	5.8	10.9	6.9
Employee	3.9	9.5	5.2
Service employee and salary employee in shops and market	17.7	16.6	17.4
Qualified employee in agriculture and fisherman	1.1	0.1	0.9
Handicraft workers and trade	15.4	10.0	14.2
Factory operators and machinery and fitter	8.5	0.7	6.7
Elementary professions	25.6	14.0	23.1
Total	100	100	100

Source: Labour Force Survey, 2012–2015, Kosovo Statistics Agency, 2016.

professional (44.3%), 16.6% were in service sector, and 14.1% in elementary professions. Men were distributed in the sector, but most of them were employed in elementary professions (25.6%), 17.7% worked as employee in services and sale, 15.4 as handicraft workers and 12.3% were professionals (Table 10.3).

Conclusions and recommendations

Kosovo is one of the sites where equality gender is at a lower level, where the state is faced with slow economic development, where there are obstacles in poverty alleviation more than states where equality gender is at a better level. Kosovo women today are considered to have a potential for developing business from a considerable number of local and international enterprises. Support to Kosovo women from family to start a business is identified as a support factor and very important to them; however, although most of the women were owners and founders of the business, they have not been released from obligations and family responsibility. Most of the women have started a business with financial support or with family support. Today, women in Kosovo have professions which mainly are focused in the education field, agriculture, and health, among others.

Therefore, these different professions have apparent wage differences. Average wages of women per month in Kosovo is about 200 euro, which is lower compared with men's wages. The maternity leave for women in Kosovo is still an apparent source of discrimination found in different process of recruitment for workplaces.

Recommendations

Businesswomen in Kosova need technical and academic support to get a higher managerial position. Moreover, the support of the state in enforcing maternity leave will ensure women give better output in their business. There is a need of harmonization of legislation of the country with European Union Directives regarding helping women in employment and other critical cases. Childcare facility should be provided in public and private institutions to increase opportunities of employing women in the private sector of business for faster development.

Ministry of Finance, in cooperation with commercial banks in Kosovo, should have policies that enable businesswomen to take credit to start their business, and help them with sustainable economic policies in different forms of microcredit with lower interest rate.

Notes

1 Program of Kosovo for Equality Gender 2008–2013.
2 Women and business: Drivers of Development, September 2011.
3 Women in venture, To Win Power, p. 7. Deloitte (2014) Albania. Member of Deloitte Touche Tohmatsu Limited.

References

Deloitte Albania (2014). SheXO Gratë në Sipërmarrje Të Fitosh Pushtet Sipërmarrja dhe Lidershipi në mjedisin Shqiptar, www.shexo_org_al_final_pages (Accessed on March 15th, 2018).

Program of Kosovo for equality gender, prepared by Agency for Gender Equality in the office of Prime Minister, https://eeas.europa.eu/sites/eeas/files/womens_participation_en.pdf (Accessed on March 5th, 2016).

The results of the Labour Force Survey 2015 in Kosova, in June 5, 2016, ASK. www.ask.rks-gov.net.

The Role of Business Development Services (BDS), SouthAfrica_Women_Sections5–7, the role Women and business: Drivers of Development, September

2011. https://www.researchgate.net/publication/215641781_The_Effectiveness_of_Business_Development_Services_Providers_BDS_in_Improving_Access_to_Debt_Finance_by_Start-Up_SMEs_in_South_Africa (Accessed on March 5th, 2016).

Women and Development, *Drivers of Development*, ifc.org 2011 TOSwomen_Sep2011, https://www.ifc.org/wps/wcm/connect/Topics_Ext_Content/IFC_External_Corporate_Site/Gender+at+IFC (Accessed on March 5th, 2016).

11 Gender inequality in higher education and employment in developing countries

Evidence from Kosovo

Luljeta Aliu, But Dedaj, and Mjellma Carabregu Vokshi

Introduction

Modern times have been characterized with women emancipation. Differentiations are encountered in many countries. In Kosovo, there are some endeavors undertaken by national, but mainly international, organizations that are trying to reinforce gender mainstreaming, gender equality, and women's empowerment across Kosovo operations, programs, and projects. In this aspect, UNDP Kosovo has been accelerating the integration of gender dimensions in all sectors and strengthening its performance for women and men. Additionally, there is a solid legal base. One of the documents is the UNDP Gender Equality Strategy 2014–2017, that puts an emphasis on protecting women's social, economic, political, and cultural lives in a context of sustainable livelihoods (United Nantions Development Program 2014).

Usually, in developing countries, most of the HEIs are being confronted with an increasing gap between the quality of graduates and the requirements of the society, business, and industry, for more flexible workforce and competence in contemporary developments (Shiroka-Pula, Dedaj and Aliu 2014). Therefore, two components are subject of this study: gender level of graduation and employment. The study analyzes the gender level of graduates at all three study levels at the University of Prishtina 'Hasan Prishtina' and the correlation in employment in Kosova in the following decades:

- 1986
- 2000/ 2002
- 2011/2012
- 2015/2016

The study is undertaken by considering gender equality not just as a dimension of economic empowerment, but also as a moral imperative, fairness, and equity. It includes many scopes: political, social, and cultural. Gender equality, however, is also a key factor in self-reported well-being and happiness across the world (OECD 2012).

Research methodology: The paper has been prepared through literature and theoretical analysis, as well as secondary research. Data used are from Statistical yearbook for Kosovo, 1989; reports and database of Statistical Office of Kosovo for the period 2000–2016.

Research limitation

This study focuses on the higher education graduates, where University of Prishtina – UP, from 2014, University of Pristhina 'Hasan Prishina,' was the only public university in Kosovo until 2011, while there were some other private higher education providers established mainly after 2004, that have started with first generations. Therefore, University of Prishtina represents most student graduates from other higher education providers – mainly private are not included in the study. Further studies could include graduates also from these institutions, as well as studies to be focused on the education level of employees.

Literature review

Women empowerment in the economic aspect is seen as a prerequisite for sustainable development mainly in developing countries. Empowered women and gender equality are considered catalysts for economic development, leading to highest returns of development investments. As regard the education of women, primary education is not anymore complex issue for most of the world countries, but when it comes to secondary and tertiary education, more efforts in the level of policy-making are needed to ensure and foster the quality of education (OECD 2012).

Normative guidelines are established by international agreements for states that agreed to work on fighting gender discrimination in the education form early stages. '*The UNESCO convention against Discrimination in Education (1960), The United Nations Convention on the Elimination of All Forms of Discrimination against women (1979) and the 1975 EEC Directive on Equality of Treatment between Man and Women workers*' (Levinson, Cookson and Sadovnik 2013), aimed to influence governments to work and foster gender equality in training and education.

At the global level, gender parity was reached in 1990, but still significant variation remains for different countries, where gender disparities tend to be stronger with restriction in the laws and cultural norms for female participation in the public sphere, especially in the less developed countries (Hendley and Charles 2016). These sociocultural changes and the shifts in the labor market structure such as segregation in occupation also impact the incentives in the individual base to attend higher level of schooling (Buchmann, DiPrete and McDaniel 2008). The article titled 'Does Gender Inequality Reduce Growth and Development? Evidence from Cross-Country

Regressions' (Klasen 2000) shows that 'gender inequality in education does impede economic growth.' Consequently, it impacts in two different ways: directly – by distorting incentives – and indirectly – through investments and population growth. The problem facing is that though the trend of women graduates is increasing, it is not followed by the same trend in employment, in comparison to their counterparts.

There are some reasons leading to this mismatch of education – work transition inequalities. Work and family balance is crucial for women that leads to inequality and gap on the labor market. On the other hand, some studies show that significant progress was made on narrowing the gap among gender. According to authors (Buchmann, DiPrete, and McDaniel 2008), progress is seen in the increase of women in the labor force.

Differences are obvious as women deal with the unavoidable and unpaid work such as housework and childcare on a daily basis. Actions toward alleviating and solving this problem are made by governments at different levels by promoting policies that support sharing of responsibility of family and work life: the policies offer facilities for public childcare, family-friendly conditions at workplace, equal entitlements for parental leaves, and so forth.

The research (Klasen and Lamanna, The Impact of Gender Inequality in Education and Employment on Economic Growth: New Evidence for a Panel of Countries, 2013) shows that the gender gaps in education and employment is shrinking. Anyway, there is enough place for improvement, where governments all around the world can play important role in promoting gender equality by developing proper policies and giving equal opportunity of public services. This would create the basis for the governments to have a more active role, and not just monitoring and evaluating policies on the gender dimensions (OECD 2012).

Research results

Characteristics of period 1986

The University of Prishtina – UP, was the only university in the territory of Kosovo, that was established in 1970 until after 2002. After 2002, private HEIs started to be established, without the PhD programs. The UP initially had four faculties: philosophy, law, engineering, and medicine. Then in 1990, the number of faculties was increased to 13, and 7 higher schools were attached to the university. Some of the higher schools operated in different cities of Kosovo. In 1991, all academic Albanian staff was dismissed within six months, and the teaching continued in the parallel system in private houses due to the political situation, where the Serbian regime occupied the university and only Serbian students were allowed to study. This situation continued in the period 1992–1998, and a parallel education system was created. It was self-financed. Additionally, in 1992, the academic staff of all other levels of education, from primary schools to high schools, were dismissed within a day (23,000 academic staff) (Statistical Office of Kosovo 2001). Of course, this situation had impact on the quality of the education, the results of which are still seen.

Gender graduates and employment

The political situation in Kosovo was not stable. Therefore, males had a higher participation in the higher education, that is the only higher education provider – University of Prishtina. Table 11.1 shows number of graduates divided by gender and percentage.

Table 11.1 shows the gap between the female and male graduation; of 3,034 graduates, only 931 were females, that is, 30.6% of total graduates were females. The population in the approximate period was 1.9 million (Statistical Office of Kosovo, 'Statistikat për Arsimin në Kosovë 2001' 2001). Almost same trends were followed as regards to the employment. The ratio between employed male and females was not equal as it was in the case of graduates. Female employment was 22%, and male employment was 78% (Statistical Office of Kosovo 1989). Figure 11.1 shows the gender gap in terms of graduates and employment.

Figure 11.1 shows that the gender employment gap is significant in both graduates and employment. The education aspect is a bit better than employment, where employment gap among gender is even higher. According to the statistics, public sector was the main employer for women.

Table 11.1 Graduates of year 1986 in Kosovo

Gender/ Status	*Female*	*Male*	*Total*
HE graduates in no.	931	2,103	3,034
Ratio in percentage	30.6%	69.4%	100%

Source: Statistical Annual book for Kosovo, 1989

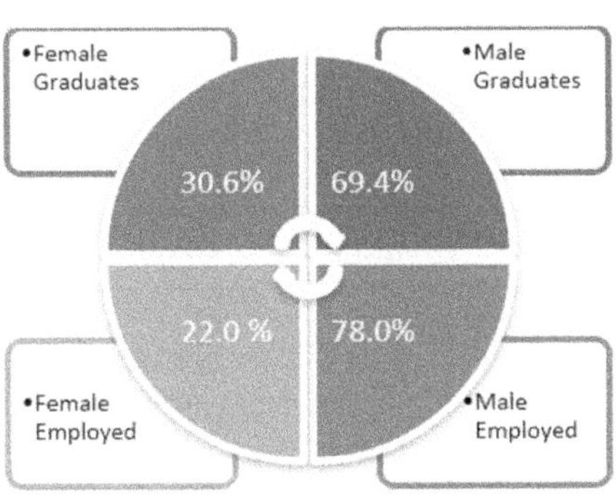

Figure 11.1 Gender graduates and employment in percentage in 1986.

Characteristics of period: 2000/2001

This was an after-war period between Kosovo and Serbia that ended in mid-1999. Almost everything was destroyed and needed to start from scratch. Besides enormous material damages, there was considerable loss of human life. According to the report from Statistical Office of Kosovo – Statistics for Education in Kosovo 2001 – population was around 2 million. However, Kosovo had a rare characteristic that could be considered as an advantage and have an impact on the study – the population was very young. One-third of its population was under 15 years old, while half was under 25 years. Only 5.5% of the total population was above 65 years (Statistical Office of Kosovo 2001).

On the other hand, as regard to the employment, given the economic situation in a post-war country, creation of new job places was quite tough. It was not able to create enough working places to absorb the labor force. Hence, the unemployment rate was tremendously high, in the difficult time when the economy was already diminishing. The main feature of the economy was the remittances that were the main fuel of the economy. Also, today remittances remain the main source of income for many households.

Gender graduates and employment

Since the country had a very young population, participation in education has been impacted. Table 11.2 presents data of women graduates in HE in academic year 2000–2001 in different HE levels, including higher schools that were part of the University of Prishtina.

The data revealed that females are more concentrated in the higher schools of the University of Prishtina, that are in the main cities of Kosovo, and not only in the capital Prishtina. The number of female graduates was higher compared to male, but only at the higher schools (belonging to the fifth level of the National Qualification Framework of Kosovo). The rest of the statistics was in favor of males. If we look at the gender ratio, female and male graduates in academic year 2000/2001 were 42% and 58%, respectively. In comparison to the previous analyzed period (1986), the percentage of women graduates increased by approximately 12%. In this

Table 11.2 Higher education graduates including higher schools in the academic year 2000/2001

Gender Graduates/Level of Graduation	*Female*	*Male*	*Percentage*
Higher school (mainly pedagogical)	385	315	55%
Bachelor	317	600	35%
Master	8	41	16%
Doctoral	6	17	26%
Total ratio	42.0%	58.0%	100%

Source: Statistical Office of Kosovo, 'Anketa mbi Fuqinë Punëtore 2002,' Prishtina, 2004.

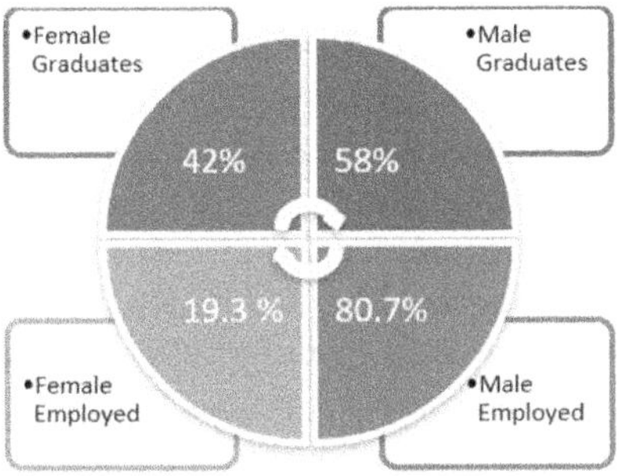

Figure 11.2 Gender analysis: HE graduates at UP and employment in %, year 2000/2002.

context, a progress is seen in equalizing gender inclusion and graduates in the tertiary education.

Regarding the employment, there were many differences. Data show that the percentage of the women employment in the postwar period decreased in comparison to the analyzed period of around 15 years ago – year 1986. Even the number of graduates increased; the women employment in 2002 decreased to 19.3%, while male employment represents the majority, at 80.7% (Statistical Office of Kosovo 2004) of total employment.

As Figure 11.2 shows, women are 'marginalized' in both graduation and employment. The situation for women graduates improved slightly in the period 2000–2002, while for the employment it was into the case. There is even an increased employment gap between females and males.

Characteristics of period 2011/2012

The University of Prishtina is still the main catalyst for the preparation of educated workforce for social needs. Although the number of higher education providers has largely increased with the establishment of tens of private higher education provider, there were only two other public universities established: University of Prizren 'Ukshin Hoti' in 2010, and University 'Haxhi Zeka' in Peja in 2011 (Shiroka-Pula, Dedaj and Aliu 2014). However, for the reporting years there were no graduates from these universities. Another important component introduced in this period was the Quality Assurance component that was introduced by the Kosovo Accreditation Agency – KAA. The agency was established by the Ministry of Education, Science and Technology (MEST), in accordance with the Law on Higher Education – LHE (2003/14) in Kosovo, as the Agency that guarantees the quality of educational and scientific research work in Higher Education Institutions in Kosovo. Therefore, each institution/study program must be accredited by KAA as an independent authority which accredits and reaccredits public and private institutions of higher education for a limited time period (Kosovar Accredditation Agency 2016).

Gender graduates and employment

According to the report from the agency for statistics of Kosovo for year 2011/2012, the following data were revealed: 53% were female graduates and 47% male graduates. In this period females, have been more represented compared to males. In the two o previously analyzed periods, the graduation of women increased and even exceeded the number of male graduates at all the three levels. The difference is not significant, only 6% in favor of females. From the data revealed, it is concluded that the position of women in the inclusion of the HE has changed in the positive way; thus, over the years, it has had an impact on the improvement of the women position in the social and political sphere. Nevertheless, the employment issue remains a problem for the entire society. Kosovo is facing an enormous high unemployment rate postwar, and it is a continuing challenge for the politicians and population. The total level of employment according to the report of Statistical Office of Kosovo (2012) was 50.6%, of which 21.1% were females, and 78.9% were males. Unbalanced gender employment is still present.

Figure 11.3 clearly shows women's progress in education, while the stagnation in employment is significant. Despite this, legal framework has contributed to some aspects of women participation, for example, in politics, social, and economic fields. By having the main objective to fully integrate women in all aspects, unemployment remains only as objective to be fulfilled, maybe in the future.

Current situation – characteristics 2014–2015

Labor market indicators in Kosovo are the worst in Europe, and women are particularly disadvantaged. Low education levels, lack of childcare institutions, the persistence of traditional social roles, and low market demand for female labor explain the exceptionally low employment rates

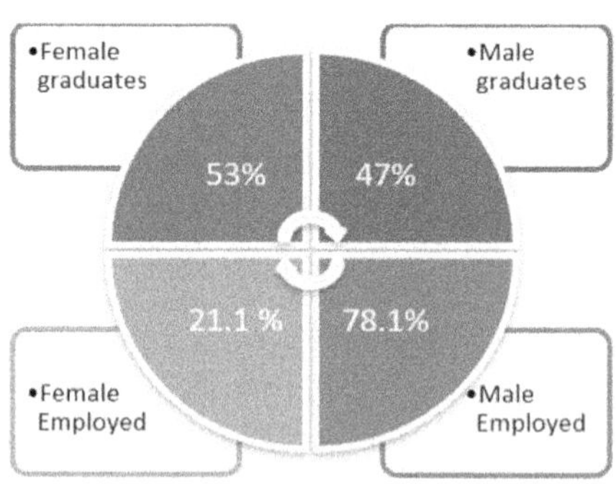

Figure 11.3 Gender analysis: HE graduates at UP and employment in %, year 2011/2012.

Table 11.3 Number of graduates at the University of Prishtina 'HasanPrishtina' in the academic year 2014/2015

Gender/Level	*Female*	*Male*	*Percentage*
University level	3,520	2,505	58.4%

Source: Statistical Office of Kosovo, 2016, Prishtina.

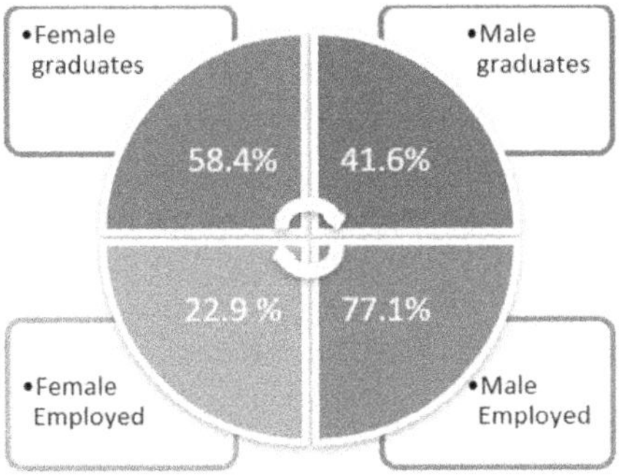

Figure 11.4 Gender analysis: HE graduates at UP and employment in %, year 2014/2015.

of women. Education is a major determinant of labor market outcomes (Worldbank 2012). On the other hand, no employment plan exists in Kosovo, and the institutions struggle to implement strategic documents. Development of public infrastructure, including roads, rail, energy supply, and electricity distribution, has been the key governmental activity expected to positively affect economic development and employment, mainly for men in the construction sector. A strategy was developed for Women's Economic Empowerment for 2011–2013, but no budget was allocated, and it has not been implemented (Färnsveden, Mustafa and Farnsworth 2014). The gender graduates show the positive trends of increasing. Table 11.3 shows the number of graduates divided in gender base for the academic year 2014/2015.

From these data, we can conclude that the ratio between gender graduates is higher for females than for males: 58.4% and 41.6%, respectively. In comparison to the previous studied period 2011/2012, where the percentage of female graduates was 53%, not much difference is seen, with an increase of approximately 5%. As regard to the women employment, little progress was made. Female employment is envisaged to be almost at the same level at 22.9%, compared to 77.1% of male employment. The progress is 1.8% for around four years.

Figure 11.4 shows a comparison of the gender differences on graduates and employment, where the correlation is positive, but with very little progress on employment.

Conclusion

Although many efforts have been made for gender equality, there are still some obstacles that need to be overcome. The link between the gender graduates and employment for the studied periods has not been strong in the past decades. Even the study periods were quite stretched, as the study included different social and political situations of Kosovo: from being under the Serbian occupation (period of 1986) to right after the war period (2001/2002); after becoming an independent country (independence declared in 2008) 2011/2012; and the trend of 2014/2015.

Huge differences were in the first studied period of year 1986 of the gender graduates, continuing with an increase of the women inclusion in the higher education. Even though, percentage of male graduates was still higher, but it started to decrease the gap among gender graduates. This positive trend continued over years and during the year 2009/2010 percentage of women graduates exceeded percentage of male graduates at the University of Prishtina "Hasan Prishtina". An increasing situation is still evident, where the percentage of female graduates is around 58%, while male graduates belong to around 42% of the total graduates during year 2014/2015.

The employment is still the main problem of the society (Figure 11.6). According to the analyzed periods, almost no improvement is shown in the women employment compared to males. The difference is very big. In the first analyzed period, women employment in ratio was 22%, and then after the war period it decreased by nearly 3%. Then some progress was seen from 1986 to 2012. The percentage in 2015 exceeded that of the first analyzed period (1986) by less than 1%, where women employment was only

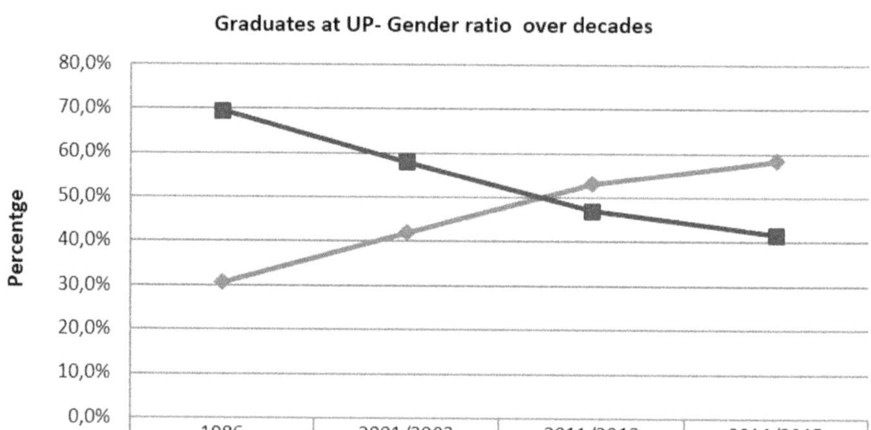

	1986	2001/2002	2011/2012	2014/2015
Female	30,6%	42,0%	53,1%	58,4%
Male	69,4%	58,0%	46,9%	41,6%

Figure 11.5 Graduates at UP – gender ratio over decades.

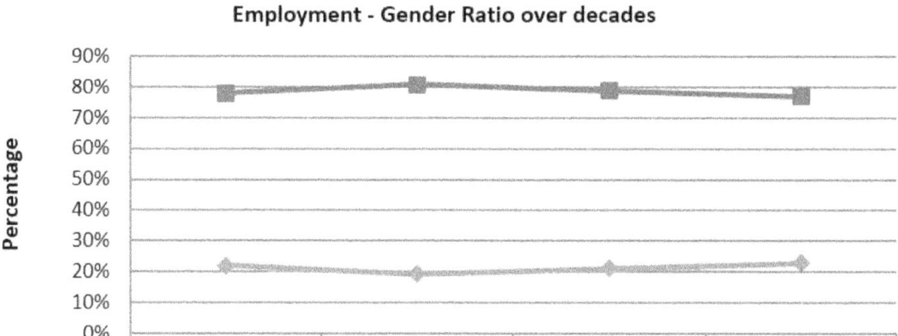

	1986	2002	2012	2015
Female	22%	19,3%	21,1%	22,9%
Male	78%	80,7%	78,9%	77,1%

Figure 11.6 Employment – gender ratio over decades.

22%, and in 2015 it was is 22.9%. It means that gender gap in labor force participation remained the same for around 30 years, thus the situation remained the same for around three decades.

Consequently, there are still many differences in the employment sector in terms of gender equality, which is slowly improving. Additionally, according to the analysis and development trends, in the upcoming decade, the gender employment ratio is not expected to become equal. Therefore, the correlation between the gender graduates and employment is not closely related.

The official data do not show the exact number of employed women due to informal economy. There are many cases that show women are discriminated and not considered equal workers as men. There are cases that shoe women work for their family businesses and not declared officially as workers, as well as they are more involved in the childcare and unpaid household tasks.

Global perspective: Women's socioeconomic disadvantage is reflected in pervasive gender inequalities in terms of earned income, property ownership, access to services, and use of time. Among those who are employed, women constitute nearly two-thirds of contributing family workers, who are employed in family businesses and farms, but receive no direct pay, and it is known that globally, women earn, on average, 24% less than men and are less likely than men to receive a pension – even the income between women and men is not balanced. Yet in all regions, women work more than men: on average, they do at least two and a half times more unpaid care and domestic work than men, and if paid and unpaid work is combined, women work longer hours than men in nearly all countries (UN Woman 2015).

Future perspective: In order to improve the current situation on closing the gender gap on labor force participation and educational attainment, certain actions are needed to be undertaken by the government. This includes addressing social and economic policies, which support/ facilitate women`s to be engaged in employment. Thus, these policies can play a significant role in fostering women's employment and education. Government should be a role model for other employers in promoting gender equality, by ensuring equal opportunity. In this regard, different international organizations can play a major role to boost women inclusion in all levels by awareness raising and lobbying for policy-changing actions. This would contribute to the improvement of gender statistics (Aliu, Luljeta, and But Dedaj. 2015. *'Decison – making in the curriculum development in higher education.'* Saarbrucken; Germany: LAP LAMBERT Academic Publishing.

References

Buchmann, Claudia, Thomas A. DiPrete, and Anne McDaniel. 2008. "Gender Inequalities in Education." *Annual Reviews*, 34, pp. 319–337.

Färnsveden, Ulf, Ariana Qosaj – Mustafa, and Nicole Farnsworth. 2014. "*Country Gender Profile – An Analysis of Gender Differences at All Levels in Kosovo.*" Prishtina: Kosovo.

Hendley, Alexandra, and Maria Charles. 2016. "Gender Inequality in Education." In Nancy A. Naples (ed.) *The Wiley Blackwell Encyclopedia of Gender and Sexuality Studies*, pp. 1–5. Hoboken, NJ: John Wiley & Sons.

Klasen, Stephan. 2000. "Does Gender Inequality Reduce Growth and Development? Evidence from Cross-Country Regressions." *World Bank Policy Research Report Working Paper No. 7.*

Klasen, Stephan, and Francesca Lamanna. 2013. "The Impact of Gender Inequality in Education and Employment on Economic Growth: New Evidence for a Panel of Countries." *Feminist Economics* (Routledge), 15, pp. 92–132.

Kosovar Accredditation Agency. 2016. Accessed 2016-28-11. www.akreditimi-ks.org/new/index.php/en/about-us/mission

Levinson, David, Peter Cookson, and Alan Sadovnik. 2013. *Education and Sociology*. New York: Routledge.

OECD. 2012. "*Gender Equality in Education, Employment and Entrepreneurship: Final Report to MCM, 2012.*" Final Report to MCM.

Pula, Justina, But Dedaj, and Luljeta Aliu. 2014. "Decison – Making in the Curriculum Development Process in Higher Education in Kosovo – Case of 'Haxhi Zeka' University." *Academic Journal of Interdisciplinary Studies* (Rome, Italy: MCSER Publishing), 3(2), p. 197.

Statistical Office of Kosovo. 1989. "*Statistical Yearbook of Kosovo*". Prishtinë: Statistical Office of Kosovo.

Statistical Office of Kosovo. 2001. "*Statistikat për Arsimin në Kosovë 2001*". Prishtina: Statistical Office of Kosovo.

Statistical Office of Kosovo. 2004. "*Anketa mbi Fuqinë Punëtore 2002*". Prishttina: Statistical Office of Kosovo.

Statistical Office of Kosovo. 2012. "*Statistical Yearbook of Kosovo*". Prishtinë: Statistical Office of Kosovo.

UN Woman. 2015. *"Progress of the World's Women 2015–2016", Transforming Economies, Realizing Human Rights.* UN Woman.

United Nantions Development Program (UNDP). 2014. *Gender Equality Strategy 2014–2017.* United Nantions Development Program, UNDP.

Worldbank. 2012. *"Kosovo: Gender Gaps in Education, Health and Economic Opportunities"*. Washington DC: World Bank.

12 The role of women in construction of sustainable and social entrepreneurship

Micilvânia Pereira de Araújo, Micilane Pereira de Araújo, Lígia de Araújo Sarmento and Emanuel Leite

Introduction

In times of intensive technological advances in the rapid access to global information, goods, and services, times of paradigm shifts regarding social welfare and the worldwide concerns with social, economic, cultural, and primarily environmental sustainability, the deconstruction of some concepts that hinder the inclusion of individuals in the productive and decisive process of social organization becomes relevant. It is in this complex scenario that this article aims to publicize and strengthen the strategic role of women in the construction of a sustainable world. We will now go through the concept of entrepreneurship that emerged in the 17th and 18th centuries in France. We will point out some differences between Social Entrepreneurship, Sector 2.5, and Social Business. These two terms are been quite often mentioned and studied. However, there are a few misuses in the employment of its definition. We will put into context Zona da Mata Pernambucana (Pernambucan Woods Zone), taking as reference the works of the Pernambucan writer Gilberto Freyre on what concerns an evaluation of the feminine.

In order to set the bases of this study, we take as parameter the experience of an organization of a group of carpet manufacturer women (*carpet manufacturer women)*, in an association in the municipality of Lagoa do Carro, situated in the Zona da Mata Norte (North both the Woods Zone) in the state of Pernambuco, that, for the last four decades, have been changing the economic reality of the region by creating jobs and a better family income. Finally, we will draw a conclusion along with a few recommendations aiming the strengthening and the spreading of this new kind of entrepreneurship where social causes are included in the development of projects. Challenges are set up. And, for the last decades, society has been claiming a bigger participation in sustainable development policies that would favor the shifting away from this suicidal path leading to a situation of scarcity of natural resources as a result of the profit-focused economic enterprises.

Short historical overview of the emerging of the term 'entrepreneurship'

The word 'entrepreneur' emerged in France around the 17th and 18th centuries with the purpose of characterizing people with an innovative spirit who stimulated economic progress through new and better forms of action. Different significations of 'entrepreneur' and 'entrepreneurship' have been used by authors in the course of time. Writer Richard Cantillon created the first definition in 1770. During the process, other authors appeared that greatly contributed in the building of these concepts, such as Israel Kirzner. In light of recent location theories, trends of the development of entrepreneurship and of the word 'entrepreneur' go across the Middle Age, the 17th century, and countless thinkers that haven't been mentioned earlier in the chapter.

With time, with other case studies, with scientific publications, and with the worldwide insertion of entrepreneurship studies in business schools and universities, this reality has been changing. Today, entrepreneurs are recognized, expected, and respected as important party in the process of innovating and creating jobs and incomes, principally in the local business. Leite scathingly criticizes Galbraith and his new global economy followers' thinking when it comes to modern enterprises, future, and entrepreneurs that are representative of the primitive capitalism in a short scale. It is important to highlight that, nowadays, rising enterprises are not landowners and raw materials proprietaries, but ideas and technology conceivers. We are now in the era of knowledge and innovation. These enterprises are small, which counters Galbraith's thinking based on the idea that only big enterprises have the conditions to survive, thus swallowing smaller enterprises.

To support this hypothesis, Leite draws the historical overview of the emergence of the processor developed by a small company of 12 employees in the 70s: Intel. In just five years, the company is transformed into a global producer of the main product of devices and now numbers 8,000 employees. According to Leite, 'Innovation is the key-word that opens the doors to the future.' He also points out the role of the entrepreneur in stating that 'entrepreneur/innovator despises the speculative investment.' Further, he notices that 'innovations create much more profit that mere commercial speculations.' Pondering this formulation, he adds that entrepreneurship 'is the entrepreneur spirit, the practice of undertaking (the act, the hard, creative, difficult and bold action), is it the result (effect) of that practice (the enterprise, the enterprising, the business),' agreeing with Peter Drucker's thinking that entrepreneurship is a 'discipline and, as such, it can be learned.'

In the 50s and the 60s, universities were surprisingly asked to answer to a market need. As a consequence of the significant increasing number of multinationals, technical education has appeared to meet the needs for skilled labor. In the 80s emerged an important and fast hardware development and more and more sophisticated software applications, starting the democratization process of access to information led by micro, small, and medium enterprises. In the same period, entrepreneurship appeared energetically when introduced as a subject in American, European, and Asian business schools. Thus, these changes stake a new era in educational entrepreneurship pedagogy: entrepreneurship is a process that can be learned and taught.

In this context, education and training are highlighted as the most important investments, since knowledge is the key element in a technology-based enterprise. This short historical overview reveals that this subject has been studied and observed over several schools around the world for some time. At a given historical period, the figure of the entrepreneur, who was considered as a bourgeois regardless of whether he was a merchant or an industrialist, was socially denied by the established powers. Several strands were created in those times of economic, social, cultural, and environmental transformation that led to the emergence of some of the entrepreneurship models geared to meet social needs. In this context, we report three definitions of 'social entrepreneur' that have been gaining strength worldwide for displaying at their core socio-environmental responsibility in economic enterprises. Those are Social Entrepreneurship, Sector 2.5, and Social Business.

Social enterprises: what are their impacts on society?

Social enterprises adopt the logic of the different economic sectors and offer quality products and services to the population excluded from the traditional market, helping to fight poverty and reduce inequality. Social inclusion, income generation, and quality of life are their main goals. However, there are some conceptual differences to address social enterprises: Social Entrepreneurship, Sector 2.5, and Social Business.

Social entrepreneurship

It is a term used to define a profitable business that at the same time allows the development of society. These enterprises use market mechanisms in order to find solutions to social problems through their main activity without forgetting profit. This type of entrepreneurship with social impact has proliferated across the country, starting with a generation of entrepreneurs whose strategy is based on sustainable values, without forgetting the ultimate goal of any organization of capitalist basis. The international non-profit organization Ashoka Entrepreneurs Network, a pioneer in the field of social innovation, offers work and support to social entrepreneurs. Established in 1980 by American Bill Drayton, Ashoka coined the term 'Social Entrepreneurship,' classifying it as a work area. Its business philosophy uses market structure to bring benefits to sectors of society that are currently excluded.

In Brazil, we can cite some examples of social enterprises, such as the pioneer in the dissemination and promotion of this type of business with social impact, ARTEMISIA, a nonprofit organization, founded in 2004 by Power Ventures, which operates with cost-effective initiatives through a given main activity, thus contributing to solving social and/or environmental problems using market mechanisms. Another example of a transformer business with social impact is the Feira Preta (or Black Fair) created in 2002, the largest fair of black culture in Latin America. In ten editions, the fair has gathered 400 artists, 500 exhibitors, 40,000 visitors, and more than R$ 2 million of currency in circulation. These are companies that operate in the market aiming to make profit, but that offer solutions to social problems of the low-income population.

Sector 2.5

There is a new kind of business booming in the world that allows entrepreneurs to unite financial sustainability and positive impact on society. It is called Sector 2.5. This type of business links the social and environmental activities to profitability in an inclusive way. These projects are at the same time social and commercial, for-profit and concomitantly related to social and environmentally sustainable development. It is considered as an intermediary between the second and third sectors, made up of companies that appear as profit-oriented and set inclusive social goals in their legal constitution. It is, therefore, a private sector driven by social and environmental awareness, but is still in construction. Brazil does not have official regulation for this type of entrepreneurship, and there are little data on the sector. Considering the report on Sustainability of the Sectorial Intelligence System (Sebrae), published in November 2013, this business model is growing in the country. According to the survey, between 20% and 30% of the companies seeking Sebrae are projects with this profile.

Sebrae has formulated some tips for those wishing to undertake in this sector:

- Understand conveniently the market you have entered or want to integrate. Search for opportunities and funding sources;
- Identify and keep the focus on the social impact from the beginning. Motivation is important and essential;
- Inquire about the aspects and characteristics of entrepreneurship, since businesses that have succeeded so far were designed by people who have previously undertaken them;
- Make your financial planning focused on business sustainability and monitor the results and impacts promoted;
- Invest in technical support, training, and continuous development.

Social business

The principle of Social Business is not financial return. It is an initiative of people and/or groups, primarily intending to improve the quality of life of those involved. In this model of 'business,' profit is not part of the process. In other words, the money invested for the project creation is returned to its investor, without interest or any other financial charges. It seeks financial self-sufficiency, that is to generate enough income to cover its own costs. In this model, no one appropriates the profits from products and services because they are reverted to payment of current costs, to reinvestment, and to innovate, encourage, and create new projects committed to social inclusion of the local community. According to Yunus (2010, pages 19 and 20), there are two types of social business:

> The first is a company with balanced revenues and expenditures, without losses or dividends, dedicated to solve a social problem. Its owners are investors who reinvest all profits in the expansion and improvement of the business. The second type is a for-profit company owned by poor people, either directly or through a fund for a predefined social cause. [...] With profits surging towards the poor, poverty is alleviated, such an enterprise is, by definition, helping to solve a social problem.

An example of Social Business that is usually attributed to the Social Entrepreneurship or to the 2.5 Sector is the Grameen Bank, the first bank specialized in microfinance, created by Professor Muhammad Yunus. The focus of Grameen is to generate a social impact from the reduction of poverty by creating business opportunities for the poorest segment of the population. According to Yunus (2010, p. 3), 97% of the 8 million borrowers are women. Dividends originated by loans were reused to expand its operations and improve its structure.

According to Yunus (2010, p. 20 and 21), seven principles are the core of social business. Those are as follows:

1. The purpose of business is to overcome poverty or one or more problems in areas such as education, health, access to technology, and environment. that threaten people and society, and not the maximization of profits;
2. The enterprise will achieve economic and financial sustainability;
3. Investors just receive back the invested amount. No dividend is paid other than the initial investment;
4. When the amount of the investment is recovered, the profit stays with the company to cover expansions and improvements;
5. The company is environmentally conscious;
6. The workforce receives market wages and enjoys better working conditions than usual;
7. Do it with joy.

Social businesses incorporate the logic of the different economic sectors and offer quality products and services to the population excluded from the traditional market, helping to fight poverty and reduce inequality. Social inclusion, income generation, and quality of life are the main objectives of social businesses, which are also cost-effective; however, there is no appropriation of profit for its members.

What are the basic differences of Social Entrepreneurship, Sector 2.5, and Social Business?

These models of organizations differ from foundations, NGOs, and co-operatives that are charitable institutions created to disburse funds from one or more donors who seek to produce benefits with their donations; they can have resources of private and government projects; they are not self-sustaining financially; they do not develop business activities that generate income; and they have no 'owner' (Table 12.1). Now, a foundation

Table 12.1 The principal characteristics

Social Enterprise	*Sector 2.5*	*Social Business*
An initiative that has social consequences.	Focus on solving social challenges.	Solving a social problem.
Created by an entrepreneur with a social vision.	To have social and environmental impact.	Unlike a nonprofit organization, it has investors and owners.
Its nature can be other than economic, or a charity, or a business initiative with or without private profit.	To have economic viability.	It is not a nonprofit organization.
Focus on low-income population	Aligned with local realities.	Focus on solving a social problem.
Intention: they have the explicit mission to cause social impact and are managed by ethical and responsible entrepreneurs.	To create social and environmental value in the community.	Generating social, economic, and environmental positive impact in the community and surroundings.
Potential scaling.	It promotes inclusion and development of people.	It may be a local, regional, national, or international enterprise such as the experience of the Grameen Bank.
Profitability.	It creates value and economic benefits; To maintain a lucrative purpose.	To create economic value exclusively to leverage the existing enterprise and / or create new social businesses.
It generates profit for the entrepreneur, investor / shareholder.	It is innovative.	It is innovative; it generates income for participants; profit reinvested in order to strengthen the enterprise and foster new social businesses.
Financially sustainable	Financially sustainable	Financial self-sustaining, or generate enough income to cover its own costs.
It generates profit for the entrepreneur, investor / shareholder.	It generates profit for the entrepreneur, investor / shareholder.	Does not generate private profit; investors receive the amount invested without any financial gain.

could be the owner of a social business by using its donations to generate the income needed for their support and at the same time create social benefits. The cooperative is owned by its members. It operates for profit and benefits its shareholders.

Considering the differences in conceptual terms and execution of actions to be Social Enterprises, Sector 2.5, and Social Business, the focus is on the new way to perceive a segment of the population considered unfit for the market, with potential to transform their reality and the community their live in, either through income and employment generation, or in the access to previously inexistent public policies concerning education, health, housing, micro-finance, or environment. It is an opportunity to innovate and undertake where a product or a service is offered as long as a social problem is being solved.

What are the possible sources of finance for social enterprises?

- Philanthropy;
- Government funding for social programs;
- Social Responsibility Fund of for-profit companies.

The point is, firstly, that these resources released for the social business will be multipliers of social enterprises that will generate income and employment, providing sustainable development and avoiding dependence policy that inhibits the creative ability of the individual; secondly, they boosts self-esteem and autonomy in their decisions. Recalling that pertinent old Chinese proverb, around 500 BC: 'Give a fish to a hungry man and you feed him for a day. Teach a man to fish and he will feed himself for the rest of his life.'

The role of engaged women in constructing sustainability

When we talk about sustainability, we engage the four inseparable pillars of this development: economic, social, environmental, and cultural. According to Sebrae data, women are commanding the opening of new businesses in the country. Representing 52% of new enterprises with less than three and a half years of activity, women are ahead. The women's entrepreneurial force is superior in four of the five Brazilian regions. Only in the Northeast they still haven't overtaken men, but they are almost there, with approximately 49% market share among new entrepreneurs.

Another important research is the concern of women in skills and access to information because they do not allow amateurism. In 49% of new enterprises, women appear to at least complete high school. Among men, this figure is 41%. The GEM survey also shows that 66% of women start a business after identifying a market opportunity, leaving aside the first motivation which was to supplement the family income or even to have an occupational activity. This change reveals a new entrepreneurial profile.

The Sebrae document also reveals that 34% of women who have business work at home, number five times higher than those of male entrepreneurs, at around 6%. Another highlight is the innovative profile of entrepreneurial identified in the survey.

According to the search Scenarios 2020 Sebrae-SP, a growing number of women entrepreneurs in São Paulo will be revealing a tie trend in the number of men and women in the labor market by the year 2020. This trend occurs in relation to Economic Active Population (PEA) – employed persons or who are looking for an occupation – in 2000, the participation of women was 42% and the projection for 2020 is 49%. Noteworthy is the number of women entrepreneurs in the form 'their own,' which are enterprises without labor employment, which, in 2000, represented 32%, and the forecast is for 47% in 2020. Another important highlight is the women's growth in the employer category, that is, entrepreneurs with employees (as), passing from 24% in 2000, to 42% in 2020.

According to the PNAD / IBGE's 1.1 million employers in the state of São Paulo (2009) and 3.3 million 'own.' Research Sebrae-SP points out that in 2020, there should be 1.5 million employers and 3.7 million entrepreneurs on their own. Thus, it is estimated that currently the entrepreneurial population of São Paulo at around 5 million people, should reach 6 million in 2020. These data indicate a trend in the growth of micro and small enterprises as an important space for individual inclusion and the generation of employment and income for women in the labor market. Selecting the Sebrae research in São Paulo was to portray a scenario analysis in the main city of Brazil. This is a national trend. However, these data are important to demonstrate the entrepreneurial force in the country, but did not specify the number of social enterprises. It is traditional entrepreneurship, that is, focused on generation of income and employment generation, but does not strip its importance in boosting the local economy.

Methodology

For this article, a brief literature review on the subject and a field research with the Association of Women Tapeceiras of car Lagoon were held in the state of Pernambuco, where we find low quality of life of its inhabitants and low participation in the state policy and decision-making, especially in relation to women. The situation of poverty in the Zona da Mata is due to the fact that the area had large plantations of sugarcane and achieved little growth by supplying only the sulcroalcooleiro complex and sustained a population of low education, low income, and long years of exploitation of slave labor in these villages. After the economic decline, many people migrated to the metropolitan area of Recife, driven by job prospect. However, if signed on the city outskirts thick the broth of the excluded in the urban area.

Pernambucan woods zone (Zona Da Mata Pernambucana): construction and evaluation of female figure in Gilberto Freyre's work

Pernambuco was one of the Hereditary Captaincy that most economically developed in times of colonization in Brazil. This economic development revolved around the planting of cane sugar, contributing to the first formation of social groups in the country. The process of organizing this society had its roots in the patriarchal and feudal economic model, marked by extreme social exclusion. The Zone of Pernambuco explore decades sugarcane monoculture, built his political, economic and social history from the traces of the power ideology and oppression, a direct consequence of concentration of income and the domain of a few families, which own large tracts of land, the landowning oligarchy, which uses the earth as a base of power.

In light of the European white man, landlord, our history was being built from the 16th century. Pernambuco contributed important chapters for this moment, but, for documentary effect, overlooks the participation of indigenous African and African descent people, whose contribution to culture is indisputable. Patriarchy also played an important domination over women. Women were expected to obey their parents, their husbands, and the clergy, simultaneously, with their bodies and their souls on hand than they needed, wanted and ordain. These social features, which date back to the Middle Ages, remained in Brazil until the early 20th century, during which many significant changes have exploded in the world. It is not hard to imagine, considering the sociocultural delay when passing the woods zone of Pernambuco, much more profound consequences on the development of their society. Domestic life in the mills and submission to their masters dragged on for many years in the last century, and unfortunately today, the submissive and obedient wife is part of sexist ideology in this region, excluding her from her rightful place in the society in which she lives.

Thus, we see clearly that the economic model of exploitation of sugarcane monoculture, where social groups were developed isolated by mills and under the baton of the masters, created an extremely conservative society that had preconceived ideas which were racist, sexist, and oppressive.

Within its stylistic paper, the literature tells us in other ways, relevant events for our historical and social education. Published in 1933, the Pernambucan Gilberto Freyre's book *Casa-Grande & Senzala* reveals the patterns of social relations held within the patriarchal system in an environment of large sugarcane mills, revealing, as it were, relations of power between master and slave, the oppressor and the oppressed, men and women. However, this study does not intend to enter into the merits of literary criticism. But, it is important to examine, albeit briefly, the narrative point of view and the place of origin of the author in his writings. The choices made for the narrative part of the look of a white man, mill owner's son, were so rich and steeped in the political domain and morally legitimized by the society in which leaned his narrative. Indeed, these do not steal the value of the work. Although some criticisms still support Gilberto Freyre, unfortunately, the events are not innocent. Anyway, these discussions are losing body, considering the importance of Casa Grande. Fernando Henrique Cardoso, a sociologist, writing the preface to the 48th edition, stated:

> (...) Yet the Freyre's work survives, and its interpretations are not repeated (which shows the insight of interpretations), as they don't keep bothering many, it takes more to ask why so much resistance to accepting and praise its positive aspects.

In Freyre's work, woman appears entirely dependent on her husband or her boss. Most of black women simply understood they owed them gratitude, as they lacked the necessary awareness of their oppression. This is a persistent leitmotif in these works where descriptions of women are prejudiced and reduce them to their body, their sexuality, or to the lack of creative thinking. This equally applies to the black slaves and to the rich and free white women. Brazilian women do not faint if we pronounce the words leg, neck, and so forth before them, as English women do (Casa Grande & Senzala, p. 313);

> White [woman] to marry, mulata to f ***, black [woman] to work
>
> (ibid p. 85)

Freyre's point of view ends up reinforcing social differences as something 'natural' in the dominant social order and as the result of the relation between the human being and the environment they live in, being a consequence of scientific models of the time which directly influenced the author. Gender relations in the patriarchal system, discussed in the literature, draw a quite stereotyped portrait of women. For example, the black characters would always go around the kitchen of the mansions cooking for their bosses, or on the street practicing prostitution. The mulatas belonged to the rooms in the big house, serving as nannies, in the sugarcane fields, or in the bedroom for they had their masters' preference.

> The good nursemaid figure that, in patriarchal times, took care of the child by nursing him, wrapping him in the hammock or the cradle, who taught him the first words in wrong Portuguese.
>
> (p. 391)

White women wouldn't have a different destiny. They would get married soon, at the age of 12 or 13, in ceremonies arranged by their families, with much older men who would fill them with children and sexual illnesses such as syphilis. They would die early because of the amount of births, always resigned to their destinies. They were narrowed to their feminine individuality, socially ignored, and, most of all, their human condition was taken away.

Who had a daughter had to marry her as child. Because after a certain age woman did not seem to offer the same flavor as virgins or maidens of 12 or 13 years old (p. 401). After 20, they were plump, soft. They created jowls. They became pale. Or they withered. (...) ugly but, fluff, with the look of man or a virago (p. 402).

Freyre will make a sketch of the patriarchal society in which a man's position is definitely consolidated in relation to the place of inferiority occupied by women, from the point of view of the slaves, from the point of view of mistresses. The work shows a clear and forceful way the thick border that separates men and women, especially black women, in the field of their minds and their sexuality, showing that way the strength and masculine power.

> What was always appreciated was that young man who would dearly be involved with women. Womanizer (raparigueiro) as we would still say now. Femeejro. Deflowerer of young girls. That wouldn't take time to impregnate black women, increasing the bevy and the paternal capital.
>
> (idem, p. 432)

Based on the modern knowledge of the gender structure, the novel outlines the way they organized the relations in this jumble of people who made up the ingenuity of sugarcane and de power structures that gave strength to this environment, but also social roles that would fit every one of these people. Black female characters took turns between the domestic affairs of big plantation house and care for the children of the boss. Other, younger, divided their time between domesticity and the production of desires.

> What the black woman of the senzala did was to facilitate depravation with their slave docility; opening their legs at the first desire of the young master. Not dire, order.
>
> (p. 425)

> Boot and woman only black
>
> (ibid p. 338);

The mistresses and *sinhazinhas* fit the house orders, mild conversations with relatives or neighbors for teas and afternoon strolls. Otherwise, the construction of male identity is through strength, virility, and stallion, holder of power – The fact that separates man's strength and the 'futility' of women.

> Attracted by the possibilities of a free life, completely loose, amid much naked woman, they settled here for pleasure or will own many European type that Paulo Prado portrays in strong traces of realism. Stallions desbragados.
>
> (p. 95)

As an everyday life chronicler, in *Casa-Grande & Senzala*, Freyre seeked to draw a social, historical, and anthropological scenario of the sugarcane mills in Pernambuco. For that, he elaborated an expanse research work on the colonial songs for children, proverbs, culinary recipes, official documents, common expressions, among others. From this material, he extracted the discursive path involving the female figure across his work: the indigenous woman, the black woman, the mulata, the maidens, the mothers, the daughters, the godmother (*comadres*), the midwifes, the witches, the nurses, the *mãe-preta* (black mother), the slave, the maids (*mucama*), the wife, the mistress (sinhá), and the young mistress (sinhazinha).

> The black corrupted the sexual life of Brazilian society, starting early in physical love – children family. But this corruption was not the black held, but the slave. Which did not take place through the African was held by indigenous slave.
>
> (p. 372)

Anyway, we can't forget that the novel was written by masculine hands:

> The "craft of the historian" is an office of men who write history in the male. Fields that address are the male action and power, even when attach new territories. Economic, history ignores the unproductive woman. Social, favors the classes and neglects the sexes. Cultural or "mental" it speaks of man in general, as sexless as mankind.
>
> (Perrot, p. 185)

It's true that, besides of the story told by men, innumerable women broke these sexist models and effectively contributed to the history of this country. However, banisse from the literary and scientific productions, they passed by those events as they were impelled, of course, by culture.

Of course, so much inequality and exclusion would not pass unpunished for years. Cities of the woods zone of Pernambuco, today, have many structural problems such as underemployment, unemployment, high social deficits, and environmental degradation. In addition, there are records of a past still fresh of child and slave labor. In the 90s, the stately profile of the old mill owners and sugar and alcohol plant did not resist to the changes of the new world economic order and soon lost power to São Paulo that united efforts to modernize the sector.

Lagoa do Carro is inserted in these contexts, past and present. It is situated in the woods zone septentrional of Pernambuco, originated as the town surrounding with sugarcane mills. Today, the city has no industrial or agro-industrial activities; services are undiversified. What prevails instead is retail trade and government services. The income transfer programs such as Bolsa Familia (*Family Allocation* seeking to reduce misery) expanded local trade and favored, to some extent, a better quality of life for its inhabitants in recent years. Still, Indicators of Social Development, HDI, and the Living Conditions Index, ICV, register worrying figures for the population. This is due to the low quality of provision of public services such as education, health, sanitation, and urbanization. These data contribute to concentration of pockets of poverty, low level of intellectual formation, and a timid participation in state politics. Gender inequality takes a legitimate air in these small towns. Patriarchy is no more an economic model, nor resisted the strength of slave families. However, the marks left by them still insist on playing places of power between men and women. Unfortunately, we cannot close the book of Freyre and think of a story of ancient times only. An important part of it is still alive among us, not in the economic model, but what is the most precious in our people and in the way women are still subjugated in this country.

Results

The Experience of Social Development of Lagoa Do Carro Pond Municipality of Craftswoman: Characterization of The Region

The Pernambuco Woods Zone consists of 43 municipalities, covering an area of 8,738 km^2, corresponding to 8.9% of Pernambuco state territory. The main economic activity in the region focuses on sugarcane monoculture. In addition to the evil land concentration, another negative effect of this type of culture was the drastic reduction of small farms (sites) from family farmers who planted subsistence crop such as cassava, yam, sweet potato, beans, and corn, some fruit trees, which served as basal power livelihood. This practice has worrying reflection on household food security in preserving the biodiversity of the region. At the beginning of the 60s, Peasant Leagues emerged, fighting for workers' rights, better working conditions, and agrarian reform. This is the most significant fight of movement in that period. Several leaders were killed and expelled from the country during the military dictatorship in Brazil.

Even with all political and economic pressure, many rural associations linked to the trade unions have been strengthened and play an important role in the present day when we face a major crisis of the sugarcane industry. In addition to the trade unions, they have emerged as social movements struggling for agrarian reform. Today, the region has a number of projects and settlements of farmers and family farmers.

This is a region known for its long history of popular struggles, with representation of numerous social organizations which somehow allows for popular participation through their associations, municipal councils, boards, committees, and others to find solutions to their problems. There is a significant number of cooperatives, NGOs, associations, and strictly economic nature of enterprises as well as enterprises with social features. It is in this scenario that the municipality of Lagoa do Carro is located. The municipal area covers 59.5 km^2 and is 00:06% of the state of Pernambuco, located 60 km from the capital, access to which is made by PE-005, BR-408, and the PE-090. The council was created on 01/10/1991, by State Law No. 10,619, formed by the district headquarters and the town of Caramuru. According to the 2010 census IBGE, the total resident population is 16,007 inhabitants. Male inhabitants totaled 7,854 (49.07%), and 8,153 were women (50.93%). The formal economic sectors are manufacturing, trade, services, and public administration, the latter being the main source of employment and income. The Municipal Human Development Index – HDI is 0.609. The county ranks 55th with this index in the state ranking.

The Craftswoman: It All Started Like This...

Countering this logic, in May 1975, a group of women from Lagoa do Carro started an enterprise that would make the municipality become a national reference. The carpet manufacturer women, Josefa Inácio da Silva (20 years of experience) and Maria Lucineide Oliveira Melo (15 years of experience), tell us that it all started when Terezinha Lira came to live in Lagoa do Carro. She already had experience in that job for she had worked in the Timbi fabric in the city of Camaragibe, in the suburbs of Recife: 'when she settled in the city, she started teaching us tapestry. She brought the raw materials, wool and tissues, and we span' (Photos 12.1 and 12.2)

After mastering of technique, the major obstacle in the beginning of the activity were the middlemen who paid a derisory price, but resold the product for a much higher value. This situation, according to Josefa Ignacia, continued throughout the 70s and part of the 80s. This reality has changed the economic, social, and cultural life of the city that became known nationally as 'land of the carpet.' Economic because it has become one of the main municipal income. Social because it included a group of women who end up involving their daughters in learning the technique. Cultural to put women in a prominent role in society, starting slowly and then gradually

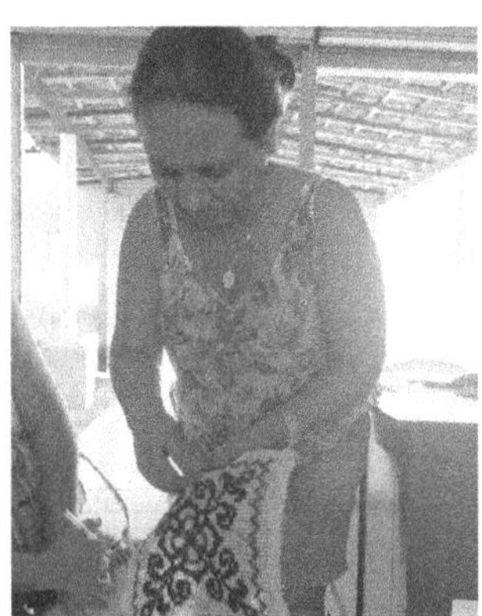

Photo 12.1 Salesperson.

Photo 12.2 Products.

showing reduction of prejudice on the part of government and, especially, their husbands and partners.

Hence arose the passion for making manuals carpets. There were 60 pioneering women who did their work on the sidewalk of their homes. To resolve this challenge in 1989, the master Isabel Gonçalves, born in the Lagoa do Carro, initiated the creation of the Association of Lagoa do Carro Tapeceiras (Astalc), in March, of this type of social organization in the region. The association is even older than the city itself, before District of Carpina.

Twenty-six years ago, this space was the meeting point of carpet manufacturer women for meetings, production, and marketing. The physical space was one of the donations from the then governor of Pernambuco, Miguel Arraes de Alencar, located on the edge of the PE 90, Km 08, car Lagoon. It is open to the public from Sunday to Sunday. Even during the visitation, the carpet manufacturer women do not stop their production, interacting with the public about the points, the screens, and the countless colors used (Photos 12.3 and 12.4).

The chief and the oficineiras carpet manufacturer women produce a tapestry following the most diverse styles such as embroidered with motifs of Portuguese tiles, floral and modern geometric shapes, with lights and shadows in points and us. They also make runners, cushions, bags, and doorstops. Among the master carpet manufacturer women are Lagoa do Carro is Luiza Costa, Terezinha Lira, Mauzé carpet, bay, and Creuza Maria de Barros.

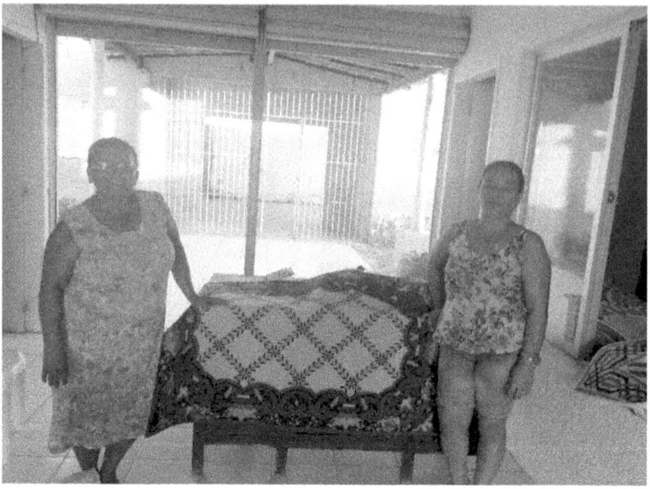

Photo 12.3 Women Entrepreneurs.

Photo 12.4 Astalc.

Astalc currently has 35 (thirty-five) women members. However, 38 women take turns in double shifts at headquarters, in two shifts. The pieces that are for sale are products of various carpet manufacturer women. Each pair is the sell-off of the report. There is a monthly contribution to the Association, which ensures the minimum expenditure for infrastructure (water, electricity, and cleaning). The raw material (wool and fabric) is purchased via association that achieves a more competitive value.

In 1997, in partnership with the Municipality, was held the first Fair Carpet. The carpet manufacturer women from Lagoa do Carro have participated in events in cities such as São Paulo, Minas Gerais, Rio de Janeiro, and Brasilia.

The carpet manufacturer women from Lagoa do Carro have a stand for the sale of its parts annually in Fenearte (National Fair of Craftsmanship) that, in 2015, held its 16th edition. The event's main aim is to promote cultural and craft production not only in Pernambuco, but throughout Brazil. The Fenearte consolidated most craft fair in Latin America. This is an important showcase for disclosure and contact; however, there is a great weakness in the aftermarket. This state event is the most lucrative for the artisans, according to Josefa Inacio: 'my husband says I have nothing to do in the association, he wanted to do I was just a housewife. But then it began a reform at home and lacked money to the kitchen. I did the whole kitchen makeover with the money received in Fenearte and shut his mouth.'

The estimated income women carpet manufacturer women revolves around R$ 700.00 / month, with two sales points: The Association and Pernambuco Crafts Center. The minimum wage in Brazil today is R$ 788.00 (US$ 222.00). Even with all lack of disclosure, space for marketing, management, technology, innovation, and training, these women, housewives, can have an income equivalent to the minimum wage in the country, demonstrating the potential of this economic activity. Since this is a handmade, manual, and exclusive product, the pieces also add an important social and cultural value (Photos 12.5 and 12.6).

Photo 12.5 One of our products.

Photo 12.6 Carpets.

The knowledge gained from past generations follows perpetuating the heredity of a people, a city, through the beautiful handmade carpets produced, thus registering a culture incommensurable in terms of domestic and international crafts. According to Maria Lucineide and Josefa, the carpet manufacturer women are finding a lot of resistance from young women to learn the craft of tapestry, as they do not believe in its economic viability. This finding puts at risk the disappearance of a technique that has become the symbol of a city.

The obstacles are major to give continuity and visibility to the enterprise:

1 Lack of municipal incentive with event promotion (fairs, travel);
2 Disclosure via social media;
3 Training in design, management, information technology;
4 IT equipment;
5 Contact phone;
6 Low participation in national and international fairs.

Conclusions

Multiple models of social enterprises as a strategic tool for sustainable local development enable the inclusion of people in situation of social vulnerability in a participatory, creative, and conscious process. It is this transformation that gives the ability to innovate, reinvent, and build a social, environmental, cultural, and economically healthier environment.

The challenges are placed, and the society in recent decades has been charging governments and private companies more involved in sustainable development policies that favor the changes of committed economy only to the capital, since this model leads to an extreme shortage of resources natural.

These women scattered to the four corners of the world, from different social classes, conscious or not of their transforming role in a predominantly patriarchal society marked by injustice and gender inequality, can overcome these inequalities in search of a more just and equitable society. Thus, go for the reduction of the consequences that this difficult scenario carries such as domestic violence, emotional and economic dependency, exclusion from public power space, controlled freedom, among other exclusion situations.

It is in this arduous journey that we find women ahead, occupying more and more important places in the private or public power spheres because of their higher sensibility and inclination to embrace social causes. Besides fighting for their personal cause, they carry out their important role as social entrepreneurs, seeking a development model based on the inclusion, the valorization, and the participation of excluded minorities.

Considering the researched material, the parameters have been raised about the experiences of women scattered organizations in the world and the experience of women carpet manufacturer women of Pernambuco; it is clear the effort of these women, even in the economic environment of hostility and violation of their most legitimate rights, insists on figuring how productive people, to the time when, more timidly persistent, are creating conditions for the improvement of the environment they live in. Thus, these women, mothers, wives, grandparents show that they also know to undertake and help support their homes while dodging the misery around and leading the place where they live in the direction of social justice. Josefa Maria Ignacia Lucileide said, 'We have four important things for our work. The first is like our office, the second is the need of money, thirdly comes our technical capability and last available labor because most women would learn the craft of tapestry but are idle because there is no demand for work.'

Recommendations

- Create alternative spaces for dialogue and dissemination of this new form of entrepreneurship that will make all the difference in the medium- and long-term sustainable development.
- Establish a network of social enterprises to multiply the successful experiences and identify, study, and develop policies; to empower the subjects in the process, build new values and paradigms, influence the design and implementation of social projects, and, above all, maintain a capital committed to this change and other alternatives in which the experience can reveal.
- Understanding education as a strong ally for the promotion of these new paradigms because sustainable development should be the guiding

criterion for the lives of thousands of young people of this country. The school can help to understand that these ideas cause great social impact, generate knowledge of the environment in which young people live, encourage creative power, sharpen self-esteem, generate a feeling of belonging, and foster local economic development. Thus, in addition to promoting scientific knowledge, the school stands as the space of creation and empowerment of people at the time that effectively contributes to the reduction of inequalities in this country.

- Higher education institutions, the Ministry of Education (MEC), the state's education departments, municipalities and the federal district, boards of education, and other opportunities for citizen participation should be mobilized toward the construction of a national core curriculum that meets new demands of education, aimed at social entrepreneurship. MEC fits also create new undergraduate and graduate students and encourage study grants for research in and outside the country.
- Promote congresses, encourage the publication of scientific papers to feed databases, and build a vast literature on the subject.

References

Yunus, Muhammad. *Creating a social business: how economically viable initiatives can solve the great problems of society.* Translation: Leonardo Abramowicz. Rio de Janeiro: Elsevier, 2010.

www.administradores.com.br/noticias/negocios/setor-2-5-uma-nova-forma-de-empreender-e-gerar-impacto-social/83980/ (Accessed on 3 August 2015).

www.ancora.org.br//textos/011-jansen-mafra.html (Accessed on 25 August 2015).

www.artemisia.org.br (Accessed on 4 July 2015).

www.brasil.gov.br/cidadania-e-justica/2012/02/empreendedorismo-social-gera-lucro-e-desenvolvimento (Accessed on 11 July 2015).

www.brasil.gov.br/economia-e-emprego/2015/04/negros-sao-maioria-entre-empreendedores-mulheres-tambem-ampliam-participacao (Accessed on 18 June 2015).

www.cidades.ibge.gov.br/painel/historico.php?codmun=260845&search=%7Clagoa-do-carro&lang= (Accessed on 18 July 2015).

www.condepefidem.pe.gov.br/c/document_library/get_file?p_l_id=18784251&folderId=22058690&name=DLFE-106004.pdf (Accessed on 25 August 2015).

www.correiocidadania.com.br/index2.php?option=com_contete&do_pdf=1&id=3069 (Accessed on 25 August 2015).

http://ec.europa.eu/teledelegations/brazil/index_en.htm (Accessed on 22 August 2015).

http://exame.abril.com.br/pme/noticias/mulheres-sao-maioria-entre-os-novos-empreendedores (Accessed on 18 June 2015).

www.feirapreta.com.br/ (Accessed on 22 July 2015).

http://inei.org.br/aceleradora25/o-que-eo-setor-2.5 (Accessed on 30 June 2015).

www.lagoadocarrope.com/#!nossa-cidade/c5ro (Accessed on 8 August 2015).

www.onordeste.com/onordeste/enciclopediaNordeste/index.php?titulo=Associa%C3%A7%C3%A3o+das+Tapeceiras+de+Lagoa+do+Carro,+Pernambuco (Accessed on 13 August 2015).

www.pnud.org.br/arquivos/ranking-idhm-2010.pdf (Accessed on 25 August 2015).

http://redeglobo.globo.com/como-sera/noticia/2015/06/negocios-de-impacto-social-possibilita-novas-formas-de-empreender.html (Accessed on 6 July 2015).

www.redemulherempreendedora.com.br/noticias/geral/cresce-a-participacao-das-mulheres-nas-atividades-empreendedoras-no-estado-de-sao-paulo (Accessed on 26 June 2015).

www.spm.gov.br/assuntos/mulher-e-trabalho (Accessed on 26 June 2015).

Index

Note: **Bold** page numbers refer to tables; *italic* page numbers refer to figures and page numbers followed by "n" denote endnotes.

For Product Safety Concerns and Information please contact our EU representative GPSR@taylorandfrancis.com
Taylor & Francis Verlag GmbH, Kaufingerstraße 24, 80331 München, Germany

www.ingramcontent.com/pod-product-compliance
Ingram Content Group UK Ltd.
Pitfield, Milton Keynes, MK11 3LW, UK
UKHW011006180926
475701UK00004B/596

* 9 7 8 1 0 3 2 0 8 6 0 3 3 *